The Health of Canada's Youth

Views and Behaviours of 11-, 13- and 15-year-olds from 11 countries

Alan J. C. King
Beverly Coles

Published by authority of the Minister of National Health and Welfare

Également disponible en français sous le titre
Nos jeunes, leur santé
Opinions et comportements des 11, 13 et 15 ans
au Canada et dans 10 autres pays

© Minister of Supply and Services Canada 1992
Cat. No. H39-239/1992E
ISBN 0-662-19373-3

Table of Contents

Preface 1

Chapter 1 — Introduction 3
A. Background of the study 3
B. Purpose of the study 3
C. Guiding framework 4
D. Design of the study 4
E. Participating countries 4
F. Sampling plan 4
   1. Target groups 4
   2. Mean ages of respondents 5
   3. Data collection 5
   4. Canadian questionnaire 6
      a. Core questions 6
      b. Optional topics 6
G. Topics for analysis 6
   1. Health-risk factors 6
   2. Exercise/Leisure-time activity 6
   3. Nutrition and dental care 6
   4. Ailments and medication 6
   5. Relationships with others 6
   6. Relationships between health-risk factors 6

Chapter 2 — Use of Tobacco, Alcohol and Other Drugs 7
A. Introduction 7
B. Tobacco use 7
   1. Prevalence of experimentation 8
   2. Prevalence of current use 9
   3. Parents' smoking habits 10
C. Alcohol consumption 11
   1. Alcohol use 11
   2. Prevalence of experimentation 11
   3. Prevalence of current use 12
   4. Trends in the consumption of alcohol by Canadian youth 13
   5. Parents' alcohol use 14
D. Other drug use 15
E. Summary 17

Chapter 3 — Exercise and Leisure-time Activities 19
A. Introduction 19
B. Exercise 19
   1. Number of times students exercise per week 19
   2. Hours of exercise per week 20
   3. Participation in sports clubs 21
   4. Encouragement from others to participate 22
   5. Participation by others close to them 23
   6. Expectations regarding exercising at age 20 24
   7. Perceptions of fitness 24
   8. Attitude toward physical education classes 26
   9. Reasons for participating in physical activity 26
C. Leisure-time activities 26
   1. Watching television 26
   2. Watching movies on a VCR 26
   3. Playing computer games 29
D. Summary 29

Chapter 4 — Nutrition, Diet and Dental Care 33
A. Introduction 33
B. Healthy foods 33
    1. Fruit 33
    2. Raw vegetables 34
    3. Whole wheat and rye breads 35
    4. Milk and milk products 35
C. Less healthy foods 37
    1. Candy and chocolate bars 37
    2. Potato chips (crisps) 38
    3. French fries 38
    4. Hamburgers, hot dogs and sausages 39
    5. Soft drinks with sugar 40
    6. Coffee 40
D. Overall dietary patterns 41
    1. Fibre 41
    2. Fat 42
E. Dental care 44
F. Summary 46

Chapter 5 — Physical Ailments and Medication 47
A. Introduction 47
B. Ailments 47
    1. Headache 47
    2. Stomach ache 47
    3. Backache 47
    4. Feeling low (depressed) 48
    5. Bad temper (irritability) 48
    6. Feeling nervous 49
    7. Difficulty getting to sleep 49
    8. Feeling dizzy 50
C. Use of medication and pills 50
D. Summary 52

Chapter 6 — Social Adjustment 63
A. Introduction 63
B. Relationship with parents 63
C. Relationship with peers 64
D. Self 67
E. Attitude toward school and teachers 70
F. Summary 74

Chapter 7 — Relationships between Health-risk Factors 87
A. Introduction 87
B. Predicting health-risk behaviours 88
    1. Smoking 88
    2. Liking school 89
    3. Being an outsider 89
C. Interrelationships 90
D. Summary 92

Chapter 8 — Summary and Recommendations.. 95
  A. Introduction 95
  B. Smoking, alcohol and drug use 95
  C. Physical activity 95
  D. Leisure time 96
  E. Nutrition.. 96
  F. Ailments.. 96
  G. Social adjustment 96
  H. Relationships among health-risk factors 96
  I. Developing theory to guide health promotion intervention...................................... 97

Appendices... 99
  A. Sampling procedures.. 99
  B. Regression and factor analysis... 101
  C. Tables 121
  D. Brief descriptions of 11 participating countries 193

Bibliography... 197

List of Tables
1.1   Population and period of compulsory education for study countries 4
1.2   Mean ages of respondents.. 5
1.3   Date of administration and gross and net sample sizes 5
2.1   Respondents who indicated they do not smoke.. 7
2.2   Proportion of students who smoke and don't smoke whose father smokes every day........... 11
2.3   Proportion of students who smoke and don't smoke whose mother smokes every day 11
2.4   Proportions of students who drink at least every week and those who don't,
      whose father drinks daily 16
4.1   Students who eat high-fat foods at least once a day 43

List of Figures
2.1   Percentages of students who have tried smoking at least once........................... 8
2.2   Percentages of students who say they smoke 9
2.3   Percentages of students who say their father smokes at least from time to time 10
2.4   Percentages of students who say their mother smokes at least from time to time..... 10
2.5   Percentages of students who have tasted alcohol 12
2.6   Percentages of students who drink alcoholic beverages at least every week 13
2.7   Percentages of students who say they have been drunk at least once 14
2.8   Percentages of students who say their father drinks at least from time to time 15
2.9   Percentages of students who say their mother drinks at least from time to time 15
2.10 Percentages of Canadian students who have used illegal substances
      at least once, by gender 16
3.1   Percentages of students who exercise at least four times a week out of school 20
3.2   Percentages of students who exercise once a week or less.................................. 21
3.3   Percentages of students who exercise four or more hours a week out of school..... 22
3.4   Percentages of students who are members of a community sports club 23
3.5   Percentages of students who are members of a school sports team 24
3.6   Percentages of students whose father often encourages them to take part
      in physical activities in their spare time.. 25
3.7   Percentages of students whose mother often encourages them to take part
      in physical activities in their spare time.. 25
3.8   Percentages of students whose father takes part in physical activities 'every week'............... 26
3.9   Percentages of students whose mother takes part in physical activities 'every week' 27
3.10 Percentages of students whose best friend takes part in physical activities 'every week'........ 27
3.11 Percentages of students who say 'definitely yes' they will be physically active
      at about 20 years of age.. 28

3.12	Percentages of students who think they are 'very fit' and 'fit'	28
3.13	Percentages of students who like physical education classes at school	29
3.14	Percentages of students who watch television 2-3 hours and 4 or more hours per day	30
3.15	Percentages of students who watch VCR movies 1-3 hours and 4 or more hours per week	31
3.16	Percentages of students who play computer games 1-3 hours and 4 or more hours per week	32
4.1	Percentages of students who eat fruit once a day or more	34
4.2	Percentages of students who eat raw vegetables once a day or more	35
4.3	Percentages of students who eat whole wheat bread or rye bread once a day or more	36
4.4	Percentages of students who drink whole and/or 2% milk once a day or more	37
4.5	Percentages of students who eat candy or chocolate bars once a day or more	38
4.6	Percentages of students who eat potato chips (crisps) once a day or more	39
4.7	Percentages of students who eat french fries once a day or more	40
4.8	Percentages of students who eat hamburgers, hot dogs or sausages once a day or more	41
4.9	Percentages of students who drink soft drinks once a day or more	42
4.10	Percentages of students who drink coffee once a day or more	43
4.11	Percentages of students who eat fibre-rich foods once a day or more	44
4.12	Percentages of students who brush their teeth once a day or more	45
5.1	Percentages of students who have had headaches 'often' in the last six months	48
5.2	Percentages of students who have had stomach aches 'often' in the last six months	49
5.3	Percentages of students who have had backaches 'often' in the last six months	50
5.4	Percentages of students who have felt depressed 'often' in the last six months	51
5.5	Percentages of students who have been bad tempered 'often' in the last six months	52
5.6	Percentages of students who have felt nervous 'often' in the last six months	53
5.7	Percentages of students who have had difficulty sleeping 'often' in the last six months	54
5.8	Percentages of students who have felt dizzy 'often' in the last six months	55
5.9	Percentages of students who have taken medicine or pills for a cough in the last month	56
5.10	Percentages of students who have taken medicine or pills for a cold in the last month	57
5.11	Percentages of students who have taken medicine or pills for a headache in the last month	58
5.12	Percentages of students who have taken medicine or pills for a stomach ache in the last month	59
5.13	Percentages of students who have taken medicine or pills for difficulty in sleeping in the last month	60
5.14	Percentages of students who have taken medicine or pills for nervousness in the last month	61
6.1	Percentages of students who talk to their parents often about ideas and things that interest them	64
6.2	Percentages of students who find it easy to talk to their father about things that really bother them	65
6.3	Percentages of students who find it easy to talk to their mother about things that really bother them	66
6.4	Percentages of students indicating they and their parents always or mostly agree about how they should spend their free time	67
6.5	Percentages of Canadian students who agree with various statements indicating relationship with parents	68
6.6	Percentages of students who say they have been picked on at least once	69
6.7	Percentages of students who say they have picked on someone else at least once	70
6.8	Percentages of most common reactions to being picked on	71
6.9	Percentages of students who have more than one close friend	72
6.10	Percentages of students who find it easy to talk to friends of the same sex about things that really bother them	73
6.11	Percentages of students who find it easy to talk to friends of the opposite sex about things that really bother them	74
6.12	Percentages of students who spend time with their friends four or more days a week outside school hours	75
6.13	Percentages of students who responded 'very happy' or 'quite happy' to "How do you feel about your life at present?"	76

6.14   Percentages of students who responded 'very often' or 'rather often' to
            "Do you ever feel lonely?" 77
6.15   Percentages of students who say it is 'very important' to have free time
            to spend on their own 78
6.16   Percentages of students who say they 'often' or 'sometimes' feel like an outsider 79
6.17   Percentages of Canadian students who agree with various statements
            concerning self-esteem 80
6.18   Percentages of Canadian students who agree they need to lose or gain weight 81
6.19   Percentages of students who believe their teachers think their school work
            is 'very good' or 'good' 82
6.20   Percentages of students who indicate they like school 83
6.21   Percentages of students who agree there are 'one' or 'several' teachers they fear 84
6.22   Percentages of students who agree there are 'one' or 'several' students they fear 85
7.1   Factors that predict smoking in 15-year-olds 88
7.2   Factors that predict 'liking school' 89
7.3   Factors that predict 'feeling like an outsider' 90
7.4   Relationships among health factors for Canadian 13-year-old girls 91
7.5   Relationships among health factors for Canadian 13-year-old boys 92
7.6   Relationships among health factors for Scottish 13-year-old girls 92
7.7   Relationships among health factors for Scottish 13-year-old boys 93
7.8   Relationships among health factors for Finnish 13-year-old girls 93
7.9   Relationships among health factors for Finnish 13-year-old boys 94

Preface

In 1982, a Cross-National Survey on Health Behaviours in School-Aged Children was initiated by researchers from three countries: England, Finland and Norway. Shortly thereafter, the project was adopted by the World Health Organization for Europe as a WHO Collaborative Study. In winter 1983-84, the first WHO Cross-National Survey was carried out in these three countries as well as in Austria. In 1985-86, the second WHO Collaborative survey was conducted with the participation of 11 countries.

Meanwhile, Canada had also undertaken two similar surveys (*Canada Health Knowledge Survey* and *Canada Health Attitudes and Behaviours Survey*) in the same period, and the successful dissemination of results of those surveys came to the attention of the World Health Organization. In 1987, Dr. Gordon Mutter of Health and Welfare Canada was invited to share the Canadian findings and dissemination process with European health researchers and to investigate the possibility of participating in their health survey program. Canada was subsequently given the special status that enabled it to participate in the research program.

European countries deal with many of the same youth health concerns as we do in Canada and, therefore, their efforts to develop research and programs to respond to these concerns can provide much useful information to support our efforts to reduce health-risk behaviour. Canada can benefit from collaboration with our European colleagues both in conducting research and developing health policy.

The following are the principal investigators who make up the research group at the present time: Anselm Eder, Austria; Danielle Piette, Belgium; Lassa Kannas, Finland; Rozsa Mandoki, Hungary; Candace Currie, Scotland; Ramon Mendoza, Spain; Jean-Pierre Abbet, Switzerland; Chris Smith, Wales; Barbara Woynarowska, Poland; Ulla Marklund, Sweden; and Bente Wold, Norway. Tapani Piha of the WHO Regional Office for Europe acts as liaison to the project.

Health and Welfare Canada contracted the Social Program Evaluation Group at Queen's University to conduct the survey and to prepare this report. Gordon Mutter, Mary Johnston and Hélène Cameron of Health and Welfare Canada gave advice and direction throughout the project. Professors Alan Roberston and Sandy Gibbons contributed to the design and conducted the pilot phase of the project. Matthew King was responsible for data entry, data summarization, programming and the preparation of the appendices. The research assistant/clerical team consisted of Maxine Leverett, Allison MacDuffie, Manuel Uhm, Heather Stanton and Jeff Leonard; Myrt MacRae conducted the communication and financial aspects of the project. Dr. Judith De Wolfe, School of Nursing, Queen's University, and Dr. Brian A. Wherrit, Department of Paediatrics, Queen's University, assisted the authors by providing background information for chapters 4 and 5 respectively. Hazel Fotheringham, Judith Whitehead and André Déry were responsible for the editorial work. Christian Labarthe designed the publication. Wendy Warren was research coordinator for the project.

The primary audience for the report is health professionals and health educators. The findings are presented in a clear, straightforward manner with the more detailed statistical analysis designed to support the findings in appendices.

This report does not necessarily represent the position of Health and Welfare Canada on basic health issues. The final responsibility for the interpretation of the findings presented in this report and the implications suggested rests with the authors.

AK and BC

Chapter 1

Introduction

A. Background of the study

There is ample evidence that Canadian youth engage in health-related behaviours that put them at risk. Health professionals and educators have long sought strategies that would improve the fitness of young people and convince them to avoid using harmful addictive substances. In addition, the schools have provided opportunities for these professionals to educate young people in appropriate health behaviour. Nevertheless, more information about the health, knowledge, attitudes and behaviour of youth is required, and more powerful strategies to ensure the long-term health of young Canadians need to be developed.

During the past 10 years, a group of researchers in Europe has worked together to collect information about the health status of the children in their countries. The original European collaboration involved only three countries: England, Finland and Norway. Shortly after the first survey in 1982, the project was adopted by the World Health Organization (WHO), European division, as a collaborative study. In the winter of 1983-84, the first WHO cross-national survey was conducted in the three original countries as well as in Austria. In 1985-86, a second similar survey was carried out with 11 countries participating. In 1989-90, the third cross-national survey was conducted in 16 countries, including Canada. The research has enabled participating researchers to conduct analyses that shed further light on the factors that influence health-related behaviours.

How did Canada become involved in a WHO-sponsored series of comparative studies on the health behaviours of children in Europe? In the early and mid-1980s, Health and Welfare Canada sponsored two large surveys on the health, knowledge, attitudes and behaviours of Canadian youth in grades 4, 7 and 10 (King et al., 1984; King et al., 1985). These studies were used to identify particular health issues and encouraged the development of initiatives to respond more comprehensively to them. The findings of these studies were shared with colleagues in Scandinavia, and representatives of Health and Welfare Canada were invited to participate in discussions of the European studies. Canadian health officials were quick to identify the advantages of being involved in cross-cultural studies of the health behaviour of young children, and were asked to join the team of European researchers now known as WHO/HBSC (Health Behaviour in School-age Children). This joint effort provided the opportunity to examine the behaviour of young Canadians in a much wider context through the use of questionnaires asking identical questions.

The two Canadian studies (King et al., 1984; King et al., 1985) have been influential in part because the responses of young people were compared across provinces and territories. If a province or territory obtained a comparatively low score the tendency was to develop programs in response to the concern. Similarly, if the responses of young Canadians were compared with those of other countries, the deficiencies and strengths of Canadian programs would be evident. Canada, therefore, was pleased to take part in the 1989-90 WHO survey to enable us to compare Canadian youth with their counterparts in other countries. This comparison allows us to explore factors that contribute to health-risk behaviours and identify health-promotion strategies that have been particularly useful in responding to them.

B. Purpose of the study

The major objective of this international comparative approach to the collection of health-related information about young people is to stimulate health promotion and health education activities. We see health promotion as the process of enabling the individual and the community to increase control over factors that influence health. To accomplish this goal, studies such as this are needed to gain insight into and to increase our understanding of young people's health-related attitudes, behaviours and knowledge. The information can then be used to develop recommendations for health promotion and education initiatives. First, it will increase our understanding of the extent of and factors associated with health-risk behaviour; second, and perhaps more important, it will direct us toward strategies and interventions that will reduce the health-risk behaviour of young people.

Surveys will be administered at four-year intervals to show changes in health behaviours and identify factors that might have contributed to these changes. An effort will be made to relate changes in the health behaviours of young people to national policies, health promotion initiatives and health curriculum interventions.

Although this report contains analyses of preliminary data that will further our understanding of the health behaviours of young people, it is designed primarily to provide information about the health status of youth to Canadian health professionals and educators in government and private settings.

C. Guiding framework

The team of researchers that developed the survey instruments did not work with a single unified theory of health behaviours. However, the research design draws heavily from the behavioural and social sciences, and when selecting the items the researchers were guided by a broad scientific perspective. This might be called a "socialization" perspective in that it reflects the influences young people respond to in their day-to-day behaviours.

Increasingly clear is that adolescent behaviour is strongly influenced by shared values and that conceptual models that attempt to explain health-related behaviours in primarily volitional terms or to minimize the influence of others restrict interventions to ones focusing on the individual. In Chapter 6, we illustrate the importance of relationships with parents, peers and teachers in the adoption or rejection of health-risk behaviours. In Chapter 7, however, we use the findings to tentatively test a theoretical framework that might prove useful as a basis for developing health interventions. Although the framework did not guide selection of survey items, the information collected through the surveys was sufficiently comprehensive to allow assessment of the exploratory model.

D. Design of the study

The study was designed to simulate a longitudinal study by surveying three age groups — 11-, 13- and 15-year olds. The questionnaire was prepared to address common health behaviours and attitudes. WHO issued a Manual of Protocol outlining the requirements to be observed. All countries were to include a substantial number of core questions in their surveys. In addition, researchers in each country were at liberty to select special focus questions related to a topic or topics of particular interest. The comparative analysis presented in this report is based on the core items only.

E. Participating countries

The 16 countries that participated in the 1990 survey were Austria, Belgium, Canada, Finland, France, Hungary, Iceland, Latvia, the Netherlands, Norway, Poland, Scotland, Spain, Sweden, Switzerland and Wales. Data from five countries — France, Iceland, Latvia, the Netherlands and Switzerland — were not available in time for this report; therefore, it is based on preliminary data from the remaining 11 countries. Brief descriptions of these countries, their school system and, in some cases, a few comments about the general approach to physical and health education appear in Appendix D. Table 1.1 gives the population and the period during which schooling is compulsory for each of the countries.

F. Sampling plan

The sampling plan was agreed upon by the WHO/HBSC committee and each country adhered to its requirements. The Canadian data were gathered with the intent to represent each province and territory proportionally. School boards were chosen using a systematic sampling approach to allow, where possible, for appropriate representation according to geographic area, community size and public or separate school representation. Classes were chosen randomly by the principal. Similar procedures were used in the various countries involved in the study. Specific details regarding sampling are found in Appendix A.

1. Target groups

In each country the target groups were to be representative of the national population in terms of age, gender and geographic distribution. Three age groups were targeted to simulate a longitudinal study, the median ages of which were set at 11, 13 and 15. A total of 1500 students was recommended for each age group. An even division of male and female respondents was expected because students were surveyed in randomly selected school classes. For most countries the grade level corresponding to the desired age ranges are grades 6, 8 and 10; however, where the lower age of compulsory education is 7, the grade levels are the equivalent of the Canadian grades 5, 7 and 9.

Table 1.1
Population and period of compulsory education for study countries

Country	Population	Compulsory schooling
Austria	7 600 000	6 to 15
Belgium	9 900 000	6 to 18
Canada	26 000 000	6 to 16
Finland	4 900 000	7 to 16
Hungary	10 700 000	6 to 16
Norway	4 200 000	7 to 16
Poland	38 000 000	7 to 17
Scotland	5 400 000	5 to 16
Spain	39 100 000	6 to 15
Sweden	8 500 000	7 to 16
Wales	2 900 000	5 to 16

2. Mean ages of respondents

Table 1.2 shows the mean ages of the respondents in each country discussed in this report. Three points must be considered when comparing the ages across countries. First, the class was generally selected as the unit of analysis, but sampling procedures varied slightly. Although most countries accepted that the procedure adequately represented the desired age samples, two countries selected samples that more specifically targeted the specified age group.

Second, some systems allow greater retardation of students than others; that is, children are held back only in some systems in the early years of school. The class unit in later years, therefore, has slightly different age representations.

Third, some discrepancies arose as a result of the time the questionnaires were administered. Table 1.3 gives the time of administration and the gross and net sample sizes for each country. For the net sample, students were removed from the gross sample because they were older or younger than the targeted age group, or because they had failed to complete a substantial portion of the questionnaire.

It is crucial that these three points be taken into consideration when interpreting the findings in this report. For example, a higher prevalence of some risk behaviours might be expected in those countries where the respondents are slightly older than the average. As well, the time of year the questionnaire was administered may influence levels of physical activity and dietary patterns.

3. Data collection

The classroom teachers who administered the surveys were asked to adhere to a specific set of instructions regarding administration and the respondents were guaranteed absolute anonymity in their responses. The fact that the study was sponsored by the WHO and Health and Welfare Canada appeared to have encouraged both the supervising teachers and the students to be very conscientious when completing the surveys.

Table 1.2
Mean ages of respondents

Country	Lowest	Middle	Highest
Austria	11.3	13.3	15.2
Belgium	11.5	13.5	15.4
Canada	12.1	14.1	16.0
Finland	11.7	13.8	15.8
Hungary	12.3	14.2	16.2
Norway	11.4	13.4	15.4
Poland	11.6	13.6	15.7
Scotland	11.6	13.7	15.6
Spain	11.8	13.8	15.8
Sweden	11.4	13.4	15.4
Wales	12.1	14.0	16.0

Table 1.3
Date of administration and gross and net sample sizes

Country	Administration date	Gross sample size	Net sample size
Austria	May 1990	3192	2984
Belgium	March 1990	3022	3007
Canada	Feb-May 1990	7633	5565
Finland	March-May 1990	3046	2996
Hungary	May 1990	8023	6498
Norway	Nov-Dec 1989	5111	5037
Poland	Feb 1990	4643	4613
Scotland	Feb-March 1990	4079	3934
Spain	March 1990	4393	3372
Sweden	Nov-Dec 1989	3631	3553
Wales	March-Apr 1990	6977	6724

4. Canadian questionnaire

The Canadian questionnaire was developed according to the Manual of Protocol developed by the international committee.

a. Core questions

The core questions were meant to be asked by each participating country in the same manner. These questions dealt with demographic background; smoking; alcohol and drug use; nutrition; dental care; exercise; time spent watching television, using video cassette recorders (VCRs) and playing computer games; ailments and use of medication. Also included were a few items about school and friends. However, some countries did not include all topics in their surveys.

b. Optional topics

Each country was at liberty to pursue topics of special interest. Canadian students responded to items about self-esteem, reasons for participating in sport and use of certain drugs which few other countries included. Some areas of concentration by other surveys were sleep problems, nutrition, sexuality, and AIDS (acquired immunodeficiency syndrome) and other STD (sexually transmitted disease).

G. Topics for analysis

The overall purpose of a survey of this type is to discover the patterns of behaviour adopted by youth of various ages that are considered either harmful or beneficial to their overall health. Research in recent years has provided very strong evidence that relationships exist between certain types of behaviour and good or poor health practices. Smoking tobacco, drinking alcohol, use of illegal drugs, exercise and nutrition contribute significantly not only to physical health, but also to mental health. Following are some of the topics we have chosen for analysis in this study.

1. Health-risk factors

Students were asked to respond to items about practices known to put people at risk in terms of their health — smoking tobacco, drinking alcoholic beverages, using illegal abusive substances and not using seat belts when riding in a car. Most of these topics are discussed in Chapter 2.

2. Exercise/Leisure-time activity

Chapter 3 deals with the many questions regarding the students' participation in sports and exercise — both in school and out of school. The amount of time they spend in such activities, their attitudes toward them, encouragement they receive to participate, reasons for participating and their assessment of their fitness level provide the bases for the analyses.

3. Nutrition and dental care

Students were given a list of various food items, some considered healthy, some unhealthy, and asked to indicate how often they eat or drink them. Only two items were asked about dental care directly, but foods eaten relate indirectly to care of the teeth. Nutrition is discussed in Chapter 4.

4. Ailments and medication

One item listed various ailments and conditions from which students may occasionally suffer. They were asked to indicate how often they had experienced these problems in the last six months. In addition, respondents were asked to reply 'yes' or 'no' to an item asking if they had taken medication in the past month for certain ailments or conditions. Chapter 5 is a discussion of the responses to these items.

5. Relationships with others

A vital sign of healthy teenagers is reflected in their relationships with parents, peers and teachers. Items relating to these topics were asked on all questionnaires. Chapter 6 contains a comparative analysis of these topics, and a section for Canadian students only based on self-esteem items and on items about parent relationships.

6. Relationships between health-risk factors

The most useful analysis of these data comes through analyses that relate risk factors to risk behaviours. In this report we have identified these issues and have discussed them in Chapter 7.

In the final chapter we summarize the findings and outline our recommendations.

Throughout the discussion the data are presented in figures. In many of the figures, several response categories are combined to illustrate points more clearly or facilitate comparisons. There is a corresponding table in Appendix C for almost every figure showing complete data by response alternatives. When figures include all or all but one of the response alternatives no corresponding table appears in the appendix.

Chapter 2

Use of Tobacco, Alcohol and Other Drugs

A. Introduction

Many actions taken by youth are considered to be detrimental to promoting good health. The actions given the most attention tend to be those involving the use of substances that affect the body's main systems in adverse ways, such as smoking tobacco, drinking alcohol and using other drugs.

The results of hundreds of studies undertaken throughout the world in recent years have proven that a relationship exists between smoking tobacco and several life-threatening diseases, such as lung cancer, heart disease and strokes. Since 1985, Health and Welfare Canada, through the Health Promotion Directorate, has actively promoted the goals of the National Strategy to Reduce Tobacco Use with the end goal being a total abstinence from tobacco use. Some examples of actions taken under the auspices of this program are a ban on tobacco advertising, provision of educational materials and legislation that limits areas in which people may smoke.

The relationship between alcohol consumption and various health problems is well documented. Liver disease, pancreatitis and alcoholism are debilitating illnesses caused by or aggravated by the heavy use of alcohol. Other related problems, such as drinking and driving, absenteeism from work and loss of control, are also often attributable to excessive drinking. Heavy drinking is difficult to define, but in one report, *Alcohol in Canada* (Health and Welfare Canada, 1989a), it was defined as consuming 15 or more drinks per week. Most literature related to alcohol use tends to accept some alcohol use and to recommend moderation rather than the complete elimination of alcohol.

However, legal restrictions are in place concerning alcohol consumption. Almost all countries forbid driving with a blood alcohol count over a certain level (this varies among countries; in Canada it is .08%). Laws also exist that designate the legal age at which a person is allowed to purchase and consume alcoholic beverages. Across Canada the legal age is determined provincially and ranges between ages 18 and 21; similar age restrictions apply in other countries, several of which set the age of permission at 16.

Drug use among youth commands a great deal of attention from the media, which makes it appear quite widespread. The most commonly used illegal substance is cannabis (marijuana and hashish). In the *National Alcohol and Other Drugs Survey, Highlights Report* (Health and Welfare Canada, 1990), about 23% of adult Canadians reported using cannabis at some time with 6.5% being current users. Very small percentages of the population use other drugs. However, the problems associated with drug use, especially crime and illness, have far greater social and economic consequences than the extent of drug use would seem to warrant.

In this chapter we examine the data collected regarding tobacco, alcohol and drug use among the respondents in this study.

B. Tobacco use

The effectiveness of the campaign to reduce, and eventually eliminate, tobacco use is difficult to determine. One problem encountered by those who attempt to assess its impact is the lack of corresponding data. Some studies deal with the total population, some break it down into the 15- to 24-year-old group, and some use school grade levels as the unit of analysis, but not always the same grade levels. Table 2.1 gives figures for high school students from some previous studies. Little change has occurred over the past six years.

Young people are constantly exposed to media advertising about the effects of tobacco use, and schools have implemented curricula dealing with this topic in health education courses.

Table 2.1
Respondents who indicated they do not smoke

| | Grade | | | | | |
Study	6	7	8	9	10	11
CHABS[1] 1984-85		89			74	
CYAS[2] 1988		92		80		75
WHO 1990	93		87		77	

[1] *King et al., 1985.*
[2] *King et al., 1988.*

Many Canadian studies have been conducted to assess the prevalence of smoking among Canadian youth, but it is very difficult to compare the results of these studies with those of our current study because questions are not identical and the data have been analysed for different age levels. The *Canada Health Attitudes and Behaviours Survey, 9, 12 and 15 Year Olds* (CHABS) in 1984-85 (King et al., 1985) indicated that 11% of Grade 7 students (usually age 12) and 26% of Grade 10 students (age 15) were smoking to some extent. The *Canada Youth and AIDS Study* (CYAS) in 1988 (King et al.) found that 8% of

Grade 7 students, 20% of Grade 9 students (age 14) and 25% of Grade 11 students (age 16) were smoking, at least occasionally, on a regular basis. Although the age definitions are not the same, the findings are generally relevant to the data in this study, which indicated that 7% of the Grade 6 students (age 11), 13% of the Grade 8 students (age 13), and 23% of the Grade 10 students (age 15) are smoking. The only commonality of the three studies is for the 15-year-old students in Grade 10; since 1985, smoking among these students has decreased by 3%, but this hardly indicates a trend.

For this study respondents were asked if they had ever smoked tobacco (even one cigarette, cigar or pipe), how often they smoke at present, and the degree to which their mother and father smoke.

1. Prevalence of experimentation

All countries that participated in this study asked similar questions about smoking. Figure 2.1 presents the percentages of respondents who have tried smoking at least once, by gender. In every country there is a dramatic increase in the number of students who have tried smoking between age 11 and age 15. At all age levels far more youth in

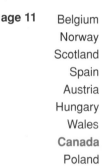

Figure 2.1
Percentages of students who have tried smoking at least once

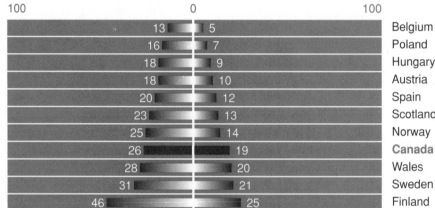

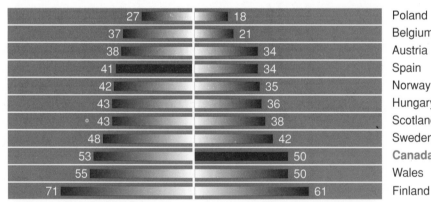

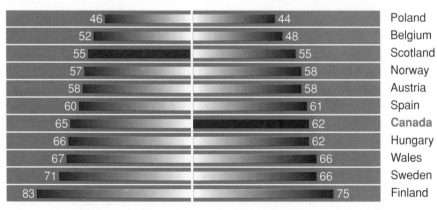

8

Finland have tried smoking than in any other country. Canadian youth tend to fall in the middle in this measure.

2. Prevalence of current use

As we see in Figure 2.2, far fewer students smoke regularly. Students were asked to indicate how often they smoke at present and were given four response choices: 'I do not smoke', 'every day', 'at least once a week, but not every day' and 'less than once a week'. Figure 2.2 shows, for each country, the total percentage of respondents who indicated they smoke at least occasionally.

Although few 11-year-old students smoke to any extent, slightly more Canadian, Scottish and Welsh girls of this age do so. Canadian boys of 11 years of age tend to smoke a little more than most of their peers, but not as much as boys in Hungary and Poland.

More 13-year-old Canadian and Finnish girls smoke occasionally than girls in other countries. By age 15 Canadian girls are in the middle brackets.

The difference in the rate of increase between Canadian boys and girls is quite pronounced; just over three times as many boys smoke at age 15 as at age 11, but almost six times as many girls do. In all but one of the survey countries one quarter or more of the girls are smoking by age 15. The exception is Poland where girls tend to have low smoking rates at each age level. In several countries, including Canada, more girls than boys are smoking by ages 13 and 15. This phenomenon has been indicated in other studies as well (Health and Welfare Canada, 1989d; A pack of trouble, *Toronto Star*, October 22, 1991).

Figure 2.2
Percentages of students who say they smoke*

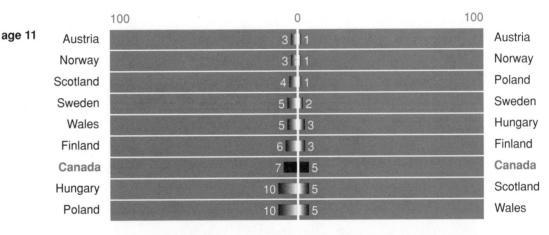

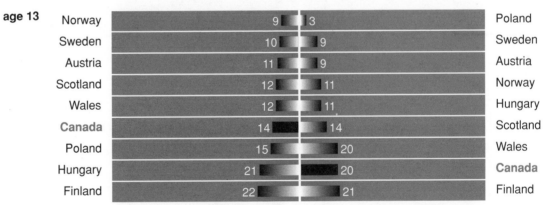

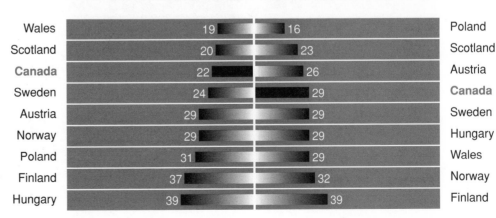

* Percentages based on responses to 'Every day', 'At least once a week, but not every day', 'Less than once a week'. See Table 1 in Appendix C.

3. Parents' smoking habits

Canada, Austria, Belgium and Spain asked students to comment on their parents' smoking habits. Response choices were 'Yes, usually every day', 'Yes, from time to time', 'No, he/she has stopped smoking', 'No, he/she has never smoked' and 'I don't know'. Figure 2.3 gives the percentage of boys and girls who say that their father smokes either 'every day' or 'from time to time'. Figure 2.4 gives the same information for the respondents' mothers. These questions were not asked of 11-year-old Canadian students; thus, we present the data for ages 13 and 15 only. Tables 2 and 3 in Appendix C give complete response data.

Canadian students indicate that fewer of their fathers smoke than do students in the other three countries. In Spain, Belgium and Austria about one half of the fathers smoke. The picture is quite different for mothers. For the most part, according to our respondents, fewer Spanish mothers smoke than in the other countries. Roughly one third of the mothers in Belgium and Canada smoke; slightly more smoke in Austria.

An analysis was conducted to determine if students who indicate that their father or mother smokes every day are more likely to smoke. Tables 2.2 and 2.3 show that for both boys and girls more of the students who smoke indicate their parents smoke daily than do the students who do not smoke. This is especially noticeable for both 13- and 15-year-old Canadian girls and for 15-year-olds of both genders in Austria.

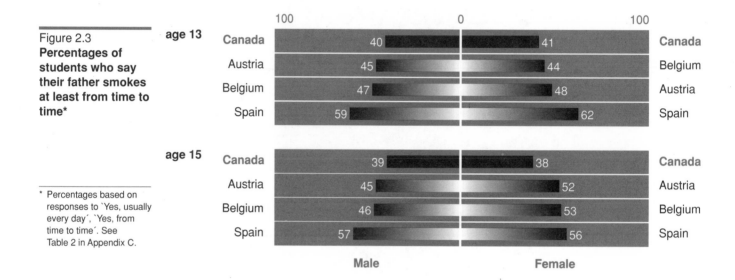

Figure 2.3
Percentages of students who say their father smokes at least from time to time*

* Percentages based on responses to `Yes, usually every day´, `Yes, from time to time´. See Table 2 in Appendix C.

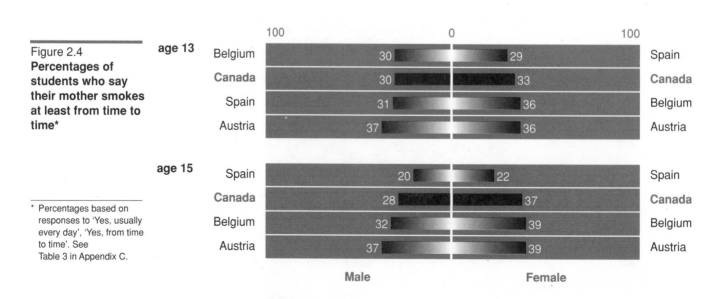

Figure 2.4
Percentages of students who say their mother smokes at least from time to time*

* Percentages based on responses to 'Yes, usually every day', 'Yes, from time to time'. See Table 3 in Appendix C.

C. Alcohol consumption

From earlier studies it can easily be seen that the laws governing the use of alcohol are not being observed. Representatives of the WHO Health Behaviour in School-age Children committee acknowledge that this is the situation in several countries. According to the Traffic Injury Research Foundation 59% of fatally injured drivers in Canada in 1985 had a blood-alcohol level over .15% (Health and Welfare Canada, 1989a, p. 23). A 1986 Gallup Poll indicated that 4% of 12- to 14-year-olds and 22% of those 15 to 17 used alcohol weekly or more often (Health and Welfare Canada, 1989a, p. 15). For these reasons it is important to monitor the use of alcohol among our youth continually and to establish educational strategies to deal with the problem.

1. Alcohol use

It is interesting to note some of the national differences in drinking patterns across countries. In a survey of 32 industrialized countries, which included all of the countries in this survey, Canada placed 21st in terms of alcohol sales in litres per person age 15 and over (Health and Welfare Canada, 1989a, p. 5). Spain, Hungary, Austria and Belgium were higher (6th, 7th, 9th and 12th respectively) and the remaining six countries were lower. Between 1978 and 1985 there was some indication of a shift toward more moderate drinking habits among Canadians; this trend seems to be continuing.

Alcohol is readily available and youth are attracted to its use through advertising and peer pressure. Questions regarding alcohol use were included on the surveys of all countries. Students were asked to respond 'yes', 'no' or 'I don't know' if they had ever tasted an alcoholic beverage. For the item asking them to indicate how often they drink beer, wine and liquor, the liquor category was described differently in some countries, for example, as 'spirits', or it was divided into two categories, 'cider' and a specific liquor, such as 'vodka'. All countries also asked students if they had ever had enough to drink to become really drunk. This item was asked in a comparable manner across countries.

2. Prevalence of experimentation

In Figure 2.5, we see that by age 11, three quarters of Canadian boys and 70% of the girls have tasted alcohol. By age 15, these figures both rise to 94%, obviously leaving a very small minority of youth who have either never tasted alcohol or don't know if they have. More students in each age group in Wales and Scotland have tasted alcohol than in all the other countries, and fewer in Norway. By age 15 the number rises substantially for both genders.

Table 2.2
Proportion of students who smoke and don't smoke whose father smokes every day

Country	Student smokes/ does not smoke	Age 13		Age 15	
		M	F	M	F
Austria	Yes	18	14	43	35
	No	8	6	24	21
Belgium	Yes	15	10	20	29
	No	10	6	20	18
Canada	Yes	21	28	28	35
	No	11	16	20	25
Spain	Yes	22	15	26	37
	No	14	8	27	33

Table 2.3
Proportion of students who smoke and don't smoke whose mother smokes every day

Country	Student smokes/ does not smoke	Age 13		Age 15	
		M	F	M	F
Austria	Yes	16	14	41	41
	No	10	7	26	21
Belgium	Yes	17	12	20	37
	No	11	6	20	17
Canada	Yes	22	29	29	40
	No	11	17	20	25
Spain	Yes	24	10	21	37
	No	17	11	28	34

3. Prevalence of current use

Students were asked how often they drink various types of alcohol — beer, wine, liquor and, in several countries, cider. The response choices were 'every day', 'every week', 'every month', 'less than once a month (seldom)' or 'never'. For each country that included this item the different types of alcohol were combined to determine the extent to which respondents drink any alcohol. Figure 2.6 indicates the percentages of students who drink some type of alcoholic beverage at least

every week. The proportions are relatively small for students at age 11, but increase substantially by age 15 when almost half of the boys in Wales are drinking regularly. About one quarter of the 15-year-old girls in Canada, Belgium, Scotland and Spain also drink regularly, but this figure rises to 35% for girls in Wales. These results indicate that in Canada, and in other countries, drinking habits are being established at quite early ages, far below the legal age limit.

To examine the responses indicating the prevalence of use of beer, wine and liquor see Tables 5, 6 and 7 in Appendix C. More boys tend to drink beer than any other type of alcohol. Hungarian boys are an exception; almost all drink wine to some extent. For the most part more girls drink wine. More 13-year-old Finnish and Swedish girls drink beer and more 13-year-old Austrian and Canadian girls drink liquor. At age 15 more Canadian and Swedish girls drink beer and more Finnish girls drink liquor.

Figure 2.5
Percentages of students who have tasted alcohol*

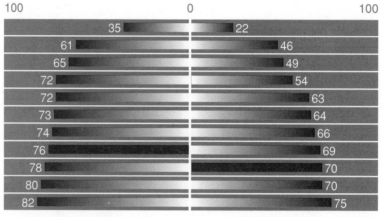
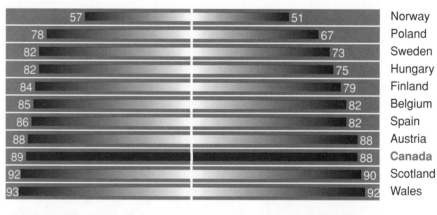

* See Table 4 in Appendix C.

Male   Female

Figure 2.7 shows how many respondents indicated they have been drunk at least once. The figures are quite high. The Canadian figures are particularly high for 15-year-old students, three fifths of whom admit to having been drunk at least once. This places Canadian girls near the top of the range, and the boys near the median, on this item.

A certain segment of Canadian youth appears to be adopting drinking habits that can lead, if intensified, to poor health and problem behaviour. The number of students who drink alcohol regularly is relatively low, but when compared with young people in other countries Canadian youth rank near the top in their consumption of beer and liquor. However, the implication from the figures on drunkenness is that many youth are experimenting with alcohol, at least on some occasions, to the extent that they overindulge and become drunk.

4. Trends in the consumption of alcohol by Canadian youth

Several Canadian studies, including CHABS and CYAS, have explored the use of alcohol by Canadian youth; however, it is difficult to determine any trends between the former studies and this study because results have been presented by different age groups and for total population rather than gender. The best sources, at this time, for comparative data are the Addiction Research Foundation studies that have been conducted every two years since 1979 with

Figure 2.6
Percentages of students who drink alcoholic beverages at least every week*

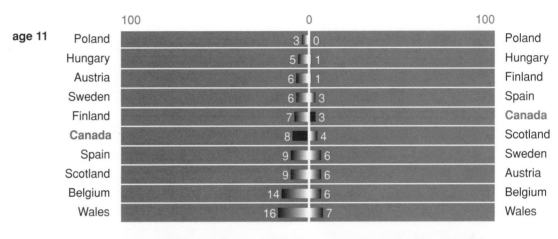

age 11

	Male	Female	
Poland	3	0	Poland
Hungary	5	1	Hungary
Austria	6	1	Finland
Sweden	6	3	Spain
Finland	7	3	Canada
Canada	8	4	Scotland
Spain	9	6	Sweden
Scotland	9	6	Austria
Belgium	14	6	Belgium
Wales	16	7	Wales

age 13

	Male	Female	
Poland	5	1	Poland
Hungary	6	2	Hungary
Finland	9	7	Sweden
Spain	14	7	Spain
Canada	14	7	Austria
Sweden	17	8	Finland
Austria	17	11	Canada
Scotland	17	13	Belgium
Belgium	18	15	Scotland
Wales	20	16	Wales

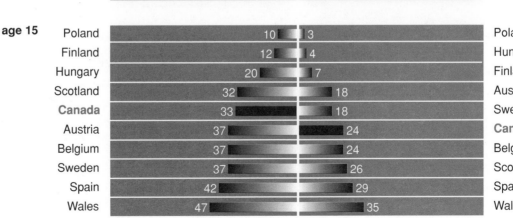

age 15

	Male	Female	
Poland	10	3	Poland
Finland	12	4	Hungary
Hungary	20	7	Finland
Scotland	32	18	Austria
Canada	33	18	Sweden
Austria	37	24	Canada
Belgium	37	24	Belgium
Sweden	37	26	Scotland
Spain	42	29	Spain
Wales	47	35	Wales

Male   **Female**

* Percentages based on responses to 'Every day', 'Every week'. See Table 8 in Appendix C.

Ontario students. Figures from the 1991 report indicate that the number of youth using alcohol has steadily decreased. In 1979, 77% said they used alcohol; by 1989 this figure had fallen to 66% and by 1991, to 39% (Smart et al., 1991).

5. Parents' alcohol use

In Canada, Austria, Hungary and Spain students were asked if their parents drink alcohol. The response choices were 'Yes, every day', 'Yes, from time to time', 'No, he/she stopped drinking alcohol', 'No, he/she never drank alcohol' and 'I don't know'. Canada asked only those aged 13 and 15; therefore, the figures include data for those age groups only. (See Tables 10 and 11 in Appendix C for full details.) In Figures 2.8 and 2.9 we show the responses, by gender, of those who say their father and mother drink alcohol. Obviously, large proportions of adults drink alcohol at least from time to time. Three quarters of the Canadian students indicate their father drinks compared with close to 90% of the students in Austria and Hungary. Fewer students, especially in Spain, say their mothers drink.

Figure 2.7
Percentages of students who say they have been drunk at least once*

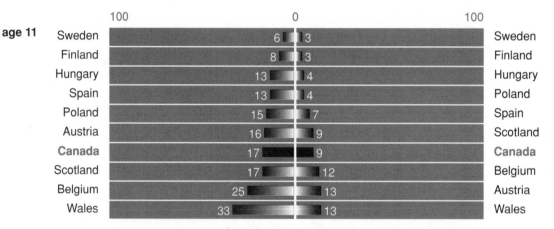

age 11

Male		Female	
Sweden	6	3	Sweden
Finland	8	3	Finland
Hungary	13	4	Hungary
Spain	13	4	Poland
Poland	15	7	Spain
Austria	16	9	Scotland
Canada	17	9	**Canada**
Scotland	17	12	Belgium
Belgium	25	13	Austria
Wales	33	13	Wales

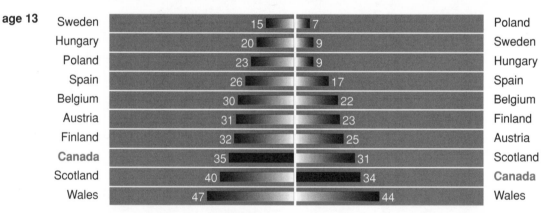

age 13

Male		Female	
Sweden	15	7	Poland
Hungary	20	9	Sweden
Poland	23	9	Hungary
Spain	26	17	Spain
Belgium	30	22	Belgium
Austria	31	23	Finland
Finland	32	25	Austria
Canada	35	31	Scotland
Scotland	40	34	**Canada**
Wales	47	44	Wales

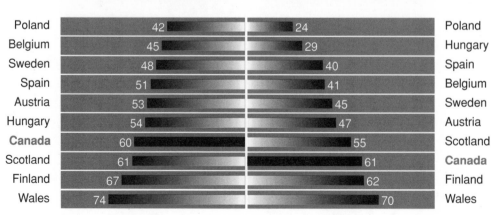

age 15

Male		Female	
Poland	42	24	Poland
Belgium	45	29	Hungary
Sweden	48	40	Spain
Spain	51	41	Belgium
Austria	53	45	Sweden
Hungary	54	47	Austria
Canada	60	55	Scotland
Scotland	61	61	**Canada**
Finland	67	62	Finland
Wales	74	70	Wales

Male **Female**

* Percentages based on responses to 'Once', '2-3 times', '4-10 times', 'More than 10 times'. See Table 9 in Appendix C.

14

To determine if there is a relationship between the drinking habits of parents and children we compiled the data in Table 2.4.

Although in a few cases the difference is slight, in every country more of the students who drink at least every week indicate that their father drinks every day. Fifteen-year-old girls in Spain appear to be the exception. By age 15, the difference in most cases is more substantial, which seems to verify that students are more likely to drink if their parents do. The same analysis for mothers indicates the same pattern, but because the number of students who drink at least weekly and say that their mothers drink daily is very small, the figures could be easily misinterpreted.

D. Other drug use

Data about the use of illegal substances are discussed only for Canadian youth. Because habitual drug use can lead to criminal acts and the long-term effects of drug use are known to have a devastating effect on good health, it is important to develop a profile of young people who are using drugs to any extent. Use of drugs that fall under the "legal" label and are used specifically for the treatment of an illness are discussed in Chapter 5. Since students were asked to respond to the question, "How often have you taken any of the following drugs?" by responding 'three times or more', 'once or twice' or 'never', we can only determine whether or not they have ever experimented with drug use; we cannot describe any aspect of current use.

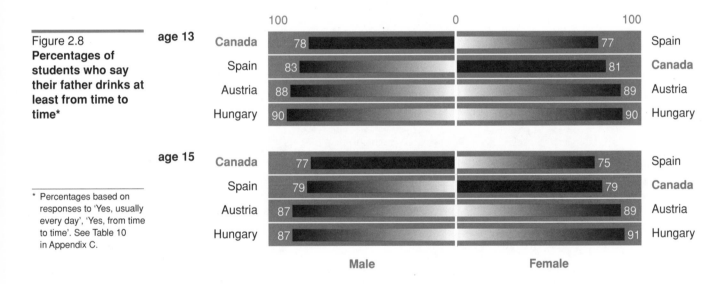

Figure 2.8
Percentages of students who say their father drinks at least from time to time*

* Percentages based on responses to 'Yes, usually every day', 'Yes, from time to time'. See Table 10 in Appendix C.

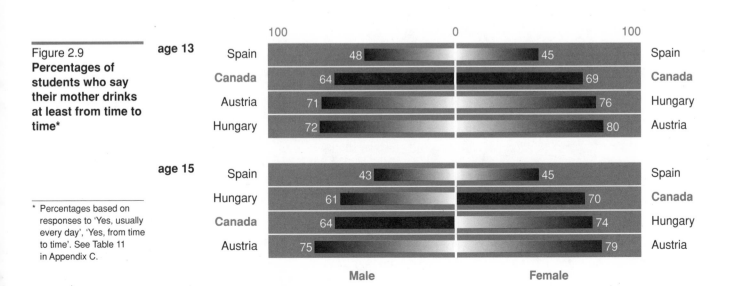

Figure 2.9
Percentages of students who say their mother drinks at least from time to time*

* Percentages based on responses to 'Yes, usually every day', 'Yes, from time to time'. See Table 11 in Appendix C.

The Canadian survey included drug items for the 13- and 15-year-olds. Students were asked to respond to a list of substances which included hashish/marijuana, solvents, cocaine, heroin, amphetamines, LSD (lysergic acid diethylamide) and medical drugs for the purpose of getting "stoned". As seen in Figure 2.10, one quarter of the Canadian 15-year-olds say they have used marijuana at least once. For the remaining items the percentages that indicate any use at all are very small, ranging between 2% and 10%. For the most part more boys are trying these substances than girls.

Table 2.4
Proportions of students who drink at least every week and those who don't, whose father drinks daily

Country	Student drinks/ does not drink	Age 13		Age 15	
		M	F	M	F
Austria	Yes	26	16	45	25
	No	15	6	35	16
Belgium	Yes	22	17	55	36
	No	21	16	39	26
Canada	Yes	26	15	36	36
	No	13	11	32	21
Hungary	Yes	10	3	31	6
	No	5	2	18	4
Spain	Yes	24	10	49	29
	No	11	7	42	32

Figure 2.10
Percentages of Canadian students who have used illegal substances at least once, by gender*

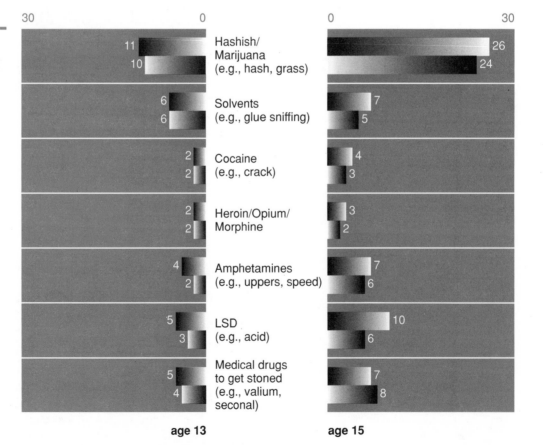

age 13   age 15

■ Male
■ Female

E. Summary

Some Canadian youth are pursuing various habits detrimental to their health. A quarter or more of our 15-year-olds are smoking somewhat regularly which, while better than in many countries, indicates that more effective programs need to be designed to address this situation. Those designing such preventive programs should be aware that more teenage girls than boys are smoking.

The proportions of young people who drink at least once a week is very high in several countries, including Canada. If the incidence of drinking were to continue to increase from age 15 into the late teens at the same rate as it does from age 11 to 15, a very large percentage of Canada's youth would be drinking regularly by that time. The economic effects of excessive drinking and the adverse social, physical and psychological effects to individuals of excessive drinking could be of great concern.

The extent of drug use is difficult to assess from these data. The sample included only youth in school. The findings do indicate that drug use does not appear to be as large a problem in the schools as media sources indicate. Our information, which corresponds with other national findings, indicates that very small percentages of youth attending school use drugs other than marijuana.

Chapter 3

Exercise and Leisure-time Activities

A. Introduction

In 1973 in Canada, Participaction began a physical activity promotion program prompted by the then much-quoted statement that the average 60-year-old Swede was in better condition than the average 25-year-old Canadian. Physical fitness, through Participaction, the Department of National Health and Welfare, and the Ministry of State for Fitness and Amateur Sport has since been strongly promoted in Canada. In a report entitled *Because They're Young: Active Living for Canadian Children and Youth*, Fitness Canada described "regular participation" as:

- Regular participation in physical activity for children and youth refers to daily involvement of at least 30 minutes in one or more sessions. Participation may be either structured or "playful", and participation goals may range from the subjective pursuit of joy and pleasure through movement to such objective and focused outcomes as skill acquisition, physical fitness, or the satisfaction of psycho-social and bio-physical needs. (Government of Canada, 1989, p. 33)

People who exercise and take part in physical activity throughout their lives enjoy better physical and mental health. Also, for the most part, those who become motivated through extensive participation in their teens are more likely to include exercise in their schedule as they age. Most people exercise less as they mature. Educators need to be aware of the point at which youth turn away from regular exercise so that interventions can be implemented to encourage continued participation.

The Canadian questionnaire, along with those of several other countries, emphasized physical exercise, sports and leisure-time activities by including many items related to these topics. The questionnaires were not administered at the same time in each country, which may have slightly affected responses to questions about physical activity. In this chapter we discuss exercise and sport separately from leisure-time activities.

The degree to which students participate in exercise and sport, the amount of time they spend on them, the encouragement they receive and from whom, the participation rate of those close to them, why they enjoy participating in physical activities and their attitude toward physical education classes are the topics covered. Several of these issues were not included in the survey of every country.

Youth participate in a wide variety of activities in their spare time, such as volunteer work, part-time jobs, music and other lessons, and club and other organization activities. However, in this report we only examine leisure-time activities in terms of television and video viewing, and video and computer games. This comparison shows the contrast between the time respondents spend being physically active and following more sedentary pursuits.

B. Exercise

In most of the countries studied, physical education is a required component of the school program (see discussion of countries in Appendix D). To determine how much voluntary physical activity young people are involved in respondents were asked how often and how long they exercise out of school. The following section deals with the number of times and the amount of time per week the students exercise.

1. Number of times students exercise per week

Students were asked how often per week they exercise outside school hours to the point they get out of breath or sweat. All questionnaires of the participating countries included this question. Figure 3.1 shows the percentage of students who exercise outside school hours four or more times a week: more Canadian and Austrian students exercise to this extent than those in other countries. There are substantial differences between countries. One constant across most of the countries is the decrease in participation by age 15, especially for girls. Sweden and Norway are exceptions; their numbers either remain relatively stable or increase slightly. Figure 3.2 shows the other side of the coin: the proportions of students who exercise once a week or less. It is easy to see that the percentages, with few exceptions, increase with age. Fewer boys than girls tend to be inactive. In many of the countries, students who decrease the time spent exercising from four or more times per week tend to exercise two or three times per week rather than eliminate exercise altogether (see Table 13 in Appendix C.)

2. Hours of exercise per week
When we compare Figure 3.3 to Figure 3.1 we note that exercising four or more times per week does not necessarily translate into four or more hours per week of exercise. Austrian youth were more likely than their peers in other countries to exercise four or more hours per week. It is interesting to note that, in almost all countries, by the time students reach age 15 the percentage that exercise four or more times per week drops, but

the proportion that exercise four or more hours per week either increases or is similar to the other two age groups. By age 15 students may be becoming more aware of the benefits of exercise, as well as enjoying the social aspects of sports and physical activity.

Figure 3.1
Percentages of students who exercise at least four times a week out of school*

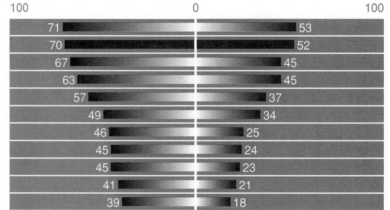
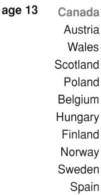
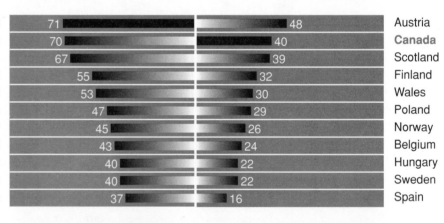
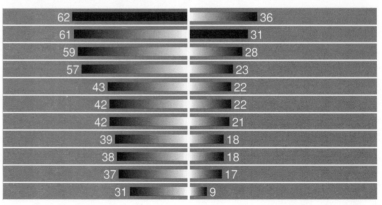

* Percentages are based on responses to 'Every day', '4-6 times per week'. See Table 13 in Appendix C.

age 11

	Male		Female	
Austria	71		53	Austria
Canada	70		52	Canada
Wales	67		45	Wales
Poland	63		45	Poland
Scotland	57		37	Scotland
Finland	49		34	Finland
Spain	46		25	Belgium
Belgium	45		24	Norway
Hungary	45		23	Hungary
Sweden	41		21	Sweden
Norway	39		18	Spain

age 13

	Male		Female	
Canada	71		48	Austria
Austria	70		40	Canada
Wales	67		39	Scotland
Scotland	55		32	Finland
Poland	53		30	Wales
Belgium	47		29	Poland
Hungary	45		26	Norway
Finland	43		24	Belgium
Norway	40		22	Hungary
Sweden	40		22	Sweden
Spain	37		16	Spain

age 15

	Male		Female	
Canada	62		36	Austria
Wales	61		31	Canada
Austria	59		28	Norway
Scotland	57		23	Finland
Belgium	43		22	Wales
Norway	42		22	Scotland
Poland	42		21	Sweden
Hungary	39		18	Belgium
Sweden	38		18	Poland
Finland	37		17	Hungary
Spain	31		9	Spain

Four hours of exercise per week does, however, exceed the minimum recommended by Fitness Canada, as noted at the beginning of this chapter. Therefore, it is useful to look at those who exercise a minimum of two hours per week. In Table 14 in Appendix C, we see that over 80% of Austrian boys of all ages and of 13- and 15-year-old Hungarian boys exercise at least two hours a week. Boys in the remaining countries are not as dedicated with roughly 60% doing so. In Canada

and Belgium, boys increase their involvement in exercise as they get older and by age 15 three quarters of them are exercising at least two hours per week. The number of girls who exercise regularly is substantially lower than for boys and is a cause for concern. The highest proportions are in Austria —between 67% and 77%, but in very few countries, including Canada, do more than half of the girls find at least two hours a week for exercise.

3. Participation in sports clubs

Students in four countries (Canada, Finland, Poland and Wales) were asked if they were members of a community sports club and, in three of these countries (Wales excluded), if they belonged to a school sports team this school year. Figures 3.4 and 3.5 give the percentages of those who said 'yes'. There is a substantial difference between the countries in the percentages of students who take part in community sports

Figure 3.2
Percentages of students who exercise once a week or less*

☐ Age 11
▦ Age 13
■ Age 15

* Percentages based on responses to 'Once a week', 'Once a month', 'Less than once a month', 'Never'. See Table 13 in Appendix C.

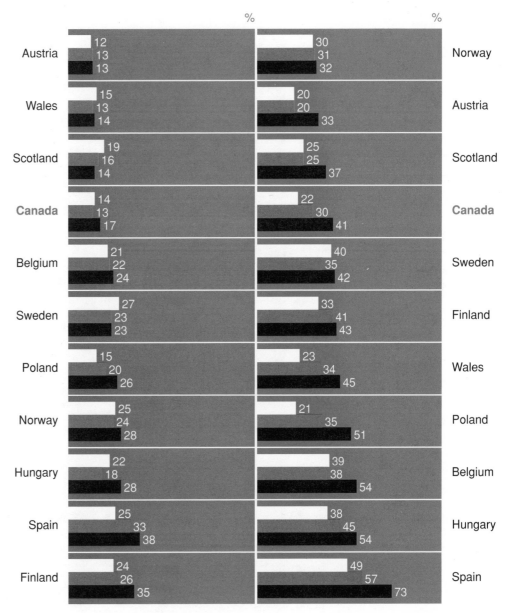

	Male		Female	
Austria	12 / 13 / 13		Norway	30 / 31 / 32
Wales	15 / 13 / 14		Austria	20 / 20 / 33
Scotland	19 / 16 / 14		Scotland	25 / 25 / 37
Canada	14 / 13 / 17		Canada	22 / 30 / 41
Belgium	21 / 22 / 24		Sweden	40 / 35 / 42
Sweden	27 / 23 / 23		Finland	33 / 41 / 43
Poland	15 / 20 / 26		Wales	23 / 34 / 45
Norway	25 / 24 / 28		Poland	21 / 35 / 51
Hungary	22 / 18 / 28		Belgium	39 / 38 / 54
Spain	25 / 33 / 38		Hungary	38 / 45 / 54
Finland	24 / 26 / 35		Spain	49 / 57 / 73

activities (Figure 3.4). More Canadian boys participate at all ages than their counterparts in the other countries. The data for girls tend to reflect the more limited opportunities, at least in Canada, for girls to be a part of a community team. Half of the 11-year-old Canadian girls belong to a community team, but by age 15 this has declined to 30%. Very few Polish girls at any age are involved in this way.

In Figure 3.5 we see that far more Canadian youth participate in school sports teams. There is a substantial drop for both genders between ages 13 and 15. Very few Finnish youth take part in school sports teams, especially at ages 13 and 15.

4. Encouragement from others to participate
Students were asked if others encourage them to take part in sport or physical activities. These 'others' are defined as mother, father, older brother, older sister, best friend and teacher.

Almost three quarters or more of Canadian youth say their fathers and mothers encourage them at least sometimes to participate in sport or other physical activities (Tables 15 and 16 in Appendix C). The exception is for 15-year-old girls, only 62% of whom indicate that their fathers at least sometimes encourage them. Figures 3.6 and 3.7 indicate to what degree students in Canada, Finland and Poland say their parents encourage them 'often'. More Canadian students say their parents do so, but the numbers are not high and decrease with age.

Figure 3.3
Percentages of students who exercise four or more hours a week out of school*

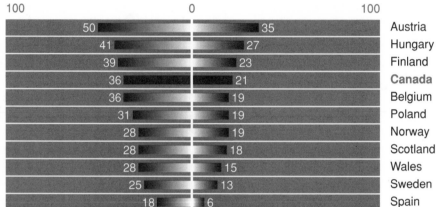

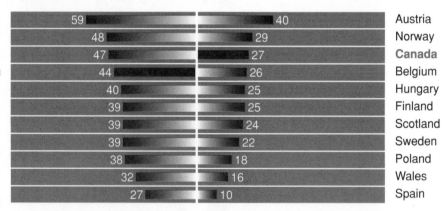

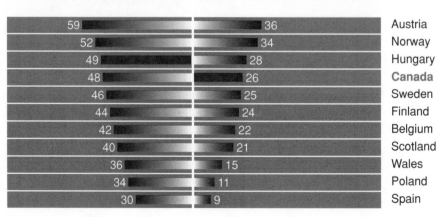

* Percentages are based on responses to 'About 4-6 hours', '7 hours or more'. See Table 14 in Appendix C.

Male   Female

5. Participation by others close to them

Students in five countries were asked if people close to them (i.e., father, mother, older brother, older sister, best friend and teacher) take part in sports or other physical activities. The response choices were 'every week', 'occasionally', 'not at all', 'don't know' and 'don't have such a person'. The purpose of this question was to provide some indication of the influence of others on the physical activity of the respondents. Consistently, for both age and gender more students in Finland than anywhere else indicate that both parents participate in exercise or sports every week (Figures 3.8 and 3.9). At the other end of the scale few Polish or Spanish students say that their parents participate. On this issue Canadian parents do not fare very well, with one quarter or fewer of the respondents reporting that their fathers exercise every week and even fewer saying their mothers exercise regularly.

Other than parents, the person who probably influences a young person more than anyone else is his or her best friend. Figure 3.10 shows that almost half or more of the boys in each country who responded to this question see their best friend as being very active physically and participating in sport or physical activity weekly. Fewer girls express this view, except in Finland where the percentages are similar to those of the boys.

Figure 3.4
Percentages of students who are members of a community sports club

■ Male
■ Female

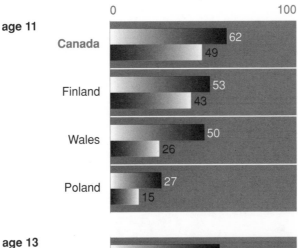

age 11

Canada	Male: 62	Female: 49
Finland	Male: 53	Female: 43
Wales	Male: 50	Female: 26
Poland	Male: 27	Female: 15

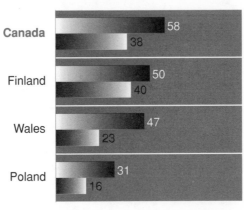

age 13

Canada	Male: 58	Female: 38
Finland	Male: 50	Female: 40
Wales	Male: 47	Female: 23
Poland	Male: 31	Female: 16

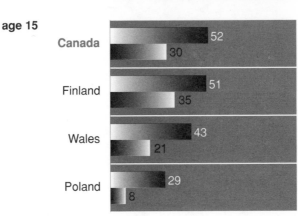

age 15

Canada	Male: 52	Female: 30
Finland	Male: 51	Female: 35
Wales	Male: 43	Female: 21
Poland	Male: 29	Female: 8

6. Expectations regarding exercising at age 20

As we see in Figure 3.11 students in Belgium are the most positive that they will be physically active at age 20, but Canadian students are close behind with three fifths of Canadian boys and two fifths of the girls intending to remain active at age 20. Boys and girls in Poland were less sure about their future participation.

7. Perceptions of fitness

In four countries (Canada, Finland, Poland and Wales) students were asked to give their perception of their fitness level. In Figure 3.12 we see that Canadian boys lead the way, with more saying they are 'very fit' than their peers in other countries. Canadian girls also express more confidence about this aspect of their life than their peers, even though fewer girls than boys in

Canada feel they are 'very fit'. Considering that Canadian students are in the top ranges of those who exercise four or more hours a week, it makes sense that Canadian youth should consider themselves 'fit' or 'very fit'.

Figure 3.5
Percentages of students who are members of a school sports team

Male
Female

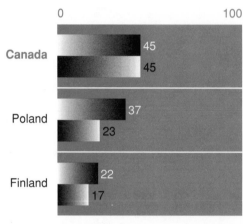

age 11

0   100

Canada 45 / 45

Poland 37 / 23

Finland 22 / 17

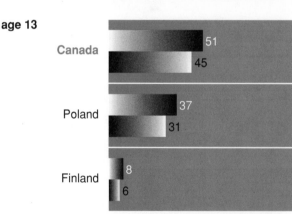

age 13

Canada 51 / 45

Poland 37 / 31

Finland 8 / 6

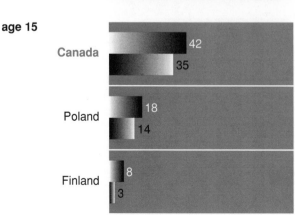

age 15

Canada 42 / 35

Poland 18 / 14

Finland 8 / 3

Figure 3.6
Percentages of students whose father often encourages them to take part in physical activities in their spare time*

* See Table 15 in Appendix C.

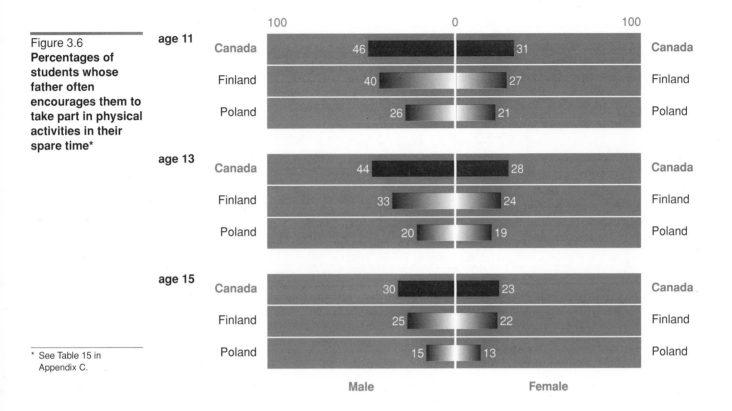

Figure 3.7
Percentages of students whose mother often encourages them to take part in physical activities in their spare time*

* See Table 16 in Appendix C.

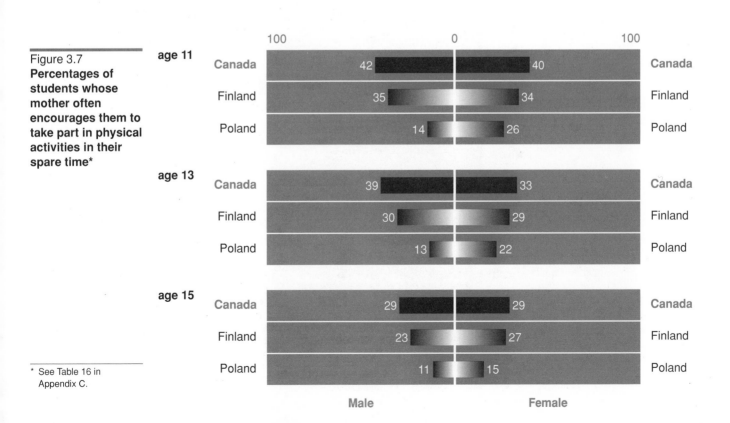

8. Attitude toward physical education classes

In five countries students were asked what they thought of their physical education classes at school. Although the figures for boys are generally high except for 13- and 15-year-olds in Spain, Figure 3.13 shows that, on the whole, fewer Canadian boys enjoy these classes than boys in the other study countries. By ages 13 and 15 fewer girls than boys in each country like physical education classes. Only in Poland do substantial numbers of both genders appear to enjoy classes.

9. Reasons for participating in physical activity

Only questionnaires in Canada and Poland included a question that listed several reasons for liking physical activity and asked students to indicate the importance of each reason. For Canadian youth the three most important reasons are 'to have fun', 'to improve my health' and 'to get in good shape'. Polish students concur with 'to improve my health' and 'to get in good shape', but

their third highest choice is 'to enjoy the feeling of using my body' (see Table 24 in Appendix C).

C. Leisure-time activities

Leisure-time activities include the out-of-school sports and exercise described earlier as well as the many other pursuits in which students are involved. In this section we examine pastimes, such as watching television, watching movies on video cassette recorders (VCRs) and playing computer games, which are far more sedentary and solitary. The questionnaires explored these topics to discover how much of students' leisure time is consumed by these activities.

1. Watching television

Watching television is obviously a popular pastime in all countries. Very few students say they never watch television (see Table 25 in Appendix C). There is, however, substantial diversity in the countries of those who watch two or more hours per day, as shown in Figure 3.14.

This ranges from as low as 36% of 11-year old girls in Norway to 87% of 11-year-old boys and 13-year-old boys and girls in Hungary. Overall, students in Hungary, Poland and Wales tend to watch television more than those in other countries and students in Norway the least. Canadians tend to fall in the middle.

Canadian girls at all three age levels spend less time watching television than Canadian boys. Although similar proportions of Canadian boys and girls watch television two to three hours a day, fewer girls than boys at all age levels watch more than four hours daily. In Canada, 15-year-olds of both sexes watch television less than do 11- and 13-year-olds.

2. Watching movies on a VCR

If watching two VCR movies a week is considered close to four hours of viewing time, VCR movie watching is not a major leisure time activity (see Figure 3.15). The percentages of students who spend four hours or more per week watching VCR

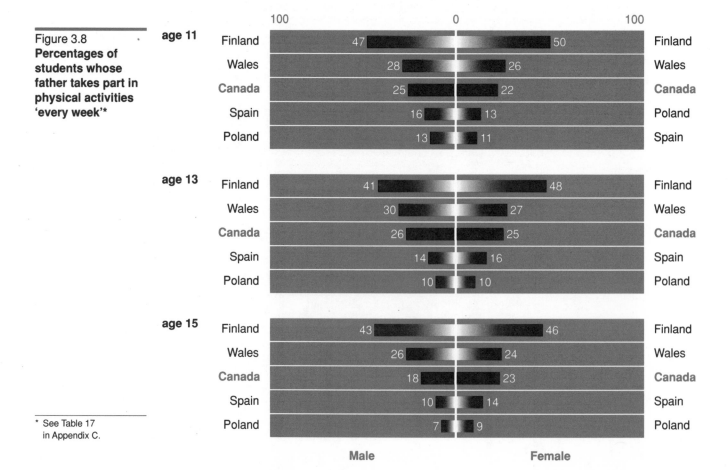

Figure 3.8
Percentages of students whose father takes part in physical activities 'every week'*

	100	0	100	
age 11				
Finland	47	50		Finland
Wales	28	26		Wales
Canada	25	22		Canada
Spain	16	13		Poland
Poland	13	11		Spain
age 13				
Finland	41	48		Finland
Wales	30	27		Wales
Canada	26	25		Canada
Spain	14	16		Spain
Poland	10	10		Poland
age 15				
Finland	43	46		Finland
Wales	26	24		Wales
Canada	18	23		Canada
Spain	10	14		Spain
Poland	7	9		Poland

Male   **Female**

* See Table 17 in Appendix C.

26

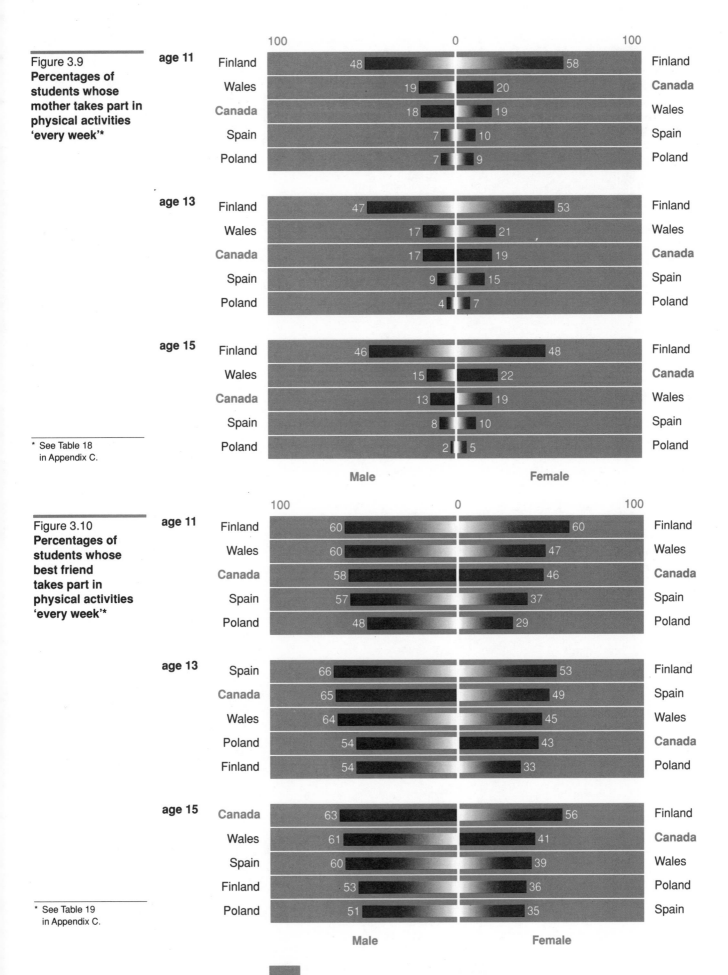

Figure 3.9
Percentages of students whose mother takes part in physical activities 'every week'*

age 11

	Male	Female	
Finland	48	58	Finland
Wales	19	20	Canada
Canada	18	19	Wales
Spain	7	10	Spain
Poland	7	9	Poland

age 13

	Male	Female	
Finland	47	53	Finland
Wales	17	21	Wales
Canada	17	19	Canada
Spain	9	15	Spain
Poland	4	7	Poland

age 15

	Male	Female	
Finland	46	48	Finland
Wales	15	22	Canada
Canada	13	19	Wales
Spain	8	10	Spain
Poland	2	5	Poland

* See Table 18 in Appendix C.

Male   Female

Figure 3.10
Percentages of students whose best friend takes part in physical activities 'every week'*

age 11

	Male	Female	
Finland	60	60	Finland
Wales	60	47	Wales
Canada	58	46	Canada
Spain	57	37	Spain
Poland	48	29	Poland

age 13

	Male	Female	
Spain	66	53	Finland
Canada	65	49	Spain
Wales	64	45	Wales
Poland	54	43	Canada
Finland	54	33	Poland

age 15

	Male	Female	
Canada	63	56	Finland
Wales	61	41	Canada
Spain	60	39	Wales
Finland	53	36	Poland
Poland	51	35	Spain

* See Table 19 in Appendix C.

Male   Female

27

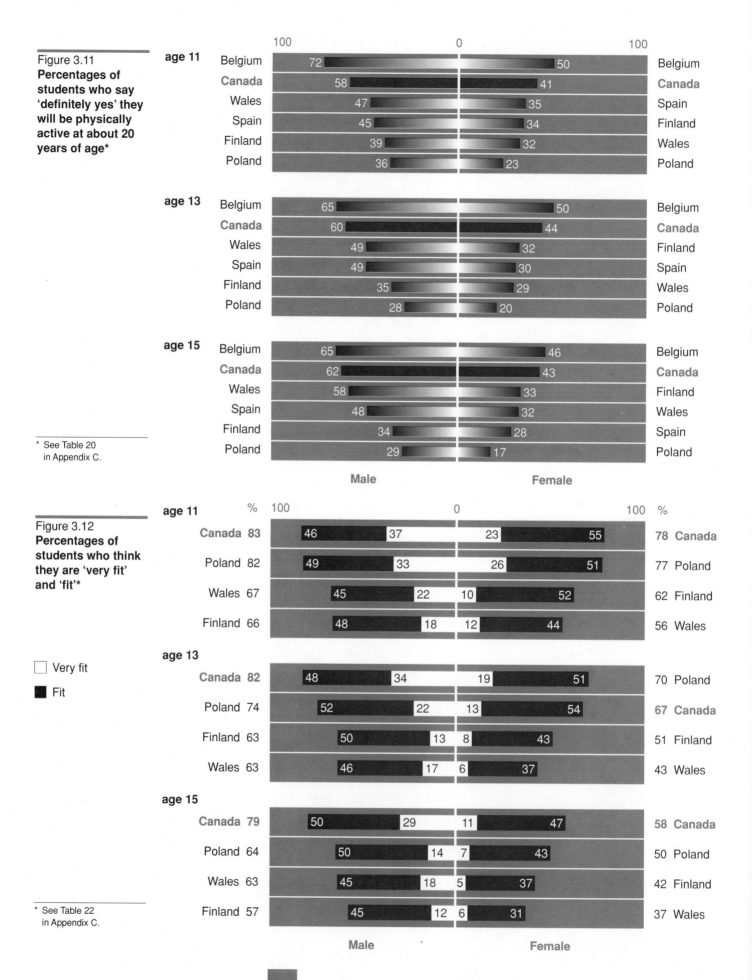

Figure 3.11
Percentages of students who say 'definitely yes' they will be physically active at about 20 years of age*

* See Table 20 in Appendix C.

age 11	Male	Female	
Belgium	72	50	Belgium
Canada	58	41	Canada
Wales	47	35	Spain
Spain	45	34	Finland
Finland	39	32	Wales
Poland	36	23	Poland

age 13	Male	Female	
Belgium	65	50	Belgium
Canada	60	44	Canada
Wales	49	32	Finland
Spain	49	30	Spain
Finland	35	29	Wales
Poland	28	20	Poland

age 15	Male	Female	
Belgium	65	46	Belgium
Canada	62	43	Canada
Wales	58	33	Finland
Spain	48	32	Wales
Finland	34	28	Spain
Poland	29	17	Poland

Male   **Female**

Figure 3.12
Percentages of students who think they are 'very fit' and 'fit'*

☐ Very fit
■ Fit

* See Table 22 in Appendix C.

age 11

	%	Fit	Very fit	Very fit	Fit	%	
Canada	83	46	37	23	55	78	Canada
Poland	82	49	33	26	51	77	Poland
Wales	67	45	22	10	52	62	Finland
Finland	66	48	18	12	44	56	Wales

age 13

	%	Fit	Very fit	Very fit	Fit	%	
Canada	82	48	34	19	51	70	Poland
Poland	74	52	22	13	54	67	Canada
Finland	63	50	13	8	43	51	Finland
Wales	63	46	17	6	37	43	Wales

age 15

	%	Fit	Very fit	Very fit	Fit	%	
Canada	79	50	29	11	47	58	Canada
Poland	64	50	14	7	43	50	Poland
Wales	63	45	18	5	37	42	Finland
Finland	57	45	12	6	31	37	Wales

Male   **Female**

movies range from a low of 6% (11-year-old Austrian girls) to a high of 37% (15-year-old Belgian boys). With few exceptions, less than 20% of all girls and less than 30% of all boys watch videos four or more hours per week. Not as many girls in any country watch VCR movies as much as boys. Canadian students tend to fall within the higher ranges of those who watch VCR movies four or more hours per week.

3. Playing computer games
On average, playing computer games takes up the time of more Canadian and Swedish youth than it does for youth in any of the other countries from which we have data (see Figure 3.16). Far fewer girls than boys play computer games, except in Sweden. On the whole, one quarter or fewer of the boys and 11% or fewer of the girls spend four or more hours per week on this activity. One notable difference can be seen for the 15-year-olds compared with the younger students; by this age far fewer are playing computer games except in Sweden. In Canada, the drop in participation

between the ages of 11 and 15 is 13% for boys and 18% for girls.

D. Summary
Overall, Canadian students appear to be interested and active in sports and physical activity. This applies especially to participation on school teams and out-of-school exercise. Canadian youth believe they are good at sports, are in fit condition and plan to continue participating in sport in the future. If we compare Canadian youth with Swedish youth as a follow-up to the Participaction

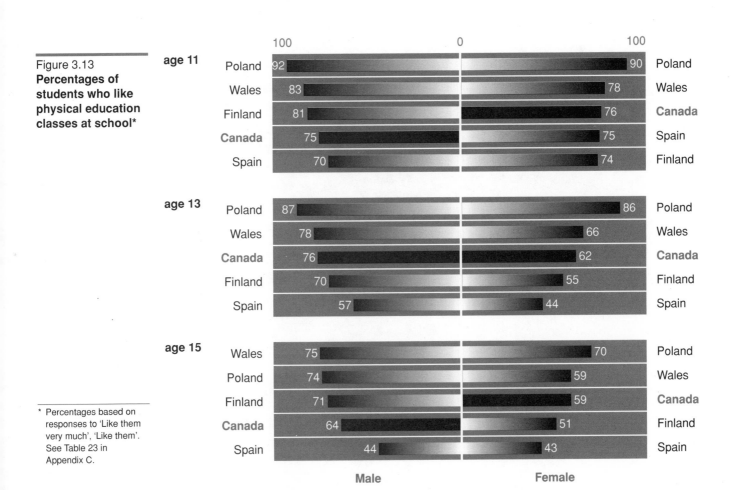

Figure 3.13
Percentages of students who like physical education classes at school*

age 11

	Male		Female	
	Poland	92	90	Poland
	Wales	83	78	Wales
	Finland	81	76	Canada
	Canada	75	75	Spain
	Spain	70	74	Finland

age 13

	Poland	87	86	Poland
	Wales	78	66	Wales
	Canada	76	62	Canada
	Finland	70	55	Finland
	Spain	57	44	Spain

age 15

	Wales	75	70	Poland
	Poland	74	59	Wales
	Finland	71	59	Canada
	Canada	64	51	Finland
	Spain	44	43	Spain

* Percentages based on responses to 'Like them very much', 'Like them'. See Table 23 in Appendix C.

29

statement, our youth fare very well on the items to which both countries responded. In the area of physical and leisure-time activities it looks as though Canadian youth are, to a large extent, maintaining a relatively good balance between active participation in physical exercise and the more sedentary aspects of leisure. Females, however, participate less, consider themselves less fit and are less likely to be physically active at age 20. It would seem that current policies are effective and should continue, but with more emphasis placed on encouraging girls to be physically active throughout their lives.

Figure 3.14
Percentages of students who watch television 2-3 hours and 4 or more hours per day*

☐ 4 or more hours per day

■ 2-3 hours per day

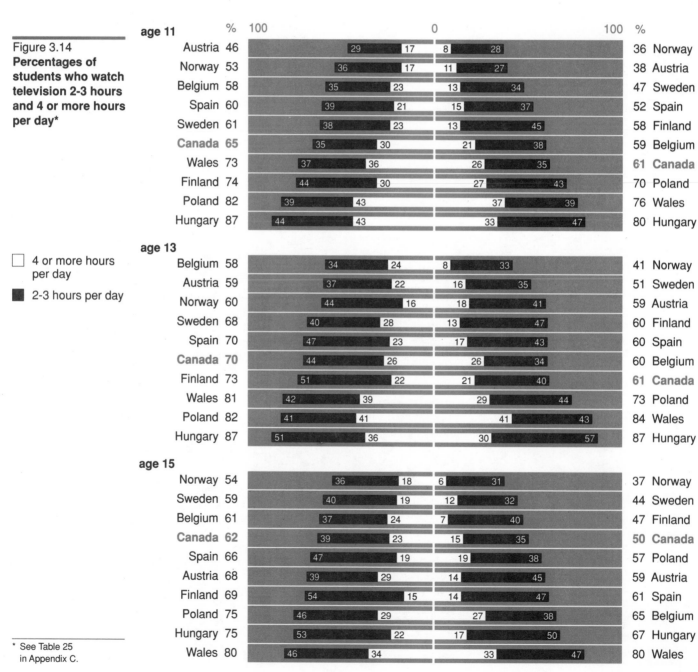

* See Table 25 in Appendix C.

Figure 3.15
Percentages of students who watch VCR movies 1-3 hours and 4 or more hours per week*

Figure 3.15
Percentages of students who watch VCR movies 1-3 hours and 4 or more hours per week*

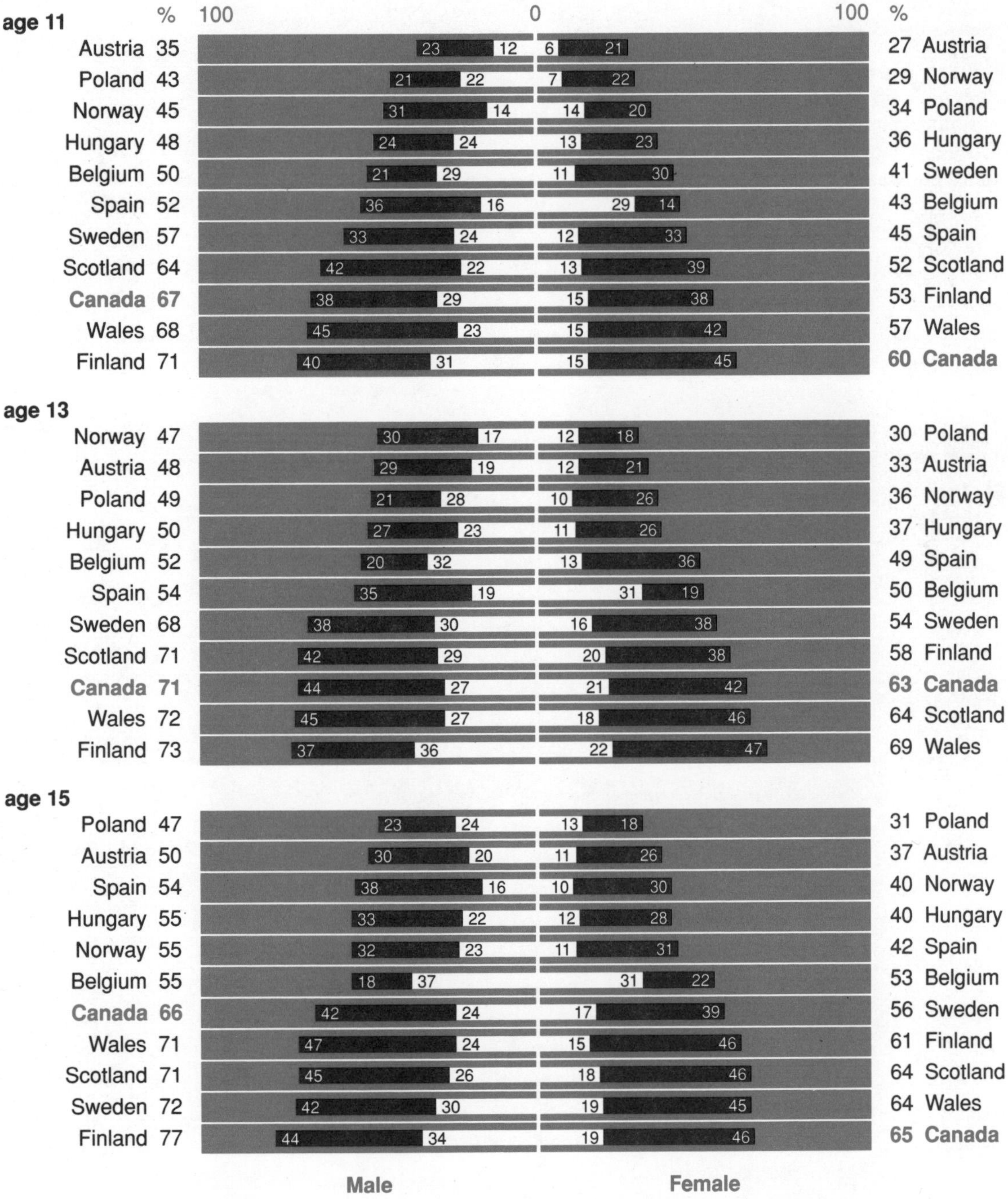

☐ 4 or more hours per week

■ 1-3 hours per week

age 11

		Male		Female		
Austria	35	23	12	6	21	27 Austria
Poland	43	21	22	7	22	29 Norway
Norway	45	31	14	14	20	34 Poland
Hungary	48	24	24	13	23	36 Hungary
Belgium	50	21	29	11	30	41 Sweden
Spain	52	36	16	29	14	43 Belgium
Sweden	57	33	24	12	33	45 Spain
Scotland	64	42	22	13	39	52 Scotland
Canada	**67**	38	29	15	38	53 Finland
Wales	68	45	23	15	42	57 Wales
Finland	71	40	31	15	45	**60 Canada**

age 13

		Male		Female		
Norway	47	30	17	12	18	30 Poland
Austria	48	29	19	12	21	33 Austria
Poland	49	21	28	10	26	36 Norway
Hungary	50	27	23	11	26	37 Hungary
Belgium	52	20	32	13	36	49 Spain
Spain	54	35	19	31	19	50 Belgium
Sweden	68	38	30	16	38	54 Sweden
Scotland	71	42	29	20	38	58 Finland
Canada	**71**	44	27	21	42	**63 Canada**
Wales	72	45	27	18	46	64 Scotland
Finland	73	37	36	22	47	69 Wales

age 15

		Male		Female		
Poland	47	23	24	13	18	31 Poland
Austria	50	30	20	11	26	37 Austria
Spain	54	38	16	10	30	40 Norway
Hungary	55	33	22	12	28	40 Hungary
Norway	55	32	23	11	31	42 Spain
Belgium	55	18	37	31	22	53 Belgium
Canada	**66**	42	24	17	39	56 Sweden
Wales	71	47	24	15	46	61 Finland
Scotland	71	45	26	18	46	64 Scotland
Sweden	72	42	30	19	45	64 Wales
Finland	77	44	34	19	46	**65 Canada**

Male   Female

Figure 3.16
Percentages of students who play computer games 1-3 hours and 4 or more hours per week*

Legend:
- □ 4 or more hours per week
- ■ 1-3 hours per week

* See Table 27 in Appendix C.

age 11

	Male %	1-3	4+		1-3	4+	Female %	
Austria	26	13	13		1	7	8	Austria
Poland	27	13	14		2	7	9	Poland
Spain	31	22	9		2	8	10	Norway
Belgium	33	20	13		2	10	12	Belgium
Hungary	37	24	13		3	10	13	Spain
Norway	38	21	17		5	9	14	Finland
Wales	55	30	25		4	12	16	Hungary
Sweden	57	33	24		5	16	21	Wales
Canada	**57**	26	31		6	16	22	Scotland
Scotland	58	31	27		11	20	**31**	**Canada**
Finland	61	30	31		11	30	41	Sweden

age 13

	Male %	1-3	4+		1-3	4+	Female %	
Poland	25	13	12		1	4	5	Poland
Belgium	32	20	12		1	6	7	Norway
Spain	34	20	14		2	8	10	Spain
Norway	38	18	20		3	7	10	Austria
Austria	40	21	19		3	10	13	Belgium
Hungary	41	28	13		4	9	13	Finland
Wales	48	26	22		2	12	14	Wales
Scotland	50	25	25		4	12	16	Scotland
Finland	54	22	32		5	14	**19**	**Canada**
Canada	**56**	29	27		1	19	20	Hungary
Sweden	68	38	30		16	38	54	Sweden

age 15

	Male %	1-3	4+		1-3	4+	Female %	
Poland	23	14	9			3	3	Norway
Spain	24	15	9			4	4	Finland
Wales	26	16	10		1	4	5	Scotland
Norway	28	14	14		1	5	6	Poland
Hungary	29	19	10		2	4	6	Wales
Finland	29	17	12		1	9	10	Spain
Belgium	31	15	16		3	8	11	Belgium
Scotland	32	15	17		5	8	**13**	**Canada**
Austria	42	20	22		1	13	14	Austria
Canada	**43**	23	20		1	20	21	Hungary
Sweden	71	41	30		17	39	56	Sweden

Male   Female

32

Chapter 4

Nutrition, Diet and Dental Care

A. Introduction

For many years Canadians have used Canada's Food Guide as the basis for sound nutritional practices. In 1990, Health and Welfare Canada released Nutrition Recommendations for Canadians and Canada's Guidelines for Healthy Eating, which appear in *Nutrition Recommendations...A Call for Action* (Health and Welfare Canada, 1990f). Canada's Guidelines for healthy eating state:

- enjoy a variety of food;
- emphasize breads, other grain products, vegetables and fruits;
- choose lower-fat dairy products, leaner meats and foods prepared with little or no fat;
- achieve and maintain a healthy body weight by enjoying regular physical activity and healthy eating; and
- limit salt, alcohol and caffeine.

The same publication indicates that Canadians over the past 10 years have adopted healthier eating patterns and have shown an increased interest in nutrition, diet and health.

Canada's Food Guide is being revised based on the Nutrition Recommendations for Canadians and Canada's Guidelines for Healthy Eating.

About one third of the respondents to the CHABS conducted in 1984-85 were not meeting the 'daily' and 'variety' criteria in Canada's Food Guide (1982) for at least one food group — particularly the fruit and vegetables category. Of the CHABS respondents, 90% or more did meet the requirements for the milk products group and the meat, fish, poultry and alternates group, and 80% or more met the requirements for the breads and cereals groups. When asked, in 1984, if they would choose a snack of candy or chips rather than raw fruit or vegetables one fifth or more replied 'most of the time'. Fibre consumption appeared to be adequate for most students in CHABS, but fat intake was considered high for at least two thirds of the respondents.

To attach meaning to the findings it is necessary to make judgments on the appropriateness of particular foods. The international survey sought information on frequency of use and not quantities consumed, making it difficult to assess quality of diet. However, we have ordered the countries based on whether the foods in question can be generally considered as healthy (e.g., fruit, vegetables, 2% milk, whole wheat breads) or less healthy (candy, soft drinks, fried foods). We can also estimate fibre and fat intake, and note whether there is still a trend toward eating candy and chips instead of more healthy snacks.

Because the items in this survey were not nearly as detailed as those in CHABS the current analysis cannot be compared meaningfully with the former study in terms of the overall dietary habits of Canada's youth. In this survey students responded to a questionnaire item that listed several foods and drinks and they were asked how frequently they eat or drink them. They were not asked about the amounts consumed, the variety of foods they regularly eat within the same food groups, nor was any aspect of a balanced diet addressed.

Students indicated how often they eat the food item listed by choosing one of the following responses: 'more than once a day', 'once a day', 'at least once a week, but not daily', 'seldom' and 'never'. Responses may have been affected slightly because the questionnaires were not administered in every country at the same time of year. The description of some food items varied from one country's questionnaire to another; for example, Canada's students were asked if they eat 'raw vegetables' and some other students simply 'vegetables'. In this case, and in others, the data from countries that defined specific foods differently were omitted from the analysis.

B. Healthy foods

1. Fruit

Canada's Food Guide has recommended for over 50 years that fruit be a major component of the daily diet. Its benefits are found in the vitamin content of many fruits, especially vitamin C in citrus fruit. In addition, most fruit contributes an intake of fibre to the diet. The recommended quantities are two to three servings per day.

In Figure 4.1 there is a wide discrepancy in the percentages of respondents who eat fruit every day, ranging from a low of 41% of 15-year-old Norwegian boys to a high of 90% of 11-year-old Polish girls. It is interesting to note the large proportions of students in several of the countries who eat fruit every day compared with the much lower proportions in Wales, Scotland, Norway and Finland. Canadian youth compare favourably with their peers. However, in all countries, both genders show a decrease in the proportions of students eating fruit every day by the time they are 15, which may reflect students expressing some independence in their eating habits as they get older.

2. Raw vegetables

According to Canada's Food Guide, vegetables should also be eaten every day as they are an excellent source of vitamins A and C, as well as several of the vitamin B components. Eating vegetables also increases fibre intake. A minimum of two to three servings a day should be included in a person's diet.

Canada's questionnaire asked only about raw vegetables. For the most part eating raw vegetables, such as lettuce, carrots, celery, cauliflower, broccoli, green peppers and others is

the best way to absorb the most benefit because some nutrients are lost when the vegetables are cooked. Eating these foods as a snack is highly recommended.

Figure 4.2 shows the percentages of respondents who indicate they eat raw vegetables at least once a day. Generally, fewer than half of the students and slightly more girls than boys eat raw vegetables. Of respondents in the survey

Figure 4.1
Percentages of students who eat fruit once a day or more*

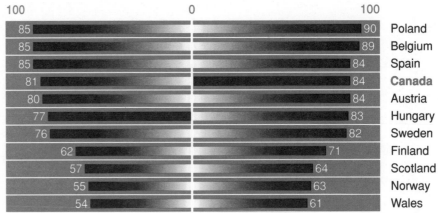
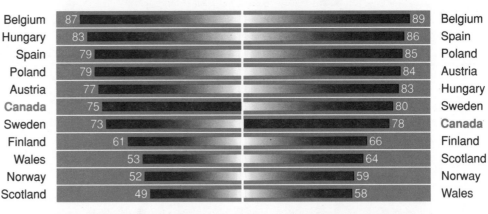
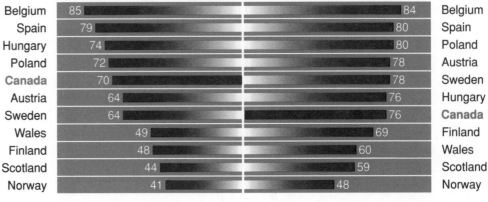

age 11

	Male		Female
Poland	85	90	Poland
Belgium	85	89	Belgium
Spain	85	84	Spain
Sweden	81	84	Canada
Hungary	80	84	Austria
Canada	77	83	Hungary
Austria	76	82	Sweden
Finland	62	71	Finland
Norway	57	64	Scotland
Scotland	55	63	Norway
Wales	54	61	Wales

age 13

	Male		Female
Belgium	87	89	Belgium
Hungary	83	86	Spain
Spain	79	85	Poland
Poland	79	84	Austria
Austria	77	83	Hungary
Canada	75	80	Sweden
Sweden	73	78	Canada
Finland	61	66	Finland
Wales	53	64	Scotland
Norway	52	59	Norway
Scotland	49	58	Wales

age 15

	Male		Female
Belgium	85	84	Belgium
Spain	79	80	Spain
Hungary	74	80	Poland
Poland	72	78	Austria
Canada	70	78	Sweden
Austria	64	76	Hungary
Sweden	64	76	Canada
Wales	49	69	Finland
Finland	48	60	Wales
Scotland	44	59	Scotland
Norway	41	48	Norway

* See Table 28 in Appendix C.

Male　　　**Female**

countries, the highest proportions of both boys and girls in Belgium, Finland, Canada and Austria eat raw vegetables at least daily.

3. Whole wheat and rye breads
The best source of fibre is from whole grain products, such as whole wheat bread and rye bread. Of course, grains also contribute many other essential nutrients, such as riboflavin, niacin, thiamin and iron as well as vitamin E.

Canada's Food Guide recommends three to five servings per day of breads and cereals.

Figure 4.3 shows the numbers of respondents who indicate they eat whole wheat or rye bread daily. Very high proportions of Hungarian students eat whole grain bread every day — 86% to 93% of all age groups. Just under half of the 11-year-old Canadian students indicate they eat whole grain bread daily, but by age 15 this figure

declines to less than two fifths. This may occur because 15-year-olds have more opportunity to choose their own food.

4. Milk and milk products
Traditionally, milk has been the foundation of nutrition; the child is fed his or her mother's milk, then animal's milk is substituted. The benefits of milk and its byproducts are manifold — calcium, vitamins A, C and D (in Canada vitamin D is

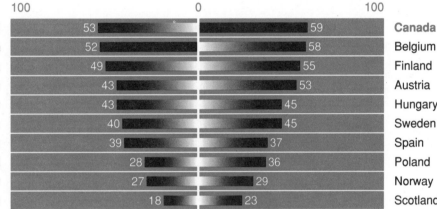

Figure 4.2
Percentages of students who eat raw vegetables once a day or more*

	Male	Female	
age 11			
Finland	53	59	Canada
Canada	52	58	Belgium
Austria	49	55	Finland
Belgium	43	53	Austria
Hungary	43	45	Hungary
Spain	40	45	Sweden
Sweden	39	37	Spain
Poland	28	36	Poland
Norway	27	29	Norway
Scotland	18	23	Scotland
age 13			
Belgium	57	62	Belgium
Finland	49	54	Canada
Canada	48	51	Hungary
Austria	48	50	Austria
Hungary	45	47	Finland
Sweden	37	43	Sweden
Spain	30	34	Spain
Poland	26	34	Poland
Scotland	23	28	Scotland
Norway	23	23	Norway
age 15			
Belgium	66	64	Belgium
Canada	49	55	Finland
Finland	41	52	Canada
Austria	39	43	Austria
Hungary	36	43	Hungary
Sweden	35	42	Sweden
Spain	30	40	Spain
Poland	19	28	Scotland
Norway	17	24	Poland
Scotland	16	20	Norway

* See Table 29 in Appendix C.

35

added to milk by law), riboflavin, niacin and animal protein.

The consumption of milk contributes greatly to the development of teeth and bones and is crucial to the young developing child. It is recommended that children up to age 11 have two to three servings per day and adolescents three to four servings. One serving of a milk product may be 250 millilitres of milk, 175 millilitres of yogurt or 45 grams of cheese.

A major concern in recent years has been the amount of animal fat consumed through milk and milk products. For this reason there are now strong recommendations that everyone over age 2 drink lower-fat milk (i.e., skim or 1% or 2%). Low-fat dairy products of every kind are now widely marketed and highly recommended.

Several countries asked about milk as a single item rather than dividing it into two parts — skim or partly skimmed milk and homogenized or whole

milk. Therefore, Figure 4.4, which shows the percentages that drink 2% or skim milk, whole or homogenized milk or a combination of both at least daily, or drink neither, has information for only five countries. Canadian and Norwegian youth drink mainly skimmed milk. In Scotland, Sweden and Wales, most youth drink whole milk. Rather surprising is the number of students who drink no milk, especially in Wales. In Canada, one fifth of the 15-year-old girls say they drink no milk.

Figure 4.3
Percentages of students who eat whole wheat bread or rye bread once a day or more*

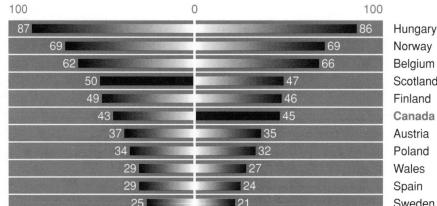
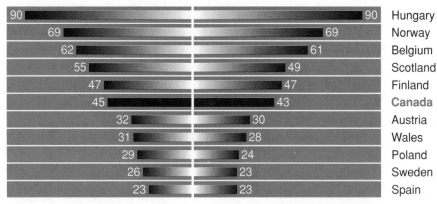

Male   Female

C. Less healthy foods

Nutritionists recommend that certain foods, because of their high content of certain elements, be eaten in moderation. Some of these elements are fat, cholesterol, sugar and caffeine. Generally, it is considered acceptable to eat almost any food as long as excessive amounts of these substances are not being consumed in the overall diet. The foods discussed below are those viewed by nutritionists as falling into the less-healthy food category from the questionnaire.

1. Candy and chocolate bars

Candy and chocolate are considered nutrition culprits because of their high sugar content and the caffeine in chocolate. Eating these products excessively supplies unnecessary "empty calories". Sugar has very few nutrients, and its caloric content is relatively high. Although the caffeine in chocolate is not in the same range as that in coffee, if a substantial amount of chocolate is eaten in conjunction with drinking coffee or cola, the caffeine intake can easily exceed the recommended levels. Figure 4.5 shows the percentages of students who eat candy or chocolate bars (or 'sweets' as designated in some countries) at least once a day. The number of Belgian, Polish and Scottish youth who do so are extremely high at all age levels. Students in Norway eat the least candy; Canada is within the lower ranges with between 18% and 30% of Canadian youth indulging in sweets daily.

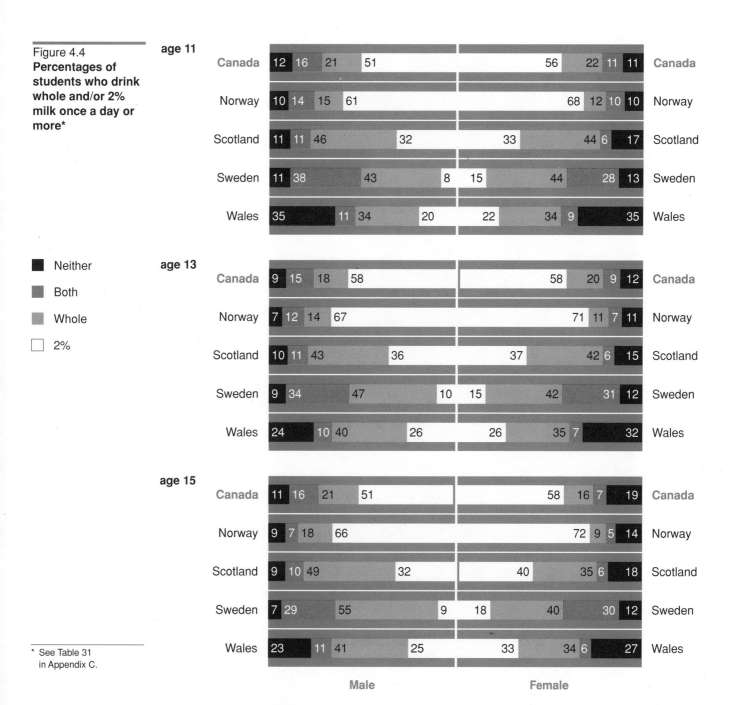

Figure 4.4
Percentages of students who drink whole and/or 2% milk once a day or more*

Legend:
- Neither
- Both
- Whole
- 2%

2. Potato chips (crisps)

Potato chips or crisps are very thin slices of potatoes deep fried until they are very crispy. There are some nutrient pluses in the potato part of this product, but because the amount of fat per piece is so high, the proportion of fat intake may easily become excessive. Potato chips are often salted to a degree that eating a substantial number gives a person more salt than recommended. Figure 4.6 shows the percentage of respondents who eat this food at least every day, and the substantial differences between the responses of the countries. In Sweden and Norway, students eat almost no potato chips, whereas in Scotland between 49% and 68% say they eat them at least daily. More respondents in Canada than in any of the remaining countries indicate they eat potato chips daily ranging from 10% of 15-year-old girls to 22% of 11-year-old boys. It is difficult to explain the extraordinarily high numbers in Scotland, but an examination of the 1988 survey results revealed similar figures.

3. French fries

French fries have basically the same properties as potato chips, except that the fat content is not quite as high per piece because more potato is used. When eaten occasionally, in moderation, french fries are quite acceptable as part of a normal diet; however, daily consumption would

Figure 4.5
Percentages of students who eat candy or chocolate bars once a day or more*

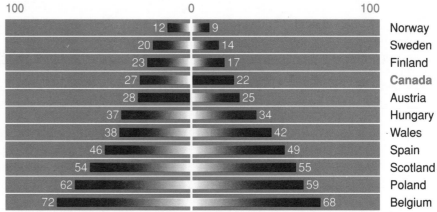

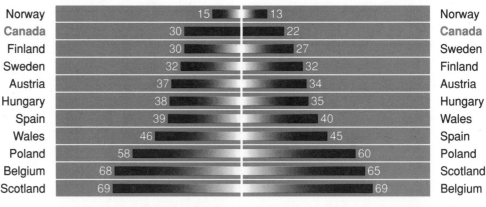

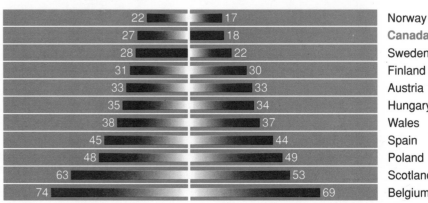

Male   Female

* See Table 33
in Appendix C.

likely increase a person's fat intake substantially. Figure 4.7 shows the percentage of respondents who say they eat french fries at least every day. Belgian students appear to eat this fried food to a much greater extent than those in any other country; Scottish and Spanish students rank a somewhat distant second and third. Few students in Norway, Sweden, Hungary and Finland eat french fries daily.

4. Hamburgers, hot dogs and sausages

Although hamburgers, hot dogs and sausage meats satisfy some of the requirements of the meat and meat alternates food group, these particular meats are proportionally very high in animal fat. Again, occasional use is not considered harmful, but daily consumption would increase fat intake to a higher than desirable level. Not surprisingly, in Figure 4.8 we see that few respondents eat these meats every day. Youth in Belgium, Scotland,

Spain and Wales (except for 15-year-olds) lead the way; 19% of 13-year-old Scottish and 15-year-old Belgian boys, and 11-year-old Spanish girls say that they eat these meats at least daily. Between 3% and 10% of the Canadian respondents stated the same, with boys in the higher brackets.

Figure 4.6
Percentages of students who eat potato chips (crisps) once a day or more*

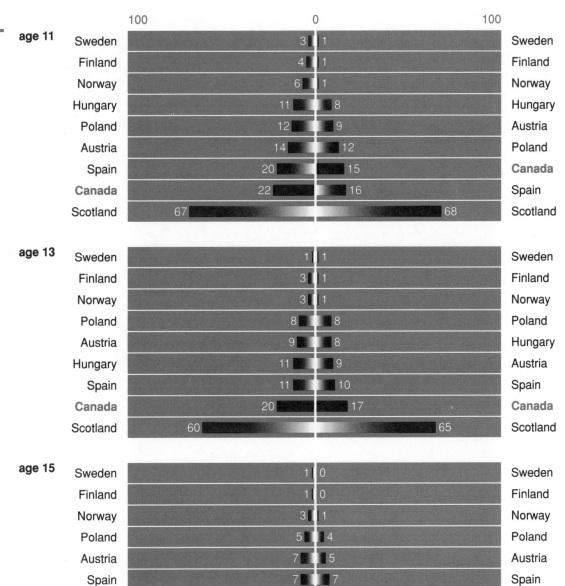

Male   Female

5. Soft drinks with sugar

Although soft drinks may be considered refreshing, they have almost no nutritional value and contain large proportions of sugar, making them very high in calories. Colas also contain caffeine. Frequent consumption of such beverages is not recommended by nutritionists. From Figure 4.9 we find that many young people in Belgium, Scotland, Wales and Canada drink sugary soft drinks every day. Far fewer students in Norway, Sweden and Finland do so. Canadian youth fall in the upper ranks for all three age groups. In all countries, with few exceptions, more boys than girls drink soft drinks daily.

6. Coffee

Coffee, which has a very high concentration of caffeine, seems to have been a staple of the North American and European diet for many years. Daily consumption of caffeine should be watched closely. The food guidelines being formulated by Health and Welfare Canada recommend that a person consume no more than 400 milligrams of caffeine a day or four 5-ounce cups of coffee. If tea, cola or chocolate is consumed, the amount of caffeine in these foods must be taken into consideration as well.

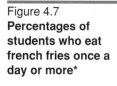

Figure 4.7
Percentages of students who eat french fries once a day or more*

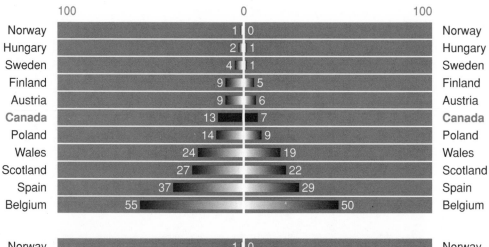

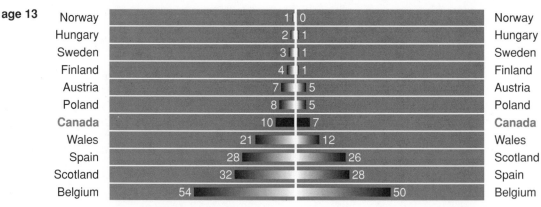

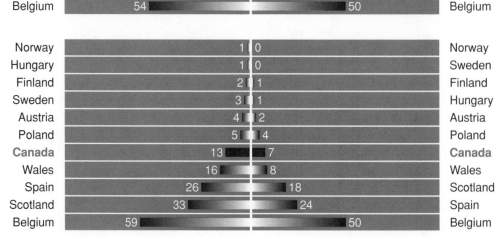

age 11

	Male	Female
Norway	1	0
Hungary	2	1
Sweden	4	1
Finland	9	5
Austria	9	6
Canada	13	7
Poland	14	9
Wales	24	19
Scotland	27	22
Spain	37	29
Belgium	55	50

age 13

	Male	Female
Norway	1	0	Norway
Hungary	2	1	Hungary
Sweden	3	1	Sweden
Finland	4	1	Finland
Austria	7	5	Austria
Poland	8	5	Poland
Canada	10	7	Canada
Wales	21	12	Wales
Spain	28	26	Scotland
Scotland	32	28	Spain
Belgium	54	50	Belgium

age 15

	Male	Female
Norway	1	0	Norway
Hungary	1	0	Sweden
Finland	2	1	Finland
Sweden	3	1	Hungary
Austria	4	2	Austria
Poland	5	4	Poland
Canada	13	7	Canada
Wales	16	8	Wales
Spain	26	18	Scotland
Scotland	33	24	Spain
Belgium	59	50	Belgium

* See Table 35 in Appendix C.

Although coffee is usually considered an adult drink, Figure 4.10 indicates that many of the young respondents in this survey have already become regular coffee drinkers. In Belgium almost one half of the respondents drink coffee daily. In Canada, small proportions (up to 11% of the 15-year-olds) drink coffee daily.

D. Overall dietary patterns

An analysis was conducted to see what percentages of students are eating fruit, raw vegetables and whole grain breads every day to determine their intake of fibre. A further analysis was done based on the responses to items about hamburgers and hot dogs, potato chips or french fries, and whole milk to calculate what percentages of students are consuming these products every

day and possibly including more fat in their diet than is recommended.

1. Fibre

Figure 4.11 shows the percentages of students who say they eat fruit, raw vegetables and whole wheat or rye bread at least once a day. Eating these types of foods regularly contributes to the overall consumption of fibre in the diet. All of the countries are not represented, either because the

Figure 4.8
Percentages of students who eat hamburgers, hot dogs or sausages once a day or more*

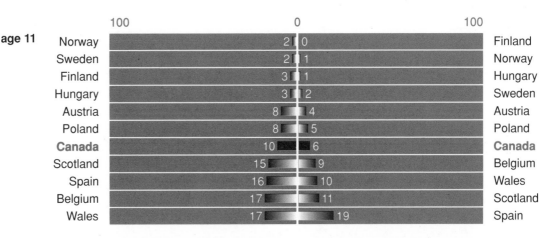

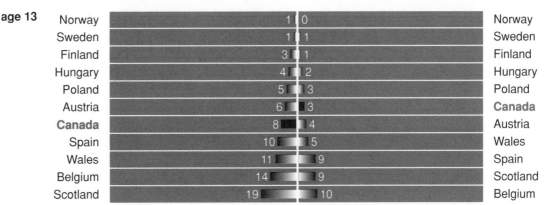

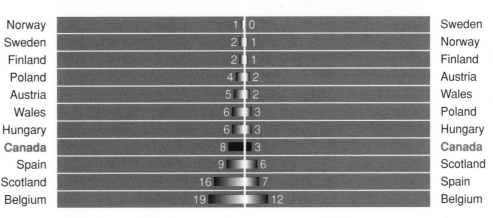

* See Table 36 in Appendix C.

41

item was missing from a country's questionnaire or it was asked in a format too different to be comparable. Generally, more of the girls tend to eat a combination of high-fibre foods every day. In each country there is a decrease by age 15 in the number of students who consume these foods daily. In no country do even half of the respondents eat fibre-rich foods daily. Youth in Belgium, Hungary, Canada and Finland do so a little more than young people in the other countries, but the benefits of increased consumption of fibre need to be stressed more in all countries.

2. Fat

Determining fat content was more difficult. Several countries omitted one or more of the items used by other countries or asked the item in a way that was not comparable. Table 4.1 shows that very few students in the countries surveyed appear to be eating an excess of fatty foods daily, with the exception, perhaps, of youth in Scotland, especially boys. Three percent or less of Canadian youth eat each of these high-fat foods every day.

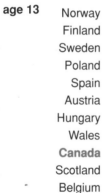

Figure 4.9
Percentages of students who drink soft drinks once a day or more*

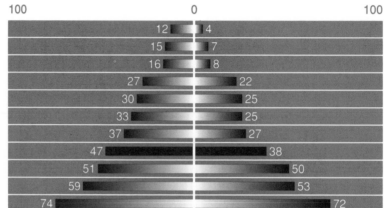

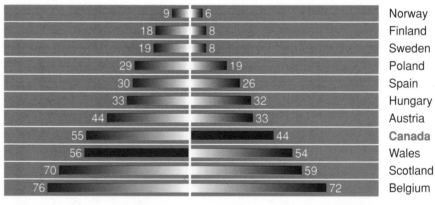

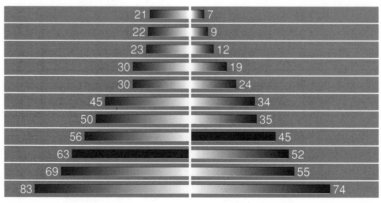

Male   Female

* See Table 37 in Appendix C.

Table 4.1
Students who eat high-fat foods at least once a day

Country	Age 11		Age 13		Age 15	
	M	F	M	F	M	F
Canada	3 %	2 %	2 %	1 %	2 %	1 %
Hungary	0	0	0	0	0	0
Norway	0	0	0	0	0	0
Scotland	8	5	9	5	7	2
Sweden	1	0	1	0	1	0
Wales	5	3	4	1	3	1

Figure 4.10
Percentages of students who drink coffee once a day or more*

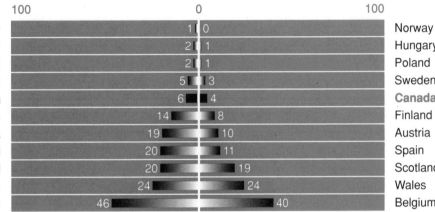

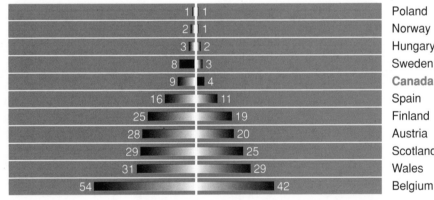

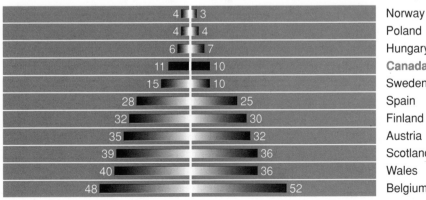

* See Table 38
   in Appendix C.

E. Dental care

Only two items in the Canadian questionnaire dealt directly with dental care. Students were asked to indicate how often they brush their teeth using the responses 'more than once a day', 'once a day', 'at least once a week, but not daily', 'less than once a week', 'never', and they were asked how often they use dental floss using the responses 'daily', 'weekly', 'seldom or never'. Most countries included the item about brushing teeth,

but very few mentioned dental floss. For several countries which did so, the responses were very high in the 'seldom or never' category. In at least one country (Wales) the use of dental floss is actively discouraged. Therefore, we have not discussed this aspect of dental care in the report, but our findings are in Table 41 in Appendix C.

Only in Sweden do fairly large proportions of youth brush their teeth more than once a day; up

to 93% of the 15-year-old girls do. In all of the survey countries more girls brush their teeth more than once a day than do boys, but for the most part, even for girls, the figures are not as high as they could be. As can be seen in Figure 4.12, no country quite measures up to Sweden in terms of brushing more than once a day. In Austria three quarters of the 11-year-old girls do so; by age 13, three quarters of the girls in Austria, Canada and Scotland are doing so and by age 15 almost 80%

Figure 4.11
Percentages of students who eat fibre-rich foods* once a day or more

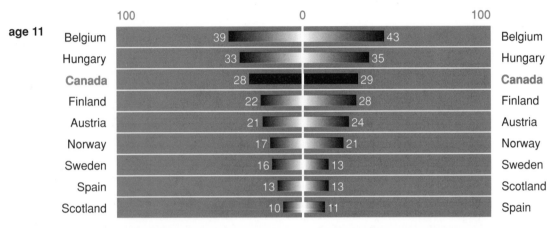

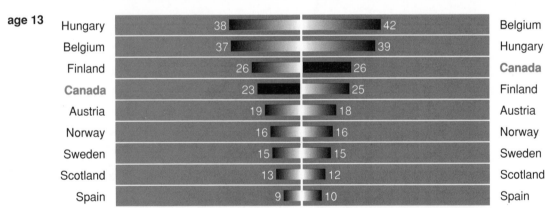

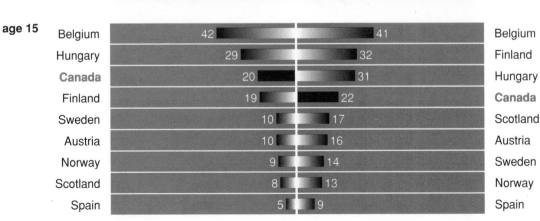

* Raw vegetables, fruits and whole wheat or rye bread.

44

of those in Austria, Wales, Hungary, Canada and Scotland brush frequently. The figures for boys never reach the 75% range, except for Sweden; only in Austria do 65% of the 11-year-old boys brush their teeth more than once a day. Whereas the percentages of brushing more than once a day increase for girls as they get older, the percentages of boys tend to decrease or remain the same, except for small changes in Canada, Hungary and Wales. When we include those who brush once a day, we see that relatively good dental hygiene is becoming established in most countries by age 15. The dental hygiene of Canadian youth improves with age and relatively few fall into the poorer categories. However, it may be advisable in most countries, Canada included, to consider strategies to encourage boys to brush more often.

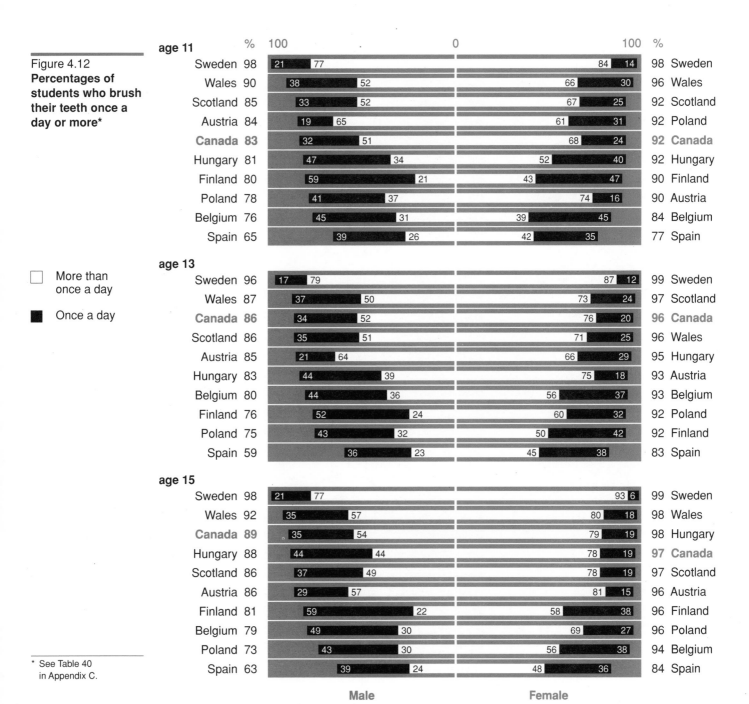

Figure 4.12
Percentages of students who brush their teeth once a day or more*

More than once a day

Once a day

Male

Female

* See Table 40 in Appendix C.

45

F. Summary

Although the data are not fully comparable, some value is gained by looking at the Canadian data from this survey in relation to the data from the 1984-85 CHABS. For the most part three quarters of the Canadian students indicate they eat fruit every day, but only one half to three fifths eat raw vegetables. Some improvement seems to be required in the diet of Canadian adolescents related to fruit and vegetables. As small percentages of Canadian youth continue to eat whole grain bread every day, hopefully they are eating cereals, beans and other grains to fulfil the daily requirements.

Milk consumption is very high. About two thirds of the young people are now drinking lower-fat milk — a good sign that they are reducing fat levels in their diets. However, attention should be given to the consumption of foods with high-fat content. Compared with their peers in other countries, Canadian students are second in consumption of fat. They also tend to drink more sugary soft drinks than their peers in most of the other countries.

Chapter 5

■

Physical Ailments and Medication

■

A. Introduction

Young people are customarily thought of as being very healthy and without many of the complaints and ailments that commonly affect adults. Yet, it is wise to be aware of the physical and emotional conditions of youth because the various symptoms they complain of can be indicative of more serious problems. The amount of literature on the topic of headaches among children and adolescents is not large; much of what is available deals with migraine headaches and their implications. However, headaches are found to be less common in children than in adults and, when present, may be in the context of another illness. Although between 5% and 10% of childhood and adolescent headaches may be attributable to emotional distress, pediatricians believe that emotional distress is evidenced more often in abdominal pain than in other physical symptoms.

A substantial amount of literature is available on adolescent depression. Dr. D. Offord et al. (1986) found that the prevalence of depression among 12- to 16-year-old children ranged from .6% with a high level to 43.9% with a low level. He stated that these findings were within previously found norms.

Adolescents are in a turbulent period of their lives. They are experiencing many new facets of life for the first time, from physical changes to pressure to achieve at school to ensure further education. Their fears can manifest themselves in many physical symptoms: depression, sleep problems, nervousness and even irritability can be signs of the strains in the adolescent's life.

Richard Ferber (1987) suggested that 10% to 15% of adolescents have significant difficulty falling asleep and another 20% to 38% have occasional difficulty. Parents are often unaware of these problems because adolescents tend to guard their privacy.

The other problems discussed in this chapter can also be indications of emotional strain or of actual ailments, such as backache as a result of physical activity or stomach ache from eating improperly. Nervousness may arise from fear of certain aspects of life the student finds difficult to face. School pressures, peer and parent relationships, even irrational fears of thunder, lightning, personal safety and death can lead to nervous reactions.

In this chapter the discussion deals mainly with the incidence of these disorders and compares their prevalence in Canada to that in the other survey countries. To ascertain to what degree young people experience some common ailments, the questionnaire presented a list of ailments to which the respondents indicated they had 'often', 'sometimes', 'seldom' or 'never' experienced each within the past six months.

B. Ailments

Students were asked to what extent they had the following health problems during the last six months — headache, stomach ache, backache, feeling low, bad temper, feeling nervous, difficulties in getting to sleep and feeling dizzy. Some of these conditions reflect physical symptoms; some, emotional.

1. Headache

The proportions of students who have had headaches 'often' in the past six months is not large; in half of the countries surveyed less than 20% of the respondents 'often' have headaches. However, as Figure 5.1 shows, respondents' experience varies. Whereas very few students in Finland and Hungary appear to have headaches, substantially more in Canada, Scotland and Wales do so. Far more girls than boys have headaches.

2. Stomach ache

Fewer youth have stomach aches but, again, as can be seen in Figure 5.2, youth in some countries appear to experience them more than others. Results are similar to those for headache — more students in Canada, Scotland and Wales have stomach aches than in Finland and far more girls than boys experience this condition. (Hungarian students were not asked this item.) Seventeen percent or less of the male and female students in any of the countries 'often' have stomach aches.

3. Backache

The incidence of backache is very low among youth overall (see Figure 5.3). It increases with age in most countries, and females obviously suffer more. More Canadian youth have backaches at all ages except for 15-year-old Belgian girls, who appear especially vulnerable to this problem.

4. Feeling low (depressed)

Feeling depressed is common to most people occasionally, but if it occurs with great regularity it can become quite a concern and inhibit a person's normal functioning. Eleven-year-old respondents usually are not experiencing this problem to a great extent, although we see in Figure 5.4 that over 10% of Canadian, Welsh, Scottish and Hungarian 11-year-old youth say they have 'often' felt depressed in the last six months. The rates

increase for the 13- and 15-year-olds, especially for girls. Canadian youth rank among the highest for this problem, but they do not feel depressed as often as Hungarian youth, particularly 15-year-old girls. The number of youth who indicate that they have experienced depression within the last six months seems to fall within the norms mentioned earlier. We have no information about the degree of depression experienced.

5. Bad temper (irritability)

Many young people discover that they, like everyone else, can be irritable, which is not considered an asset socially. However, with many of them able to admit to irritability, this may possibly aid them in being able to control their temper. From Figure 5.5 we see that more girls feel they have been bad tempered than boys, except for 11-year-old Canadians. Youth in

Figure 5.1
Percentages of students who have had headaches 'often' in the last six months*

age 11

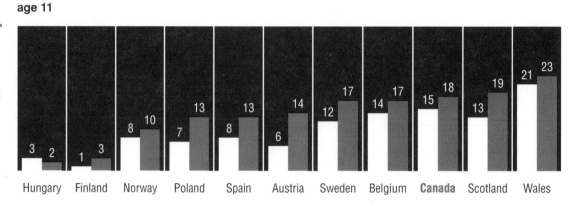

age 13

☐ Male

■ Female

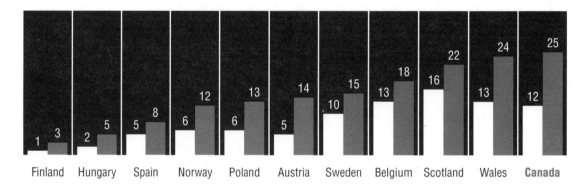

age 15

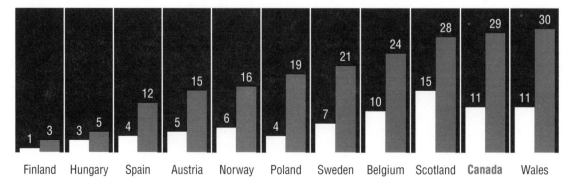

* See Table 42 in Appendix C.

Canada, Scotland, Wales and 15-year-old girls in Hungary appear to believe they are bad tempered more than most. Finnish youth are least likely to say they have been bad tempered in the past six months.

6. Feeling nervous

The differences between countries in the responses to feeling nervous are quite dramatic. In Figure 5.6 we see a steady increase from age 11 to age 15 in the percentages of females in Canada, Hungary, Poland and Spain and male respondents in Hungary, Poland and Spain who say they have often felt nervous in the last six months. Canadian youth generally fall within the middle ranges, with one fifth or less saying that they 'often' feel nervous.

7. Difficulty getting to sleep

Figure 5.7 shows that difficulty in getting to sleep is not a problem for most youth, but surprisingly it seems that 11-year-olds have this problem as much or more than the older respondents. Youth in Canada tend to experience this problem to a greater extent than their counterparts in other countries.

age 11

Figure 5.2
Percentages of students who have had stomach aches 'often' in the last six months*

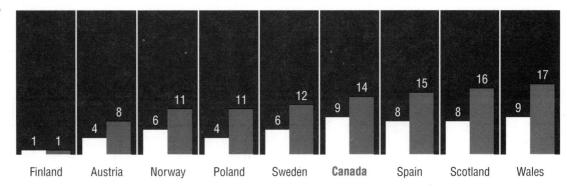

☐ Male
■ Female

age 13

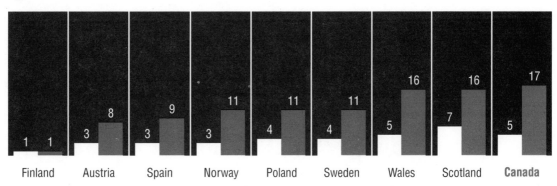

age 15

* See Table 43 in Appendix C.

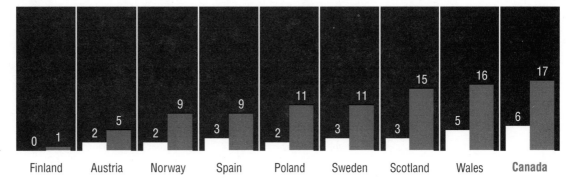

8. Feeling dizzy

Overall, very small percentages of students experience dizziness. However, Figure 5.8 shows that girls are dizzy more than boys and that Canadian students are among the highest sufferers at all age levels.

C. Use of medication and pills

Included on the questionnaire was a question about using medication for certain conditions so the extent of use could be determined among young people. In recent years there has been some concern about the increase in the use of "over-the-counter" drugs to ease the symptoms of many ailments. Students were asked to indicate 'yes' or

'no' to the question, "During the last month, have you taken any medicine or pills for the following: a cough, a cold, headache, stomach ache, difficulty sleeping and nervousness?" They were not asked to indicate dosages or strength of medication.

Quite a dichotomy seems to appear in the responses to these items; that is, substantial portions of the youth population do take medication and pills for some problems, but very

Figure 5.3
Percentages of students who have had backaches 'often' in the last six months*

☐ Male

■ Female

age 11

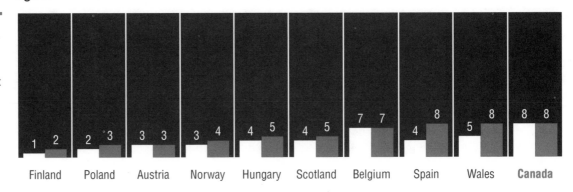

age 13

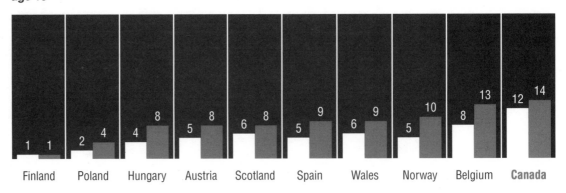

age 15

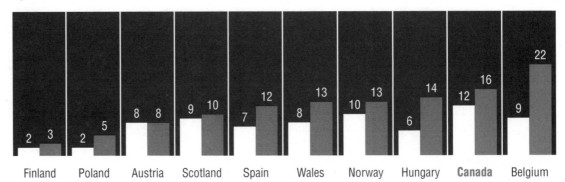

* See Table 44 in Appendix C.

few take anything for other problems. Figures 5.9, 5.10, 5.11 and 5.12 show two patterns — Canada, Scotland and Wales are consistently among the top countries in terms of the percentages of youth who have taken medication in the previous month; and girls tend to take medication more than boys. Cold and headache medications are the most common taken (Figures 5.10 and 5.11). Very few boys take pills for a stomach ache, but by ages 13

and 15, one quarter or more of the girls in most countries do so. Only in Austria are the figures consistently low (see Figure 5.12). Younger children tend to take medicine for a cough (Figure 5.9) more than older ones; parents may be the influential factor in this situation.

Very few students seem to take medication for difficulty in sleeping or nervousness. Figure 5.13 shows that 7% or less take anything for sleeping problems and Figure 5.14 reveals that up to 11% have taken medication in the previous month for nervousness. Only in Poland does it appear that this may be a concern; across all three age groups more Polish youth take medication for this purpose.

Figure 5.4
Percentages of students who have felt depressed 'often' in the last six months*

age 11

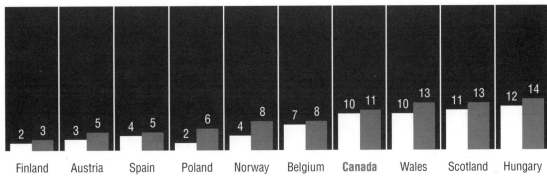

☐ Male

■ Female

age 13

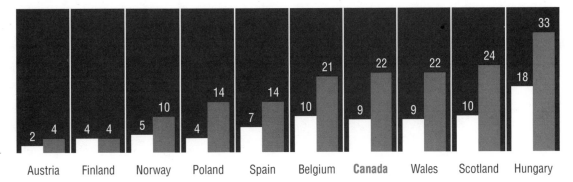

age 15

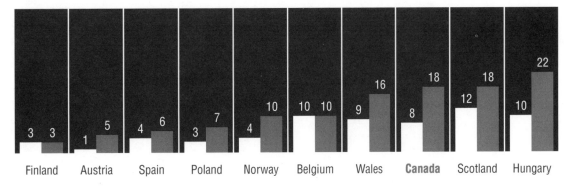

* See Table 45 in Appendix C.

D. Summary

More girls than boys have headaches, stomach aches, backaches, feel depressed, display irritability (bad temper) and feel nervous. Canadian youth are among those who experience these problems more than most. In addition, more girls than boys overall take medication to ease the symptoms of these ailments. The degree to which young people experience these ailments and take medication when they do appears to be linked to cultural definitions of disease. For example, Scotland, Wales and Canada, which have many similarities in terms of cultural influences, tend to be similar in the reporting of most ailments. The higher incidence of these conditions among Canadian youth than among students in several other countries suggests that further research on this issue is necessary.

Figure 5.5
Percentages of students who have been bad tempered 'often' in the last six months*

□ Male
■ Female

age 11

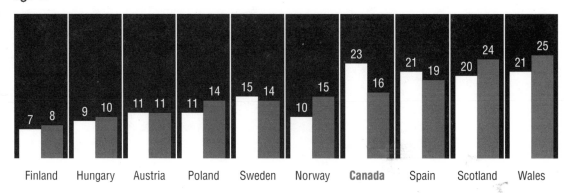

Finland Hungary Austria Poland Sweden Norway **Canada** Spain Scotland Wales

age 13

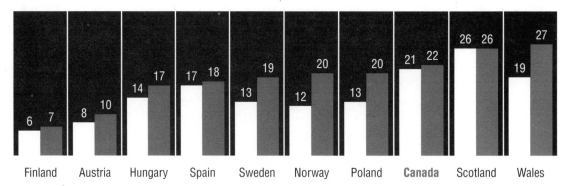

Finland Austria Hungary Spain Sweden Norway Poland **Canada** Scotland Wales

age 15

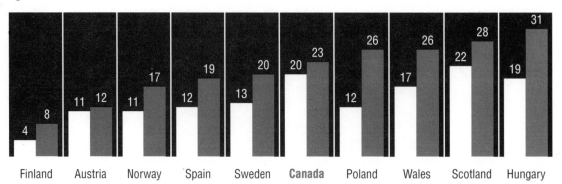

Finland Austria Norway Spain Sweden **Canada** Poland Wales Scotland Hungary

* See Table 46 in Appendix C.

age 11

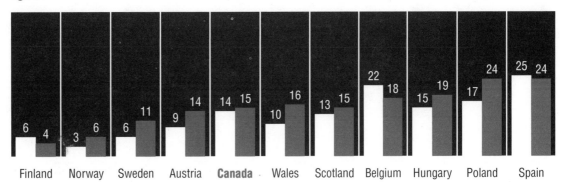

Figure 5.6
Percentages of students who have felt nervous 'often' in the last six months*

age 13

☐ Male
■ Female

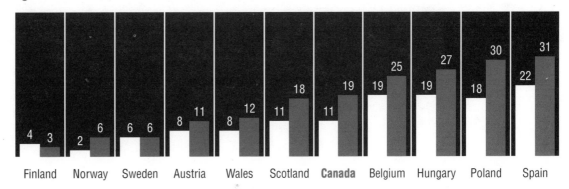

age 15

* See Table 47
  in Appendix C.

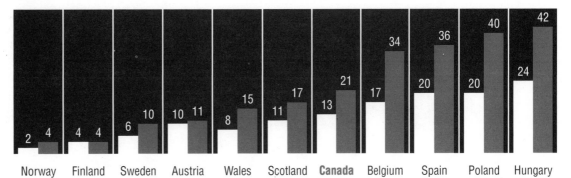

Figure 5.7
**Percentages of
students who have
had difficulty
sleeping 'often' in
the last six months***

age 11

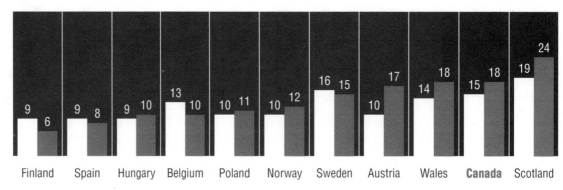

Finland — Spain — Hungary — Belgium — Poland — Norway — Sweden — Austria — Wales — **Canada** — Scotland

☐ Male
◼ Female

age 13

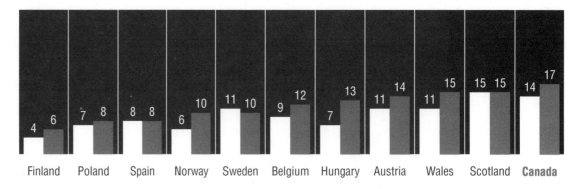

Finland — Poland — Spain — Norway — Sweden — Belgium — Hungary — Austria — Wales — Scotland — **Canada**

age 15

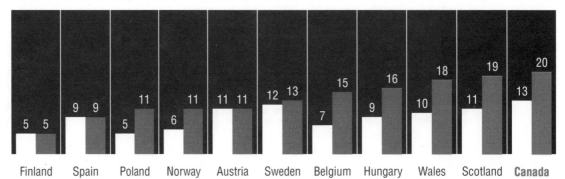

Finland — Spain — Poland — Norway — Austria — Sweden — Belgium — Hungary — Wales — Scotland — **Canada**

* See Table 48
  in Appendix C.

Figure 5.8
Percentages of students who have felt dizzy 'often' in the last six months*

age 11

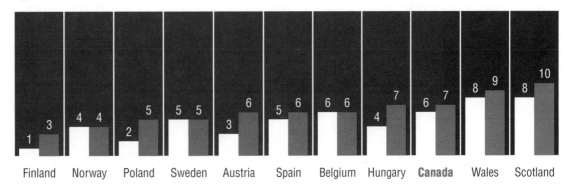

Finland	Norway	Poland	Sweden	Austria	Spain	Belgium	Hungary	**Canada**	Wales	Scotland

□ Male

■ Female

age 13

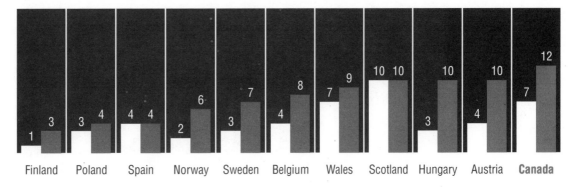

Finland	Poland	Spain	Norway	Sweden	Belgium	Wales	Scotland	Hungary	Austria	**Canada**

age 15

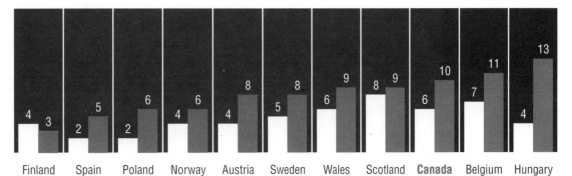

Finland	Spain	Poland	Norway	Austria	Sweden	Wales	Scotland	**Canada**	Belgium	Hungary

* See Table 49 in Appendix C.

Figure 5.9
Percentages of students who have taken medicine or pills for a cough in the last month

☐ Male
■ Female

age 11

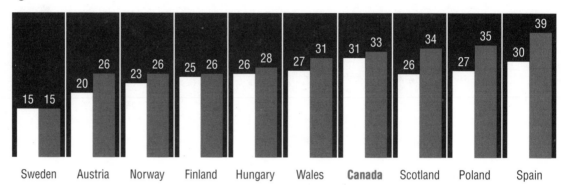

age 13

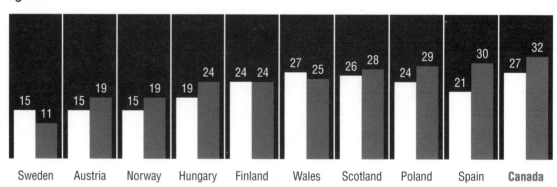

age 15

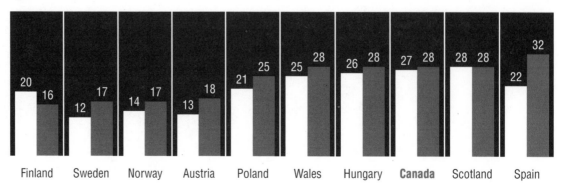

Figure 5.10
Percentages of students who have taken medicine or pills for a cold in the last month

☐ Male
■ Female

age 11

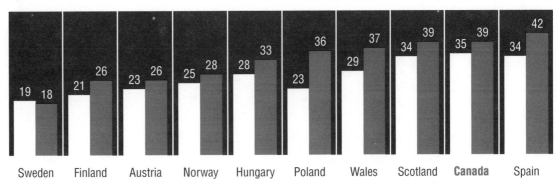

Sweden 19 18 | Finland 21 26 | Austria 23 26 | Norway 25 28 | Hungary 28 33 | Poland 23 36 | Wales 29 37 | Scotland 34 39 | **Canada** 35 39 | Spain 34 42

age 13

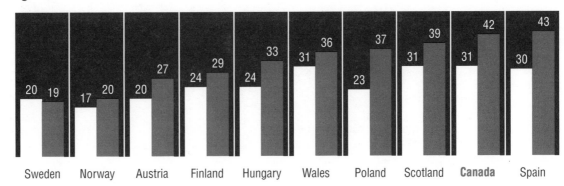

Sweden 20 19 | Norway 17 20 | Austria 20 27 | Finland 24 29 | Hungary 24 33 | Wales 31 36 | Poland 23 37 | Scotland 31 39 | **Canada** 31 42 | Spain 30 43

age 15

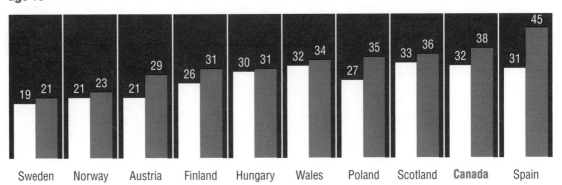

Sweden 19 21 | Norway 21 23 | Austria 21 29 | Finland 26 31 | Hungary 30 31 | Wales 32 34 | Poland 27 35 | Scotland 33 36 | **Canada** 32 38 | Spain 31 45

age 11

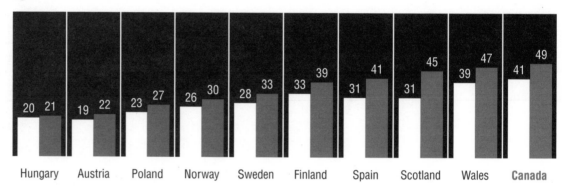

	Hungary	Austria	Poland	Norway	Sweden	Finland	Spain	Scotland	Wales	Canada
Male	20	19	23	26	28	33	31	31	39	41
Female	21	22	27	30	33	39	41	45	47	49

□ Male
■ Female

age 13

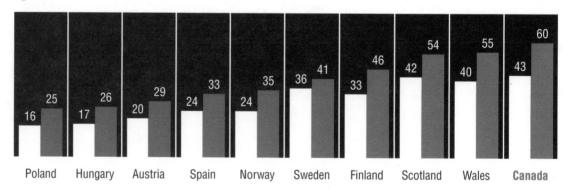

	Poland	Hungary	Austria	Spain	Norway	Sweden	Finland	Scotland	Wales	Canada
Male	16	17	20	24	24	36	33	42	40	43
Female	25	26	29	33	35	41	46	54	55	60

age 15

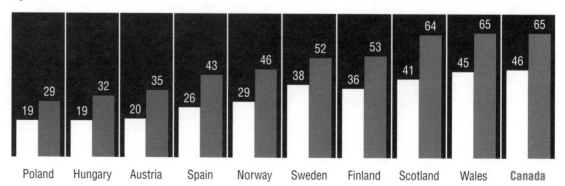

	Poland	Hungary	Austria	Spain	Norway	Sweden	Finland	Scotland	Wales	Canada
Male	19	19	20	26	29	38	36	41	45	46
Female	29	32	35	43	46	52	53	64	65	65

Figure 5.12
**Percentages of
students who have
taken medicine or
pills for a stomach
ache in the last
month**

Male
Female

age 11

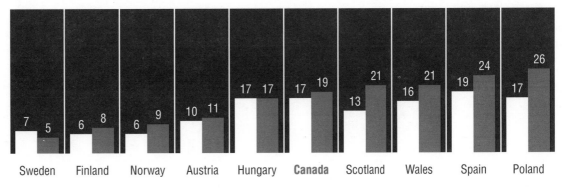

Sweden	Finland	Norway	Austria	Hungary	**Canada**	Scotland	Wales	Spain	Poland
7 / 5	6 / 8	6 / 9	10 / 11	17 / 17	17 / 19	13 / 21	16 / 21	19 / 24	17 / 26

age 13

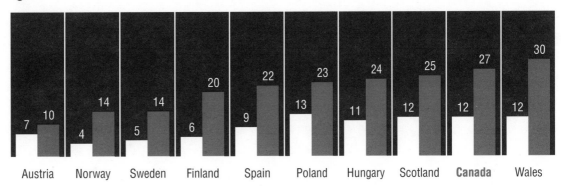

Austria	Norway	Sweden	Finland	Spain	Poland	Hungary	Scotland	**Canada**	Wales
7 / 10	4 / 14	5 / 14	6 / 20	9 / 22	13 / 23	11 / 24	12 / 25	12 / 27	12 / 30

age 15

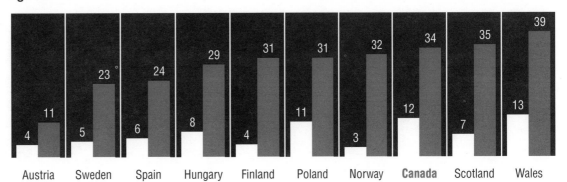

Austria	Sweden	Spain	Hungary	Finland	Poland	Norway	**Canada**	Scotland	Wales
4 / 11	5 / 23	6 / 24	8 / 29	4 / 31	11 / 31	3 / 32	12 / 34	7 / 35	13 / 39

59

Figure 5.13
Percentages of students who have taken medicine or pills for difficulty in sleeping in the last month

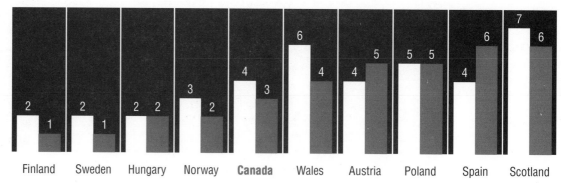

☐ Male
■ Female

age 13

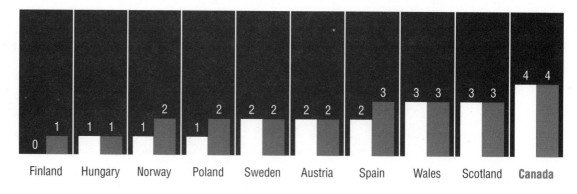

age 15

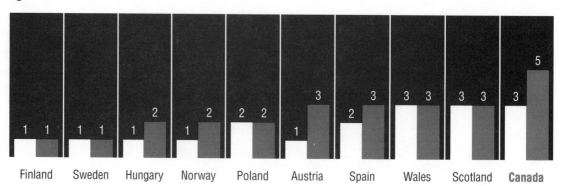

Figure 5.14
Percentages of students who have taken medicine or pills for nervousness in the last month

Male
Female

age 11

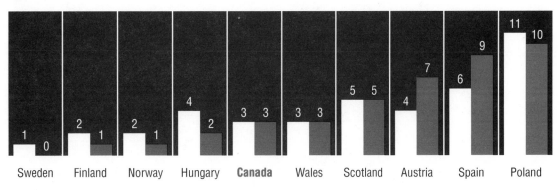

age 13

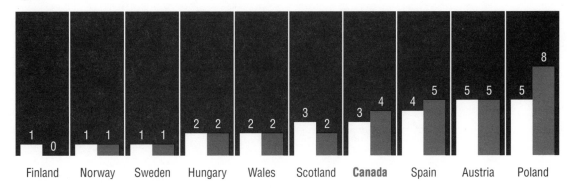

age 15

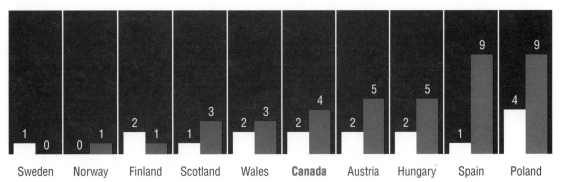

Chapter 6

Social Adjustment

A. Introduction

Although the primary purpose of the survey was to examine the physical health of youth, we also attempted to assess the extent to which they are socially well-adjusted. To do this, we asked a series of questions about students' relationships with their parents and their peers and what they thought of school. The Canadian survey included items on these themes, as well as questions regarding self-esteem.

B. Relationship with parents

In the past few years substantial changes have taken place in the structure of families — more husbands and wives are living apart and in more families both parents are working. In our 1984 review of Ontario adolescents, we found that 80% of young people lived with both parents (King et al., 1986). Just four years later the figure had dropped to 75% (King et al., 1988). How do young people adjust to these changing family structures and are there differences across countries that can inform us about such relationships?

To determine the quality of the relationships between young people and their parents, questions focused on whether or not young people could talk with their parents about issues of importance. In Figure 6.1, it can be seen that Canadian young people are very similar at age 11 to those in several other countries in terms of how often they talk to their parents about matters of interest. However, by ages 13 and 15, fewer young Canadians talk often to their parents about such issues. Young people in Scotland consistently rank the most positive on this measure. Figures 6.2 and 6.3 present the proportions of young people who find it easy to talk with their father and mother about things that bother them. The most notable point about the two figures is that both boys and girls find it easier to talk with their mother. Girls find it particularly difficult to talk with their father. In comparison to other countries, Canadian youth experience more difficulty talking with both parents; however, the differences are not pronounced between countries.

To indicate the extent to which children and their parents deal with specific issues that may be contentious, we asked the respondents if they and their parents agree about how they should spend their spare time. Figure 6.4 shows that Canadian youth at all three age levels are less likely to agree with their parents about how they should spend free time. The highest levels of agreement occur for Austrian, Belgian and Hungarian youth. Overall, compared with other countries, Canadians are less likely to feel comfortable talking with their parents and less likely to agree on specific issues.

Over the past eight years the Social Programs Evaluation Group at Queen's University has developed a scale that purports to measure the strength of the relationship between young people and their parents. For this study a seven-item version of the scale was employed. In the next chapter this scale is used to help explain the factors associated with health-related behaviour. In this chapter each of the items in a comparative format across the three age groups is examined.

Generally, Canadian youths' relationships with their parents are quite positive. This is most true for the 11-year-olds and increasingly less so for older students. For example, as can be seen in Figure 6.5, as young people get older the proportions that think their parents understand them decreases. Fewer young people in this study indicated that what their parents think of them is important compared with the 1984 adolescent experience data (King, 1986) and the 1988 CYAS study (King et al., 1988). This decline may correspond to the continuing breakdown of the family. A substantial number of young people feel their parents expect too much of them, and in the next chapter we show how conflict with parents is positively related to greater involvement in health-risk behaviours and problems with school.

Interestingly, girls are more likely than boys to say there are times when they would like to leave home and less likely to say they have a happy home life. The 13- and 15-year-old girls are also more likely to say that they have arguments with their parents. This pattern of greater strain for girls than boys is a recent phenomenon and may be related to the inability of some parents to provide the necessary supports for young women as they make their career plans. Although girls are now as likely as boys to have definitive career plans, they are more likely to select unattainable vocations and look to their peers for career guidance (King, 1986). Their uncertainty is reflected in the greater tendency to "feel useless at times" or feel they are "not as good as others". (Posterski and Bibby, 1988).

C. Relationship with peers

The importance of friendship for young people cannot be minimized. To be fully accepted by a group of peers is a fundamental component of an individual's mental health. However, membership in some groups can mean adopting health-risk behaviours such as smoking and drinking.

A Norwegian researcher, Dan Olweus (1991), has made an effort to understand the impact of bullying on young people and eloquently records the negative aspects of this behaviour. We asked two questions to determine to what extent respondents are recipients or providers of bullying behaviour. Figure 6.6 presents the proportion of young people who say they have been "picked on" across the participating countries. Overall, a substantial number of young people have been

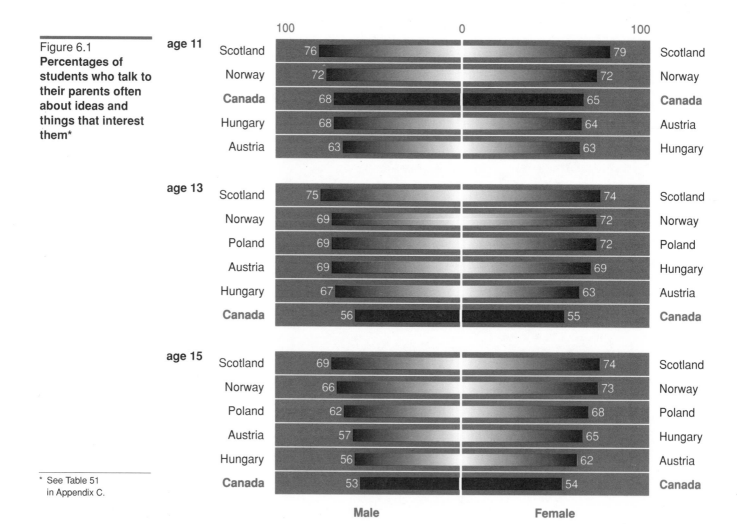

Figure 6.1
Percentages of students who talk to their parents often about ideas and things that interest them*

age 11

	Male		Female
Scotland	76	79	Scotland
Norway	72	72	Norway
Canada	68	65	**Canada**
Hungary	68	64	Austria
Austria	63	63	Hungary

age 13

Scotland	75	74	Scotland
Norway	69	72	Norway
Poland	69	72	Poland
Austria	69	69	Hungary
Hungary	67	63	Austria
Canada	56	55	**Canada**

age 15

Scotland	69	74	Scotland
Norway	66	73	Norway
Poland	62	68	Poland
Austria	57	65	Hungary
Hungary	56	62	Austria
Canada	53	54	**Canada**

*   See Table 51
    in Appendix C.

picked on and there are some interesting differences by country. In Canada, three quarters of boys and girls of all age groups surveyed say they have been picked on. With one exception (11-year-old Scottish boys), boys are more likely than girls to have been picked on. Canadian girls are more likely to be picked on than their peers in other countries. This is also true for boys at age 11, but for the other two age groups Canada is second only to Hungary.

Figure 6.7 presents the opposite side of the coin; that is, the proportion of young people who have picked on others. Again, it is relatively common in Canada at all grade levels and least common in Norway and Poland. The consistent commonalities and differences in these various analyses are worthy of examination; for example, can it be shown that young people in such countries as Norway and Poland are gentler in

some respects than young people in other countries, including Canada?

Figure 6.8 illustrates the most common responses to being picked on. Typically, there are male and female differences with girls more likely to avoid confrontations and do nothing. A higher percentage of Canadian youth, especially boys, indicated that they shout at bullies. Overall, boys

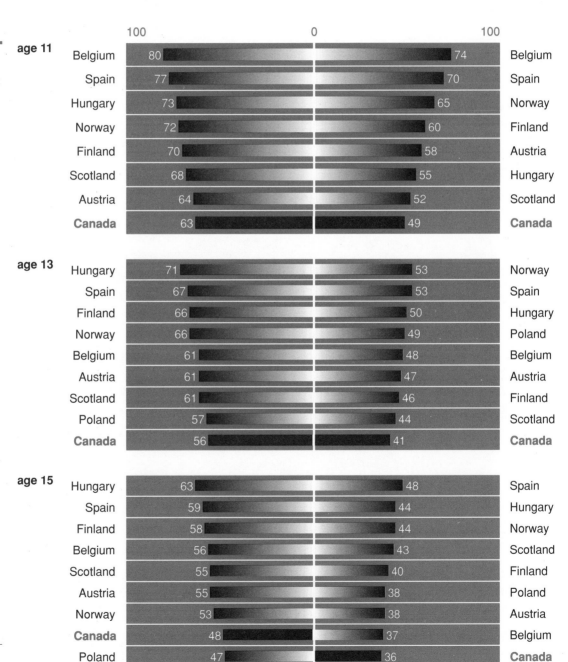

Figure 6.2
Percentages of students who find it easy to talk to their father about things that really bother them*

* See Table 52 in Appendix C.

age 11

	Male		Female	
Belgium	80		74	Belgium
Spain	77		70	Spain
Hungary	73		65	Norway
Norway	72		60	Finland
Finland	70		58	Austria
Scotland	68		55	Hungary
Austria	64		52	Scotland
Canada	63		49	**Canada**

age 13

	Male		Female	
Hungary	71		53	Norway
Spain	67		53	Spain
Finland	66		50	Hungary
Norway	66		49	Poland
Belgium	61		48	Belgium
Austria	61		47	Austria
Scotland	61		46	Finland
Poland	57		44	Scotland
Canada	56		41	**Canada**

age 15

	Male		Female	
Hungary	63		48	Spain
Spain	59		44	Hungary
Finland	58		44	Norway
Belgium	56		43	Scotland
Scotland	55		40	Finland
Austria	55		38	Poland
Norway	53		38	Austria
Canada	48		37	Belgium
Poland	47		36	**Canada**

Male **Female**

are more likely to fight (see Table 58 in Appendix C).

In all participating countries the vast majority of young people have more than one close friend (Figure 6.9). Over 80% of Canadians of both sexes and all three age groups surveyed do. In the next chapter we indicate those students who feel like an outsider and relate this feeling to their social and physical health. Austrian youth are most likely to have more than one friend and Norwegian youth least likely. Table 61 in Appendix C presents information on the sex of the respondents' closest friend. For the most part younger children have same-sex closest friends, although there are some exceptions. By age 15 a substantial number have opposite-sex close friends. The Austrians are most likely to have opposite-sex close friends and the Norwegians and Scots least likely.

Figure 6.10 indicates that girls are more likely than boys in each country to be able to talk to friends of the same sex about things that bother them. Canadian girls rank the highest in all three age groups which indicates not only how well they are socialized among peers, but also how important friends are to the decisions they make. Hungarian boys rank the highest on this measure. Interestingly, 11- and 13-year-old boys are more likely to say they can talk to members of the

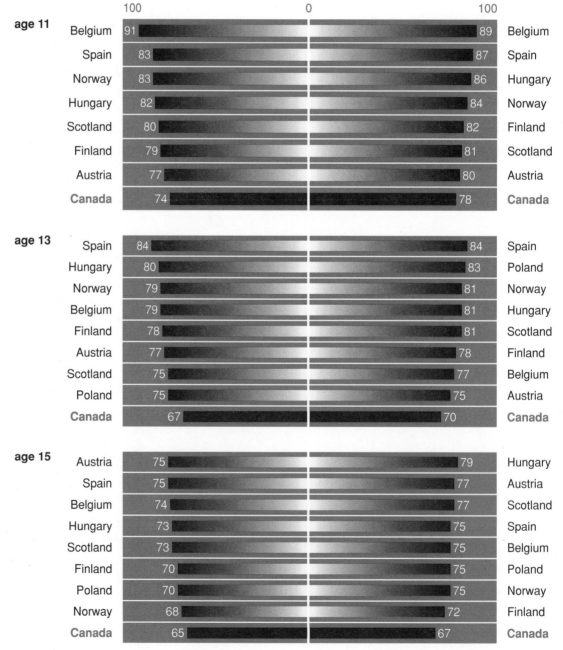

Figure 6.3
Percentages of students who find it easy to talk to their mother about things that really bother them*

* See Table 53 in Appendix C.

Male   **Female**

age 11

Male		Female	
Belgium	91	89	Belgium
Spain	83	87	Spain
Norway	83	86	Hungary
Hungary	82	84	Norway
Scotland	80	82	Finland
Finland	79	81	Scotland
Austria	77	80	Austria
Canada	74	78	Canada

age 13

Male		Female	
Spain	84	84	Spain
Hungary	80	83	Poland
Norway	79	81	Norway
Belgium	79	81	Hungary
Finland	78	81	Scotland
Austria	77	78	Finland
Scotland	75	77	Belgium
Poland	75	75	Austria
Canada	67	70	Canada

age 15

Male		Female	
Austria	75	79	Hungary
Spain	75	77	Austria
Belgium	74	77	Scotland
Hungary	73	75	Spain
Scotland	73	75	Belgium
Finland	70	75	Poland
Poland	70	75	Norway
Norway	68	72	Finland
Canada	65	67	Canada

opposite sex about things that bother them than girls; but by age 15 this is true only for four of the countries (Figure 6.11). Canadian youth usually are more comfortable than those in other countries talking to members of the opposite sex.

Although girls are more likely than boys to value the support of their friends, Figure 6.12 shows that boys are more likely to spend time four or more days a week outside school hours with their friends. Hungarian youth are the most likely to spend time more days per week with their friends and Scottish and Welsh youth the least; Canadian youth tend to be in the middle of the group.

D. Self

The degree to which young people accept who and what they are is extremely important to their social adjustment. On a positive note, in every country the vast majority of students indicate they are either very happy or quite happy about their life (Figure 6.13). Although Canadian youth ranked in the lower ranges for all three age levels, the

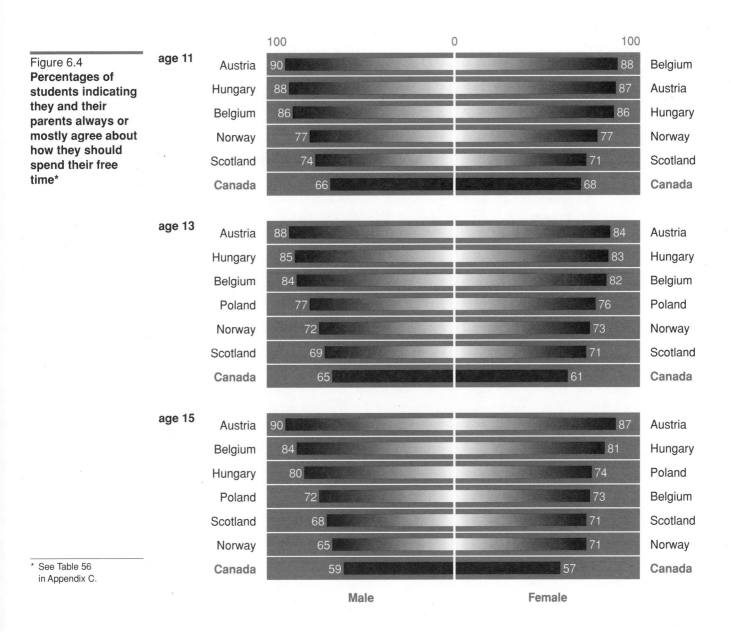

Figure 6.4
Percentages of students indicating they and their parents always or mostly agree about how they should spend their free time*

	Male (age 11)	Female (age 11)	
Austria	90	88	Belgium
Hungary	88	87	Austria
Belgium	86	86	Hungary
Norway	77	77	Norway
Scotland	74	71	Scotland
Canada	66	68	**Canada**

	Male (age 13)	Female (age 13)	
Austria	88	84	Austria
Hungary	85	83	Hungary
Belgium	84	82	Belgium
Poland	77	76	Poland
Norway	72	73	Norway
Scotland	69	71	Scotland
Canada	65	61	**Canada**

	Male (age 15)	Female (age 15)	
Austria	90	87	Austria
Belgium	84	81	Hungary
Hungary	80	74	Poland
Poland	72	73	Belgium
Scotland	68	71	Scotland
Norway	65	71	Norway
Canada	59	57	**Canada**

* See Table 56 in Appendix C.

differences are not great and the figures are relatively high for all countries. Boys were more likely than girls to say they are happy, but the differences were relatively small.

Figure 6.14 indicates the proportion of young people who answered 'very often' or 'rather often' to the question, "Do you ever feel lonely?" The proportion indicating these responses was relatively low at each age level. Girls were more likely than boys to say they are lonely which is consistent with our understanding of their greater need for friends. In all three age groups Canadian youth are more likely to say they feel lonely; the most substantial difference is among 11-year olds.

Although youths tend to spend quite a lot of time with their friends, we also wanted to know if they felt it was important to have free time to spend alone. Figure 6.15 shows the responses of those who indicated it is 'very important'. In Poland, 11-year-old youths were not asked this question, but, for those aged 13 and 15, very high proportions compared with other countries feel they need time on their own. Canadian youth rank next for this need. The differences between

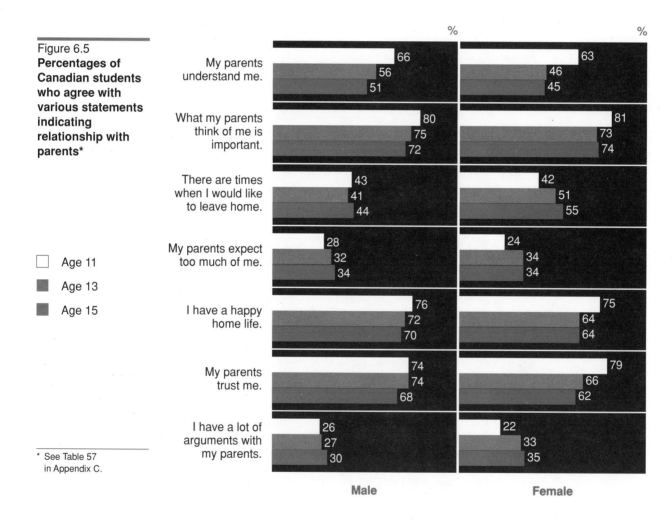

Figure 6.5
Percentages of Canadian students who agree with various statements indicating relationship with parents*

☐ Age 11
▨ Age 13
■ Age 15

* See Table 57 in Appendix C.

Canadians and those in other countries is not great except for students in Norway, very few of whom feel having time alone is 'very important'.

An important criterion for positive self-esteem is the degree to which one feels a part of the group. Figure 6.16 shows the percentage of respondents who 'sometimes' or 'often' feel like an outsider. Girls experience this feeling more than boys and

Canadian girls tend to be in the higher ranks, especially in the 'often' category. More 15-year-old Canadian boys express this view than their peers. Fewer respondents in Austria at each age level feel 'like an outsider' than in the other countries.

To measure self-esteem in this study six items related to self-confidence, decisiveness and acceptability of self, actions and appearance have

been used. Figure 6.17 presents the Canadian responses to the six items that make up the self-esteem scale. On most scale items boys consistently respond more positively than girls, particularly the 13- and 15-year-olds. Responses to these items measuring self-esteem are remarkably similar from age to age, although self-confidence declines somewhat for the 15-year-olds.

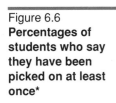

Figure 6.6
Percentages of students who say they have been picked on at least once*

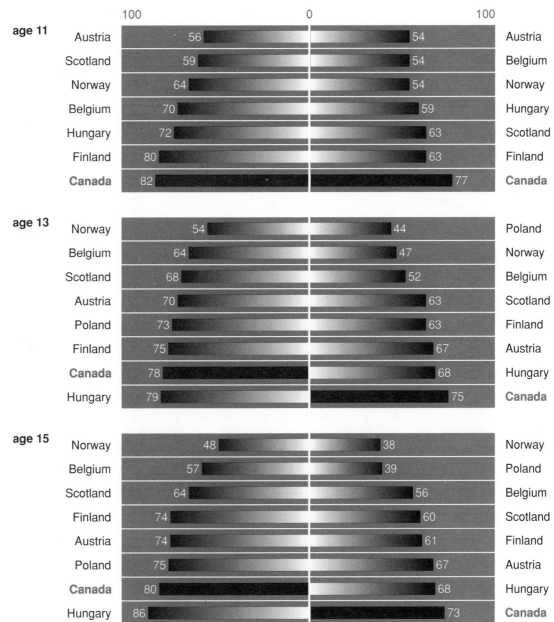

* Percentages based on responses to 'Yes, several times', 'Yes, once or twice'.

Boys are more likely than girls to think they need to gain weight (Figure 6.18) and girls are more likely than boys to think they need to lose weight. Certainly, far more girls say they need to lose weight than is indicated by their dietary patterns. Fewer girls who eat a high-fat, high-sugar diet say they need to lose weight. Girls experience greater social pressure to be thin.

E. Attitude toward school and teachers

In the next section we look at the factors that seem to influence young peoples' satisfaction with school. In this section, we focus quite specifically on the relationships they have with their teachers and how they think about school. In addition, we also indicate whether the respondents are afraid of any of their fellow students.

Figure 6.19 shows the proportion of students who believe their teachers think their school work is 'very good' or 'good'. It is important for teachers to encourage students and indicate when they are making their best efforts. An encouraging sign is that Canadian youth are more likely than those in other countries at age 15 and for the boys at ages 11 and 13 to feel that this is the case. The girls at ages 11 and 13 are also in the upper rank of

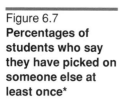

Figure 6.7
Percentages of students who say they have picked on someone else at least once*

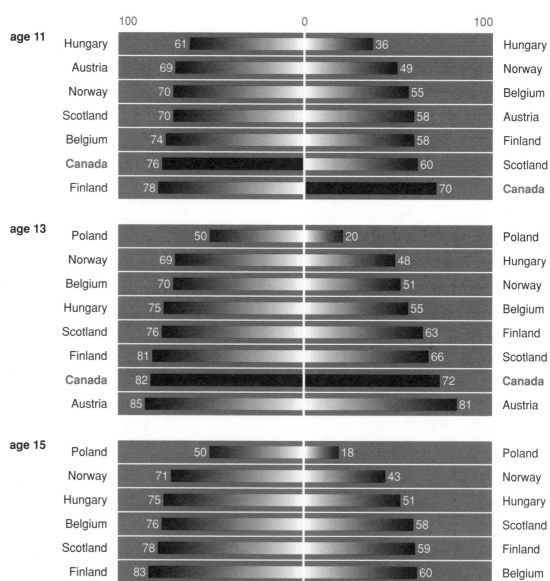

* Percentages based on responses to 'Yes, several times', 'Yes, once or twice'.

Figure 6.8
**Percentages of
most common
reactions to being
picked on***

☐ Male

■ Female

age 11　　　　　　　　age 13　　　　　　　　age 15

Do nothing and wait until they calm down

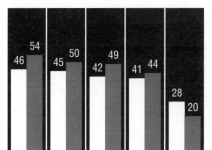

Canada　Belgium　Austria　Scotland　Hungary

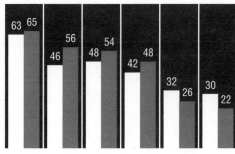

Belgium　Austria　**Canada**　Scotland　Poland　Hungary

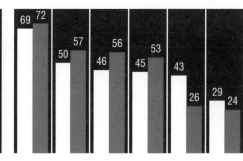

Belgium　Austria　**Canada**　Scotland　Poland　Hungary

Shout at the others

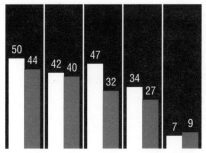

Canada　Scotland　Belgium　Austria　Hungary

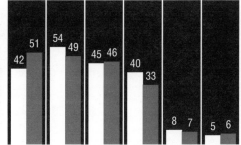

Belgium　**Canada**　Scotland　Austria　Poland　Hungary

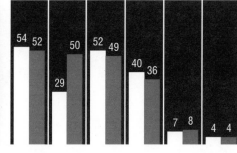

Canada　Belgium　Scotland　Austria　Poland　Hungary

Try to get away

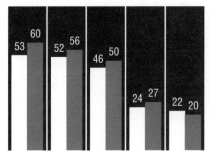

Austria　**Canada**　Scotland　Belgium　Hungary

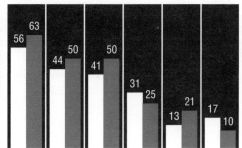

Austria　Scotland　**Canada**　Belgium　Hungary　Poland

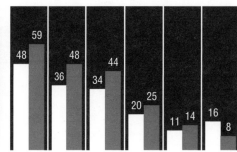

Austria　Scotland　**Canada**　Belgium　Hungary　Poland

* See Table 58
in Appendix C.

countries on this measure. In Canada, rarely are there standardized tests that might be used to assign these age groups more formally to particular achievement categories. In several other countries in the study, such standardized tests are used extensively and students are given information that places them in percentiles in relation to their peers. This is true of Sweden and Finland, and enables the students to place themselves more exactly in comparison to others and produces a more realistic distribution across the four response categories.

The relationship between the structure of a school system and students' responses to it is difficult to assess. However, both Hungary and Finland tend to have relatively structured educational systems and students from these countries are least likely to say they like school. In those systems that are somewhat more student-centred and flexible, students are more inclined to say they like school (see Figure 6.20). Nevertheless, more information is required before this relationship can be verified. Canadian youth tend to fall in the middle in the comparisons across countries on this measure, although Canadian 15-year-old girls are near the top.

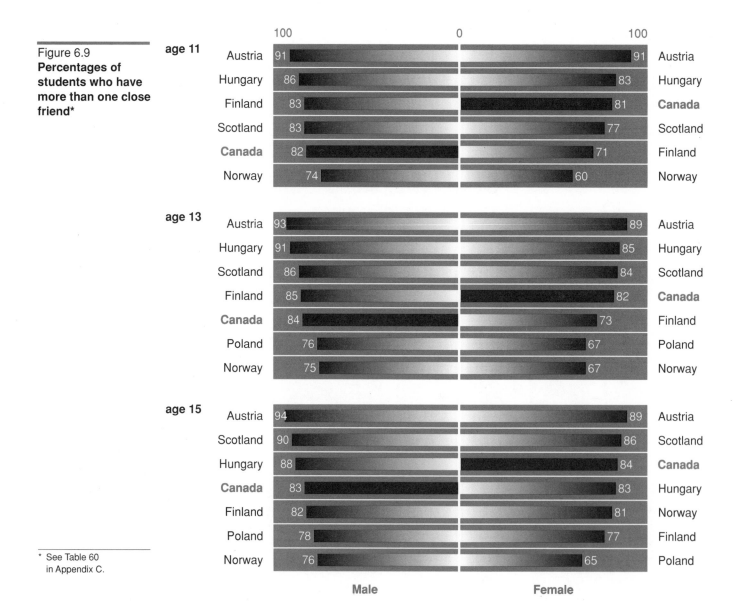

Figure 6.9
Percentages of students who have more than one close friend*

age 11

	Male		Female	
Austria	91		91	Austria
Hungary	86		83	Hungary
Finland	83		81	Canada
Scotland	83		77	Scotland
Canada	82		71	Finland
Norway	74		60	Norway

age 13

	Male		Female	
Austria	93		89	Austria
Hungary	91		85	Hungary
Scotland	86		84	Scotland
Finland	85		82	Canada
Canada	84		73	Finland
Poland	76		67	Poland
Norway	75		67	Norway

age 15

	Male		Female	
Austria	94		89	Austria
Scotland	90		86	Scotland
Hungary	88		84	Canada
Canada	83		83	Hungary
Finland	82		81	Norway
Poland	78		77	Finland
Norway	76		65	Poland

Male   **Female**

* See Table 60 in Appendix C.

Anselm Eder (1990), in measuring social integration, included the concept of 'fear of teachers'. The argument he made is that the more fearful students are of teachers, the less likely they are to be integrated into the life of the school. From Figure 6.21 we see that Canadian students tend to be in the middle of the range on this question. There is a decline in the proportion of Canadian youth who are fearful of a teacher from the age 11 to age 15 groups, and girls tend to be more fearful of their teachers than boys. The substantial proportion of young people who do fear teachers is noteworthy; certainly, it is the responsibility of the schools to make students feel accepted and not fearful. Relationships between students and teachers built around fear do not contribute to positive mental health.

School is not a very satisfying place if students are afraid of their peers. We have seen previously that

Canadian youth have two characteristics that slightly differentiate them from their peers in other countries. They tend to pick on each other a little more and tend to be a little more dependent on their friends for guidance and support. As seen in Figure 6.22, Canadian young people tend to be in

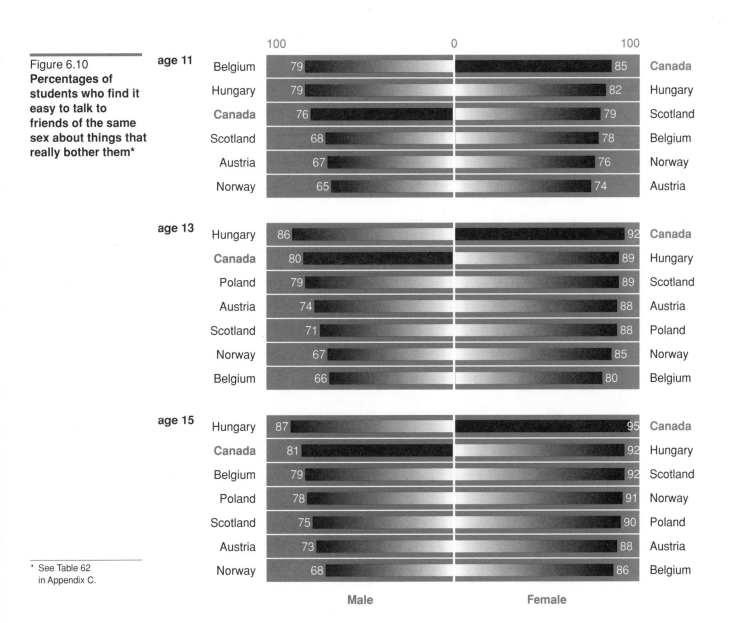

Figure 6.10
Percentages of students who find it easy to talk to friends of the same sex about things that really bother them*

* See Table 62 in Appendix C.

the upper ranks of countries indicating that they are afraid of at least one of their fellow students. This is especially notable at age 11.

F. Summary

The findings on relationships for Canadian youth illustrate a clear pattern. They are more likely to experience strain in their relationships with their parents, to look to their friends for advice on personal and career matters, and to be aggressive in relationships with each other. To have positive attitudes toward school and good mental health young people typically require a network of friends with whom to share thoughts, behaviours and offer advice, but such relationships should not be developed at the expense of positive relationships at home. The most well-adjusted young people come from supportive home environments where there is little conflict about important issues such as how time is spent. The changing nature of family life, in which more parents separate or divorce and both parents work, and parents spending less time with their children, appear to

Figure 6.11
Percentages of students who find it easy to talk to friends of the opposite sex about things that really bother them*

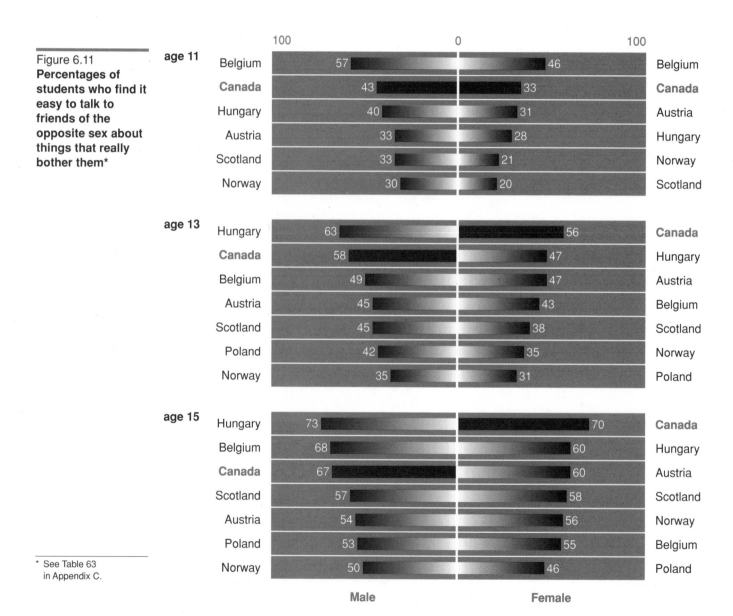

* See Table 63 in Appendix C.

74

affect the quality of child-parent relationships adversely. The school, rather than providing a necessary support system to encourage achievement and to provide the opportunities for positive school relationships, is seen by some youth as rigid and insensitive. Using friends as a primary source of meaning and purpose in life is only healthy when it encourages the appropriate behaviours. However, friends can provide reinforcement for both healthy and hazardous behaviours. The findings clearly indicate that there are differences across countries with regard to the support young people receive from school. It might prove fruitful to examine how this is achieved in the countries that are more successful.

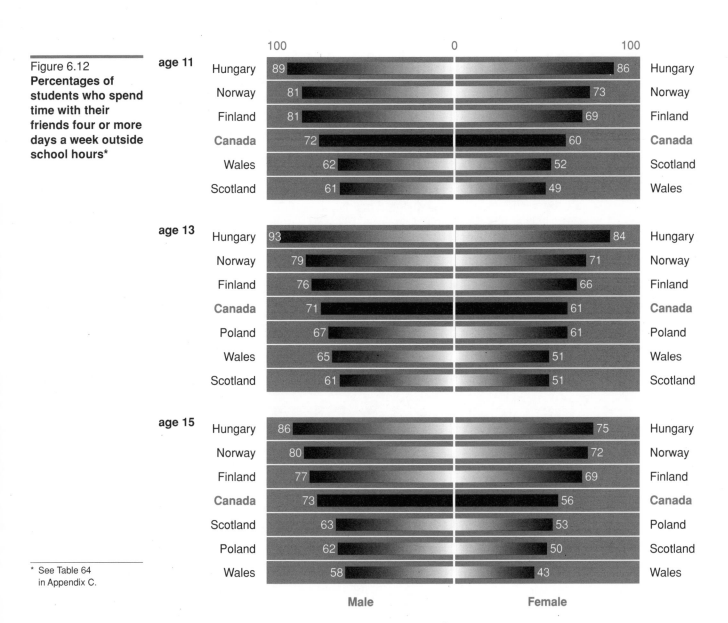

Figure 6.12
Percentages of students who spend time with their friends four or more days a week outside school hours*

* See Table 64 in Appendix C.

Figure 6.13
Percentages of students who responded 'very happy' or 'quite happy' to "How do you feel about your life at present?"*

☐ Very happy

■ Quite happy

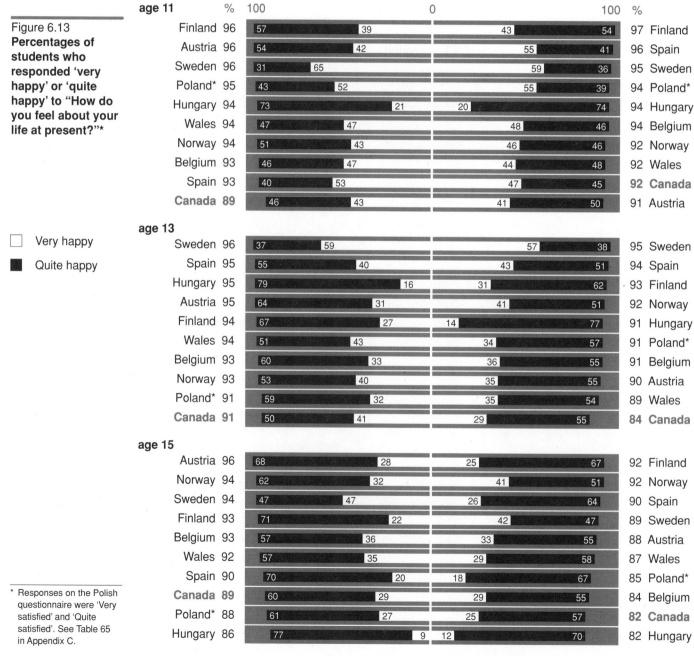

age 11	%	Male		Female	%	
Finland	96	57 / 39		43 / 54	97	Finland
Austria	96	54 / 42		55 / 41	96	Spain
Sweden	96	31 / 65		59 / 36	95	Sweden
Poland*	95	43 / 52		55 / 39	94	Poland*
Hungary	94	73 / 21		20 / 74	94	Hungary
Wales	94	47 / 47		48 / 46	94	Belgium
Norway	94	51 / 43		46 / 46	92	Norway
Belgium	93	46 / 47		44 / 48	92	Wales
Spain	93	40 / 53		47 / 45	92	**Canada**
Canada	89	46 / 43		41 / 50	91	Austria

age 13	%	Male		Female	%	
Sweden	96	37 / 59		57 / 38	95	Sweden
Spain	95	55 / 40		43 / 51	94	Spain
Hungary	95	79 / 16		31 / 62	93	Finland
Austria	95	64 / 31		41 / 51	92	Norway
Finland	94	67 / 27		14 / 77	91	Hungary
Wales	94	51 / 43		34 / 57	91	Poland*
Belgium	93	60 / 33		36 / 55	91	Belgium
Norway	93	53 / 40		35 / 55	90	Austria
Poland*	91	59 / 32		35 / 54	89	Wales
Canada	91	50 / 41		29 / 55	84	**Canada**

age 15	%	Male		Female	%	
Austria	96	68 / 28		25 / 67	92	Finland
Norway	94	62 / 32		41 / 51	92	Norway
Sweden	94	47 / 47		26 / 64	90	Spain
Finland	93	71 / 22		42 / 47	89	Sweden
Belgium	93	57 / 36		33 / 55	88	Austria
Wales	92	57 / 35		29 / 58	87	Wales
Spain	90	70 / 20		18 / 67	85	Poland*
Canada	89	60 / 29		29 / 55	84	Belgium
Poland*	88	61 / 27		25 / 57	82	**Canada**
Hungary	86	77 / 9		12 / 70	82	Hungary

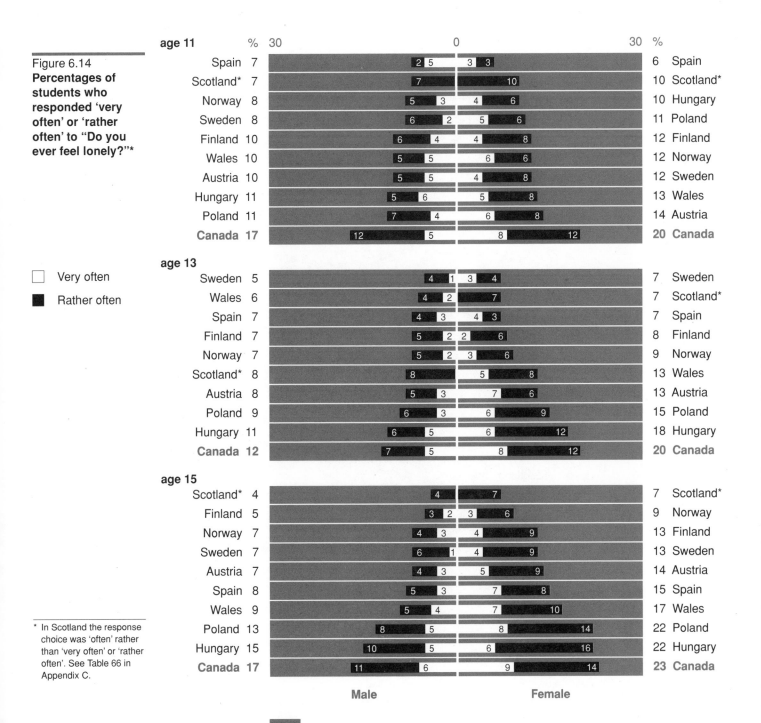

Figure 6.14
Percentages of students who responded 'very often' or 'rather often' to "Do you ever feel lonely?"*

Very often
Rather often

* In Scotland the response choice was 'often' rather than 'very often' or 'rather often'. See Table 66 in Appendix C.

age 11

	Male	Female	
Spain 7	2 5	3 3	6 Spain
Scotland* 7	7	10	10 Scotland*
Norway 8	5 3	4 6	10 Hungary
Sweden 8	6 2	5 6	11 Poland
Finland 10	6 4	4 8	12 Finland
Wales 10	5 5	6 6	12 Norway
Austria 10	5 5	4 8	12 Sweden
Hungary 11	5 6	5 8	13 Wales
Poland 11	7 4	6 8	14 Austria
Canada 17	12 5	8 12	**20 Canada**

age 13

	Male	Female	
Sweden 5	4 1	3 4	7 Sweden
Wales 6	4 2	7	7 Scotland*
Spain 7	4 3	4 3	7 Spain
Finland 7	5 2	2 6	8 Finland
Norway 7	5 2	3 6	9 Norway
Scotland* 8	8	5 8	13 Wales
Austria 8	5 3	7 6	13 Austria
Poland 9	6 3	6 9	15 Poland
Hungary 11	6 5	6 12	18 Hungary
Canada 12	7 5	8 12	**20 Canada**

age 15

	Male	Female	
Scotland* 4	4	7	7 Scotland*
Finland 5	3 2	3 6	9 Norway
Norway 7	4 3	4 9	13 Finland
Sweden 7	6 1	4 9	13 Sweden
Austria 7	4 3	5 9	14 Austria
Spain 8	5 3	7 8	15 Spain
Wales 9	5 4	7 10	17 Wales
Poland 13	8 5	8 14	22 Poland
Hungary 15	10 5	6 16	22 Hungary
Canada 17	11 6	9 14	**23 Canada**

Figure 6.15
Percentages of students who say it is 'very important' to have free time to spend on their own*

* See Table 70 in Appendix C.

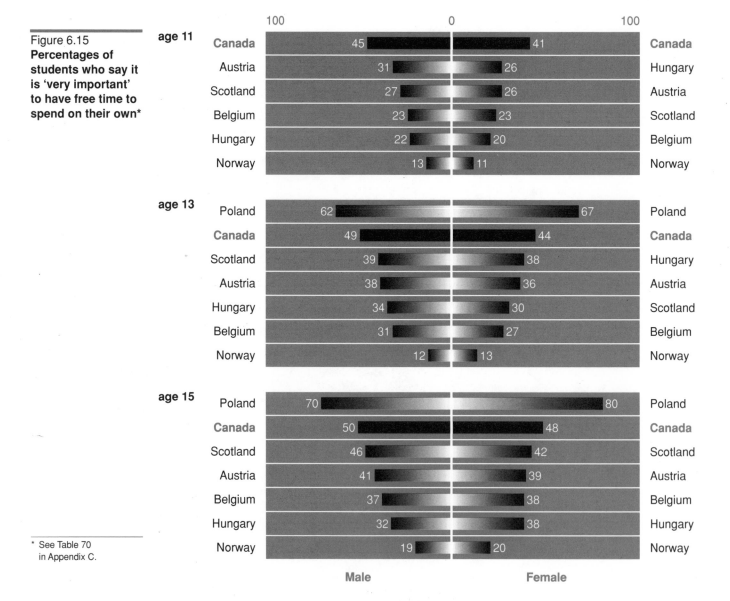

	100	0	100	
age 11				
Canada	45	41		**Canada**
Austria	31	26		Hungary
Scotland	27	26		Austria
Belgium	23	23		Scotland
Hungary	22	20		Belgium
Norway	13	11		Norway
age 13				
Poland	62	67		Poland
Canada	49	44		**Canada**
Scotland	39	38		Hungary
Austria	38	36		Austria
Hungary	34	30		Scotland
Belgium	31	27		Belgium
Norway	12	13		Norway
age 15				
Poland	70	80		Poland
Canada	50	48		**Canada**
Scotland	46	42		Scotland
Austria	41	39		Austria
Belgium	37	38		Belgium
Hungary	32	38		Hungary
Norway	19	20		Norway

Male   **Female**

Figure 6.16
Percentages of students who say they 'often' or 'sometimes' feel like an outsider

☐ Often

■ Sometimes

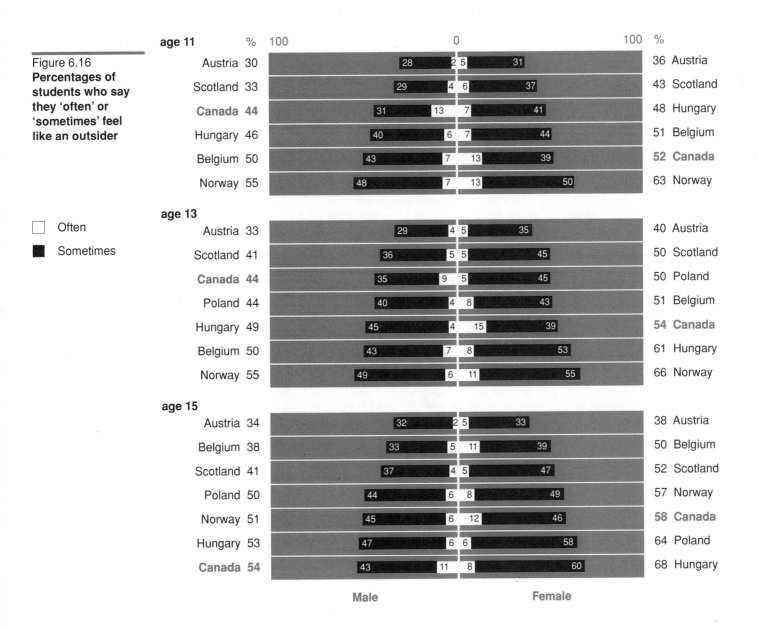

age 11	% 100		0		100 %	
Austria	30	28 · 2	5	31	36	Austria
Scotland	33	29 · 4	6	37	43	Scotland
Canada	**44**	31 · 13	7	41	48	Hungary
Hungary	46	40 · 6	7	44	51	Belgium
Belgium	50	43 · 7	13	39	**52**	**Canada**
Norway	55	48 · 7	13	50	63	Norway

age 13						
Austria	33	29 · 4	5	35	40	Austria
Scotland	41	36 · 5	5	45	50	Scotland
Canada	**44**	35 · 9	5	45	50	Poland
Poland	44	40 · 4	8	43	51	Belgium
Hungary	49	45 · 4	15	39	**54**	**Canada**
Belgium	50	43 · 7	8	53	61	Hungary
Norway	55	49 · 6	11	55	66	Norway

age 15						
Austria	34	32 · 2	5	33	38	Austria
Belgium	38	33 · 5	11	39	50	Belgium
Scotland	41	37 · 4	5	47	52	Scotland
Poland	50	44 · 6	8	49	57	Norway
Norway	51	45 · 6	12	46	**58**	**Canada**
Hungary	53	47 · 6	6	58	64	Poland
Canada	**54**	43 · 11	8	60	68	Hungary

Male   Female

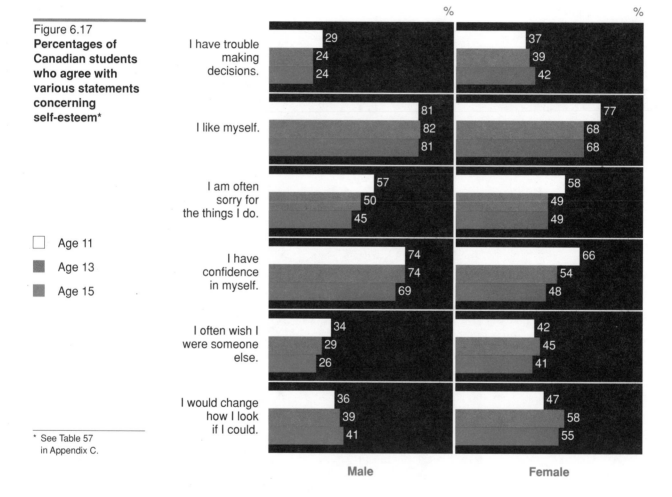

Figure 6.17
Percentages of Canadian students who agree with various statements concerning self-esteem*

Age 11
Age 13
Age 15

* See Table 57
  in Appendix C.

Figure 6.18
**Percentages of
Canadian students
who agree they
need to lose or gain
weight***

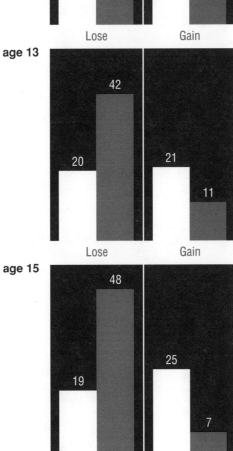

age 11

age 13

age 15

☐ Male
■ Female

* See Table 57
  in Appendix C.

Figure 6.19
Percentages of students who believe their teachers think their school work is 'very good' or 'good'*

Very good

Good

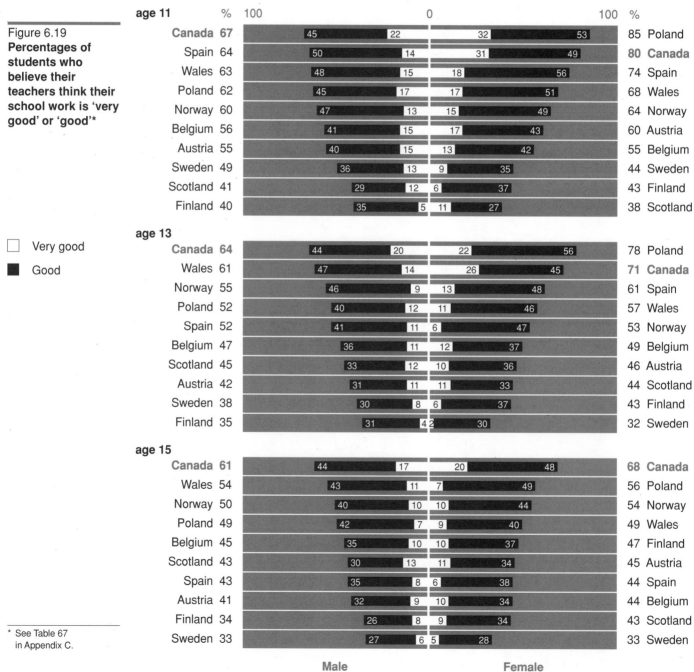

age 11

	% 100			0		100 %	
Canada 67	45	22		32	53	85	Poland
Spain 64	50	14		31	49	80	**Canada**
Wales 63	48	15		18	56	74	Spain
Poland 62	45	17		17	51	68	Wales
Norway 60	47	13		15	49	64	Norway
Belgium 56	41	15		17	43	60	Austria
Austria 55	40	15		13	42	55	Belgium
Sweden 49	36	13		9	35	44	Sweden
Scotland 41	29	12		6	37	43	Finland
Finland 40	35	5		11	27	38	Scotland

age 13

Canada 64	44	20		22	56	78	Poland
Wales 61	47	14		26	45	71	**Canada**
Norway 55	46	9		13	48	61	Spain
Poland 52	40	12		11	46	57	Wales
Spain 52	41	11		6	47	53	Norway
Belgium 47	36	11		12	37	49	Belgium
Scotland 45	33	12		10	36	46	Austria
Austria 42	31	11		11	33	44	Scotland
Sweden 38	30	8		6	37	43	Finland
Finland 35	31	4	2	30		32	Sweden

age 15

Canada 61	44	17		20	48	68	**Canada**
Wales 54	43	11		7	49	56	Poland
Norway 50	40	10		10	44	54	Norway
Poland 49	42	7		9	40	49	Wales
Belgium 45	35	10		10	37	47	Finland
Scotland 43	30	13		11	34	45	Austria
Spain 43	35	8		6	38	44	Spain
Austria 41	32	9		10	34	44	Belgium
Finland 34	26	8		9	34	43	Scotland
Sweden 33	27	6		5	28	33	Sweden

Male

Female

* See Table 67
  in Appendix C.

82

Figure 6.20
Percentages of students who indicate they like school*

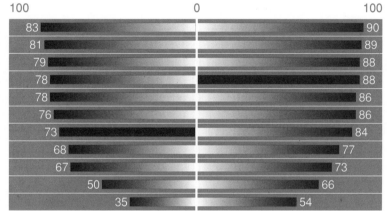

age 11

	Male		Female	
Scotland	83		90	Poland
Norway	81		89	Sweden
Poland	79		88	Scotland
Austria	78		88	**Canada**
Sweden	78		86	Austria
Wales	76		86	Wales
Canada	73		84	Norway
Spain	68		77	Belgium
Belgium	67		73	Spain
Finland	50		66	Finland
Hungary	35		54	Hungary

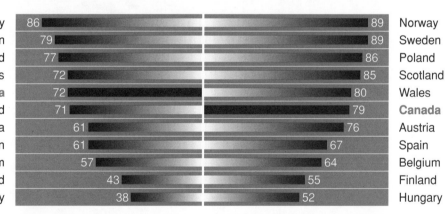

age 13

	Male		Female	
Norway	86		89	Norway
Sweden	79		89	Sweden
Scotland	77		86	Poland
Wales	72		85	Scotland
Canada	72		80	Wales
Poland	71		79	**Canada**
Austria	61		76	Austria
Spain	61		67	Spain
Belgium	57		64	Belgium
Finland	43		55	Finland
Hungary	38		52	Hungary

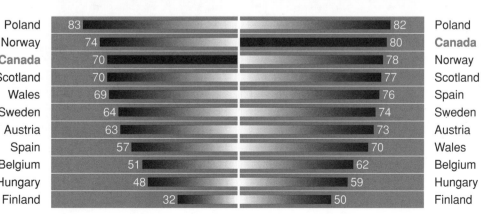

age 15

	Male		Female	
Poland	83		82	Poland
Norway	74		80	**Canada**
Canada	70		78	Norway
Scotland	70		77	Scotland
Wales	69		76	Spain
Sweden	64		74	Sweden
Austria	63		73	Austria
Spain	57		70	Wales
Belgium	51		62	Belgium
Hungary	48		59	Hungary
Finland	32		50	Finland

Male   **Female**

* Percentages based on responses to 'I like it a lot', 'I like it a little bit'. See Table 68 in Appendix C.

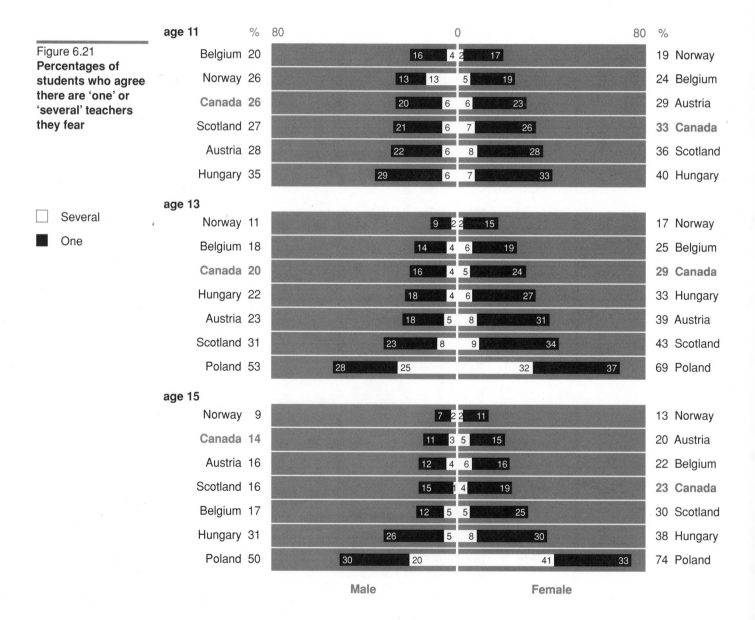

Figure 6.21
Percentages of students who agree there are 'one' or 'several' teachers they fear

☐ Several
■ One

age 11   %   80   0   80   %

Male				Female
Belgium 20	16 4 2	17	19 Norway
Norway 26	13 13	5 19	24 Belgium
Canada 26	20 6	6 23	29 Austria
Scotland 27	21 6	7 26	33 Canada
Austria 28	22 6	8 28	36 Scotland
Hungary 35	29 6	7 33	40 Hungary

age 13

Norway 11	9 2 2	15	17 Norway
Belgium 18	14 4	6 19	25 Belgium
Canada 20	16 4	5 24	29 Canada
Hungary 22	18 4	6 27	33 Hungary
Austria 23	18 5	8 31	39 Austria
Scotland 31	23 8	9 34	43 Scotland
Poland 53	28 25	32 37	69 Poland

age 15

Norway 9	7 2 2	11	13 Norway
Canada 14	11 3	5 15	20 Austria
Austria 16	12 4	6 16	22 Belgium
Scotland 16	15 1	4 19	23 Canada
Belgium 17	12 5	5 25	30 Scotland
Hungary 31	26 5	8 30	38 Hungary
Poland 50	30 20	41 33	74 Poland

Male   Female

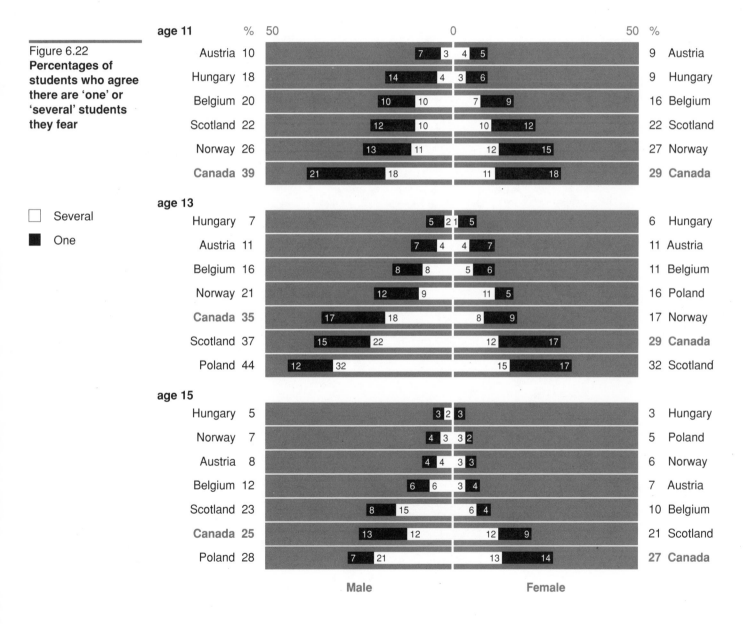

Figure 6.22
Percentages of students who agree there are 'one' or 'several' students they fear

☐ Several
■ One

age 11

	%					
Austria	10	7 3	4 5	9	Austria
Hungary	18	14 4	3 6	9	Hungary
Belgium	20	10 10	7 9	16	Belgium
Scotland	22	12 10	10 12	22	Scotland
Norway	26	13 11	12 15	27	Norway
Canada	39	21 18	11 18	29	Canada

age 13

	%					
Hungary	7	5 2 1	5	6	Hungary
Austria	11	7 4	4 7	11	Austria
Belgium	16	8 8	5 6	11	Belgium
Norway	21	12 9	11 5	16	Poland
Canada	35	17 18	8 9	17	Norway
Scotland	37	15 22	12 17	29	Canada
Poland	44	12 32	15 17	32	Scotland

age 15

	%					
Hungary	5	3 2	3	3	Hungary
Norway	7	4 3	3 2	5	Poland
Austria	8	4 4	3 3	6	Norway
Belgium	12	6 6	3 4	7	Austria
Scotland	23	8 15	6 4	10	Belgium
Canada	25	13 12	12 9	21	Scotland
Poland	28	7 21	13 14	27	Canada

Male   **Female**

Chapter 7

Relationships between Health-risk Factors

A. Introduction

In the past few years, interest in designing comprehensive health education programs has increased. Behavioural change conceptual models have been used to guide research to determine whether curriculum affects knowledge, attitudes and skills which, in turn, lead to appropriate health behaviours. Because education alone has not produced the desired outcomes, efforts have been made to introduce a comprehensive school health model, combining the school instructional program with community health services. In practice, this has come to mean targeting an array of health-risk behaviours, such as smoking, alcohol abuse, poor diet and lack of physical activity, in an integrated fashion and promoting knowledge and skills that attempt to deal with the prevention of such behaviours. This approach is combined with dental, medical and social services integrated from community agencies and reinforced in the home.

The health-belief model (Becker, 1974) has been applied on numerous occasions to guide the development of health education programs, but its dependence on the rational individual having the necessary information to make appropriate decisions has limited its utility. Since Jessor and Jessor's work (1977), linking a wide range of health-risk behaviours, a number of efforts have been made to develop broad-based theories to explain the patterning of health-risk behaviours. The theory of planned behavior (Azjen, 1985), expanding on the theory of reasoned action (Azjen and Fishbein, 1980), has more recently been used to guide the development of health programs but, as yet, the influence of cultural and social determinants are not fully incorporated into either of these theories. Concerns not well conceptualized in these theories include: high-risk behaviours may have both positive and negative consequences with regard to sexual behaviour, diet and even smoking; conditions and consequences are not always that clear; the perception of the risk depends on the way the issue is presented; individuals frequently underestimate the cumulative effects of extended use or involvement in some behaviour or its combined effect with other health-risk behaviours; and for many young people delaying gratification is difficult (Leviton, 1989).

Bandura's (1989) theory of perceived self-efficacy is particularly attractive to educators because it implies, given the right circumstances, that young people can control their behaviour, motivation and social environment; therefore, appropriate behaviour can be taught and students will adopt it. To some extent this is true, but it is becoming clear that the social environment is a very powerful influence in determining behaviours. Evidence of this can be seen in research on smoking behaviour and AIDS (acquired immunodeficiency syndrome). It appears that health-risk behaviours tend to be linked together in the same young people, because they have such a strong need to be accepted by their peers and to become independent of parents. These needs shape their behaviour and determine their actions more than future health considerations do. It may be that young people who are not fully accepted at home or in school settings turn to each other to satisfy their need for acceptance and often end up sharing sets of values and behaviours that are both physically and socially unhealthy. For some young people, then, the social environment is a stronger influence on their behaviour than is their awareness of the dangers of risky practices.

This study provides an opportunity to examine the interrelationships among health factors in a variety of settings. Two important measures not included in the surveys administered in other countries were added to the Canadian survey. The measure regarding relationships with parents is particularly important because it shapes the way young people see themselves as a result of their associations with their parents. The other measure, self-esteem, has proven to be particularly useful in understanding how young people feel about themselves in social situations. The massive data file from the 11-country study enables researchers to examine many combinations of factors. Limitations of time and space have forced us to be selective in our presentation of the findings and to choose small groups of countries similar in some respects to Canada for comparison purposes. Therefore, this chapter covers only a small segment of what is potentially available in this comprehensive study.

In the following section, we have taken three factors and have attempted to identify the other factors that predict the occurrence of the three. The first, 'smoking' behaviour', can be seen as a physical health issue. The second, 'liking school', represents adjustment in the school setting. The third, 'feeling like an outsider' is an indicator of social adjustment. In the second analysis discussed in this chapter, we look at relationships between health-risk behaviours in the selected countries.

B. Predicting health-risk behaviours

1. Smoking

Some variation occurs in smoking behaviour across countries, but there is a stable core of smokers in each country. Even when there is a strong education program, where legislation prohibits cigarette advertising and when taxes make cigarette smoking very expensive, such as in Canada and Finland, a substantial number of young people smoke. Why then do young people smoke when there is so much evidence linking smoking to serious disease in later life?

Figure 7.1 presents findings from six countries for 15-year-olds that purport to isolate the factors that predict smoking. The black dots in the figure indicate that the factor does predict smoking behaviour. (Figures 7.1, 7.2 and 7.3 have been developed from regression analyses. The procedure and all significant factors for each country are presented in Appendix B.) It is quite clear that smoking is a socially unacceptable behaviour and those 15-year-olds who smoke typically engage in other health-risk behaviours with their peers. The most pronounced of these risky activities, of course, is drinking alcohol to excess at least once. This is true in all participating countries. It is also quite common for 15-year-olds who smoke not to be involved in athletics, not to eat healthy foods regularly, and to show evidence of health problems such as headaches, stomach aches and other ailments. However, there are quite important findings related to other aspects of their lives. Girls who smoke in four of six countries also argue with or have difficulty talking with their parents, are experiencing difficulty in school, or both. Boys in four of the countries spend an excessive amount of time with their friends.

To summarize these relationships, there is a group of young smokers in all six of the countries who appear to be part of a sub-culture of health risk-takers. In all cases this is characterized by having been drunk, and also by other evident health concerns, by lack of involvement in physical activity and by poor relationships with parents. One of the ironies of these findings is that the smoker tends to have good friends and to spend a great deal of time with these friends. It would appear then that smoking is a behaviour engaged in by groups of friends who are experiencing stress at home and difficulty in school and, perhaps as a result, look to each other for support and encouragement. Unfortunately, it appears that engaging in health-risk behaviours is a condition of group membership. This makes it particularly difficult to influence these young people not to begin smoking or to stop once they have started.

Figure 7.1
Factors that predict smoking in 15-year-olds

		Belgium	Hungary	Austria	Scotland	Finland	Canada
Has been drunk	M	●	●	●	●	●	●
	F	●	●	●	●	●	●
Cannot talk to parents	M	—	●	●	—	—	—
	F	●	—	●	●	—	●
Is not involved in sports	M	—	●	—	●	●	●
	F	—	●	●	—	●	●
Poor diet	M	—	—	—	—	●	—
	F	—	●	—	●	—	—
Dislikes school or achieves poor marks	M	—	—	—	—	—	—
	F	●	—	●	●	—	●
Is usually tired in the morning	M	●	—	—	●	—	—
	F	—	—	—	—	—	—
Has pocket money	M	—	—	●	—	—	—
	F	—	—	●	—	—	●
Has health concerns	M	—	●	—	●	—	—
	F	—	—	—	●	●	●
Spends a great deal of time with friends	M	—	●	●	●	—	●
	F	—	—	—	—	●	●

2. Liking school

In our research on the factors that make school responsive to the needs of young people (King and Peart, 1990), we found evidence that the school that is accepting of young people and that attempts to recognize and respond to their needs is most satisfying to young people. In Figure 7.2, we identify the factors that predict liking school in the three age groups in four of the countries studied. Liking school is consistently related to the level of achievement attained in school. Students with good marks are far more likely to like school than those with poor marks. Interestingly, as for the smoking predictors, drinking to excess is an important predictor; young people who have been drunk are not as likely to like school. In Canada, 'relationships with parents', for the older students, is also an important predictor and those happy with their life tend to be quite happy with school. On the latter measure, the pattern is true for all age groups in Finland.

There are some implications from these findings for designing a "healthy" school — a school in which young people are likely to feel better about themselves. It is important that the school provide support and encouragement in an environment where success can be achieved and a setting where friendships can be developed and maintained. The notion of the healthy school will receive greater attention in the near future from the team of international researchers examining the health behaviours of school children.

3. Being an outsider

In Canada, increasing attention has recently been given to relationships between young people and how peer relations affect personal adjustment and performance in school. A Norwegian researcher, Dan Olweus (1991), has been studying the phenomenon of bullying behaviour for a number of years and has developed an intervention for discouraging bullying among young people. His intervention is being considered for use in Canadian school boards.

In the analysis presented in Figure 7.3, we examine the factors related to young people feeling like outsiders. It is not surprising to find that having been bullied is one of the predictors of young people feeling like outsiders in nearly all grades in three of the four countries. The outsider feels lonely, has difficulty making new friends, is often afraid of other students, but does not necessarily engage in other health-risk behaviours. This analysis also supports the contention that the school can play a role in making students feel more accepted. This can be done by making opportunities to allow friendships to develop, providing classroom settings that encourage social interaction and discouraging bullying and scapegoating behaviours.

Figure 7.2
Factors that predict 'liking school'

		Canada 11	Canada 13	Canada 15	Austria 11	Austria 13	Austria 15	Finland 11	Finland 13	Finland 15	Scotland 11	Scotland 13	Scotland 15
Good marks	M	●	●	●	●	●	●	●	●	●	●	●	●
	F	●	●	●	●	●	●	●	●	●	●	●	●
Is not tired in the morning	M	●	●	●	—	●	—	—	●	●	—	●	●
	F	●	●	●	—	●	●	●	●	●	—	—	●
Can talk to parents	M	—	●	—	—	—	●	—	—	—	●	●	—
	F	●	—	●	—	—	—	—	—	●	●	—	—
Has not been drunk	M	●	—	●	—	●	●	—	●	●	—	—	●
	F	—	●	●	—	—	—	—	●	●	—	●	—
Does not smoke	M	—	—	—	—	●	—	—	—	—	●	—	—
	F	—	—	●	●	●	●	—	—	—	●	—	●
Is happy with life	M	—	—	●	●	●	—	●	●	●	—	—	—
	F	—	●	—	—	●	●	●	●	●	—	—	—
Good diet	M	●	—	—	—	●	—	—	●	●	—	—	—
	F	●	—	—	—	—	●	●	●	—	●	—	—

C. Interrelationships

There is a long tradition of examining the relationships between health-risk factors. Typically, it has been shown that people who smoke and drink are also more likely to have poor dietary and physical activity practices. More recently, there has been an effort to draw in other measures; not only socio-economic status but also mental health, relationships with peers and parents and adjustment in school. Anselm Eder (1990) has focused on the concept of social integration, which means the extent to which young people have a network of friends and share a number of values. He has demonstrated that the need for social integration for young people can result in the establishment of groupings that may be dysfunctional in terms of health-risk behaviours, but are important in meeting young peoples' needs to be accepted. Young people who smoke, drink or engage in risky sexual activity, because it is accepted and reinforced within their peer group, are not likely to respond well to education messages that emphasize positive health behaviours.

Ramon Mendoza and his Spanish research team have analysed data from the 1986 survey involving 10 countries to determine commonalities among health-risk behaviours across countries (Mendoza et al., 1991). They found that frequent consumption of tobacco, alcohol and unhealthy food is linked to physical inactivity, dislike of school, poor marks, health problems and an active social life away from school and family. This pattern is particularly common among boys of lower class backgrounds. Health habits tend to be best among girls from higher social classes. Overall, the relationships between these factors were not as strong among girls as among boys. Both Eder's and Mendoza's work reinforces the presence of a link between health-risk behaviours and an array of other social problems.

To determine whether similar relationships exist between such factors in Canada, we conducted a factor analysis for each of the three age groups. In addition, we selected two other countries for similar analysis, Finland and Scotland. For the Canadian analysis, we were able to augment the number of factors in the analysis by incorporating a measure of 'relationships with parents' as well as 'self-esteem'. Figures 7.4 and 7.5 present the findings for 13-year-old girls and boys respectively in a simplified format. The Scottish and Finnish data for 13-year-olds are similarly presented in Tables 7.6 to 7.9. A more detailed summary of this analysis, including information for all three age groups, can be found in Appendix B.

Figure 7.3
Factors that predict 'feeling like an outsider'

		Austria 11	13	15	Scotland 11	13	15	Canada 11	13	15	Hungary 11	13	15
Has been bullied	M	●	●	●	●	—	●	●	●	●	●	—	—
	F	●	●	●	●	●	●	●	●	●	—	—	—
Can't make new friends	M	●	●	—	●	●	—	●	●	●	●	●	—
	F	●	●	●	—	—	●	●	●	●	—	—	●
Feels lonely	M	—	●	●	●	●	●	●	●	●	●	●	●
	F	—	●	●	●	●	●	●	●	●	●	●	●
Has not been drunk	M	●	—	—	—	—	—	—	—	—	—	—	—
	F	—	—	—	—	—	—	—	—	●	—	—	●
Does not drink	M	—	—	●	●	●	—	—	—	●	—	—	—
	F	—	—	—	—	—	—	—	—	—	—	—	—
Afraid of other pupils	M	—	—	●	●	●	—	—	—	●	—	—	●
	F	●	●	—	●	—	—	●	●	●	—	—	—
Low self-esteem*	M							—	●	●			
	F							●	●	●			
Feels low	M	—	—	—	—	●	●	●	●	●	—	—	—
	F	—	●	—	—	—	●	—	●	●	—	●	—
Cannot talk to parents	M	—	—	●	—	●	—	—	—	—	●	—	—
	F	—	—	●	●	—	●	●	●	—	●	●	●
Unhappy with life	M	—	—	●	—	—	—	●	●	—	—	—	●
	F	—	—	●	—	—	—	—	—	●	—	—	—

* a factor examined only in Canada

Figures 7.4 and 7.5 illustrate that seven categories of factors come together in one grouping — mental health, social health, relationship with parents, adjustment to school, health status, physical fitness and participation in sports. The items representing the factors have been presented in a positive direction to illustrate that when one positive measure is present the others are also present in a positive direction. The reverse of this is also true; that is, if a person is experiencing difficulties in one of the areas, he or she is likely to be experiencing them in all of the others. Interestingly, this grouping of factors does not touch on the traditional measures of good health such as diet, behaviour related to smoking and alcohol and physical activity; rather, it is primarily concerned with mental and social health.

For girls, the second grouping of factors is built around risk behaviours and social integration. As we have noted in the previous chapter, these young people tend to be somewhat alienated, but together they share health-risk behaviours. For the boys, the friendship side is not as important, but being involved in smoking and drinking is.

When a similar analysis was conducted for the Scottish 13-year-old students, it was found that the first grouping for both boys and girls is built around adjustment to school and includes avoidance of smoking and drinking and a positive relationship with parents (Figures 7.6 and 7.7). For the boys it also includes some positive measures of mental health and diet. The second grouping also tends to link the absence (or presence) of negative groupings of factors such as loneliness, feeling like an outsider, fear of other pupils, having been bullied, being unable to talk with father and mother, having difficulty making friends and spending little time with friends. This grouping is similar to the Canadian first grouping, but with far more emphasis on relationships with friends and treatment by peers.

As can be seen from Figures 7.8 and 7.9, the relationships between health-risk behaviours are similar for Finnish and Canadian 13-year-olds. However, for the Finnish youth, smoking and alcohol use are also included. The second factor tends to be the obverse of the first with the addition of the typical combination of spending much time with friends and drinking and smoking behaviours. This analysis reinforces the strong link that exists between all categories of positive health behaviours from diet to relationships with parents.

Figure 7.4
Relationships among health factors for Canadian 13-year-old girls

Group 1	Group 2
Mental health - rarely lonely - rarely depressed - rarely irritable - fresh in the morning - rarely get headaches - happy with life	**Risk behaviours** - smoke - drink beer - drink liquor - been drunk
Social health - positive self-esteem - rarely feel like an outsider	**Participation in sports** - not good at sports
Relationship with parents - agree about leisure time - can talk about problems with father - can talk about problems with mother - talk to parents often - overall positive relationships with parents	**Social integration** - make new friends easily - spend a great deal of time with friends - easy to talk about problems with opposite sex friends
Adjustment to school - like school - high academic achievement	
Health status - very healthy	
Physical fitness - very fit	
Participation in sports - good at sports	

D. Summary

Young people who take serious risks with their health in one area typically, but not always, do so in others. As in other studies, this study affirms the association between smoking, drinking, poor diet and infrequent physical activity. Also, youth who are alienated from school because of low levels of achievement and who experience difficulties in relationships with their parents are more likely to engage in health-risk behaviours.

Youth in this latter group tend to be drawn together and to share risk behaviours as part of earning and maintaining the right to group membership. When other health-risk behaviours, such as risky sexual activity and drinking and driving, are examined, the same youth are found to be involved. Therefore, health-risk behaviours can be seen to be imbedded in the structure of society. Educational programs containing accurate information about healthy lifestyles are necessary but so are opportunities to develop skills needed for positive relationships with peers and parents. Perhaps most important of all is the need to develop schools that are supportive of young peoples' needs — academic, social and recreational — and which discourage the formation of groups of individuals who are excluded from participating fully.

Figure 7.5

Relationships among health factors for Canadian 13-year-old boys

Group 1	Group 2
Mental health - rarely lonely - rarely depressed - fresh in the morning - happy with life	**Risk behaviours** - smoke - drink beer - drink wine - drink liquor - been drunk
Social health - make new friends easily - positive self-esteem - rarely feel like an outsider	
Relationship with parents - can talk about problems with father - can talk about problems with mother - talk to parents often - overall positive relationships with parents	
Adjustment to school - like school	
Health status - very healthy	
Physical fitness - very fit	
Participation in sports - good at sports - expect to participate in sports at age 20	

Figure 7.6

Relationships among health factors for Scottish 13-year-old girls

Group 1	Group 2
Relationship with parents - agree about leisure time	**Mental health** - rarely lonely
Adjustment to school - like school - high academic achievement	**Social integration** - rarely feel like an outsider - have not been bullied - make new friends easily - easy to talk about problems with same sex friends - easy to talk about problems with opposite sex friends - spend a great deal of time with friends
Risk behaviours - don't smoke - seldom drink beer - seldom drink wine - seldom drink liquor - seldom drink cider - seldom been drunk	**Relationship with parents** - can talk about problems with mother

Figure 7.7
Relationships among health factors for Scottish 13-year-old boys

Group 1	Group 2
Mental health - rarely irritable - fresh in the morning	**Mental health** - rarely lonely

Relationship with parents
- can talk to parents
- agree about leisure time
	Social integration
	- rarely feel like an outsider
	- have not been bullied
	- make new friends easily
	- not afraid of other pupils
	- easy to talk about problems
	    with same-sex friends
	- easy to talk about problems
	    with opposite-sex friends
	- spend a great deal of time with friends
	- have a lot of close friends

Adjustment to school - like school	
Risk behaviours - don't smoke - seldom drink beer - seldom drink liquor - seldom drink cider - seldom been drunk	**Relationship with parents** - can talk about problems with mother
Diet - rarely drink soft drinks - rarely eat sweets	

Figure 7.8
Relationships among health factors for Finnish 13-year-old girls

Group 1	Group 2
Mental health - fresh in the morning	**Mental health** - seldom lonely
Relationship with parents - can talk about problems with father	**Participation in sports** - low frequency and/or duration of participation
Physical fitness - very fit	**Physical fitness** - not fit
Participation in sports - high frequency and/or duration of participation	**Social integration** - easy to make new friends - spend a great deal of time with friends
Adjustment to school - like school	**Risk behaviours** - drink beer - drink wine - drink cider - been drunk
Risk behaviours - don't smoke - seldom drink beer - seldom drink wine - seldom drink liquor - seldom drink cider - seldom been drunk	

Figure 7.9
Relationships among health factors for Finnish 13-year-old boys

Group 1	Group 2
Mental health - rarely lonely - rarely depressed - fresh in the morning - happy with life	**Participation in sports** - not good at sports - not a member of a sports club - low frequency and/or duration of participation - don't expect to participate in sports at age 20
Relationship with parents - can talk about problems with father - can talk about problems with mother	**Physical fitness** - not fit
Physical fitness - very fit	**Risk behaviours** - drink beer - drink wine - drink liquor - drink cider - been drunk
Participation in sports - high frequency and/or duration of participation - expect to participate in sports at age 20	**Diet** drink soft drinks
Adjustment to school - like school - high academic achievement	
Risk behaviours - don't smoke - seldom drink beer - seldom drink cider - seldom drink liquor - seldom been drunk	
Health status - very healthy	

Chapter 8

Summary and Recommend- ations

A. Introduction

The primary purpose of this study is to examine the health behaviours and attitudes of young Canadians in comparison with those of young people from 10 other countries. Caution has been taken in attributing cause to differences between countries because it is not always easy to understand the cultural and political factors that precipitate such differences. However, young Canadians have been found to be substantially different from those in other countries with regard to some health-risk behaviours and these differences may suggest areas of concern that should be dealt with by health programs. At the same time, commonalities in health-risk behaviours that exist across countries indicate that some problems are deep-rooted and more intensive efforts to respond to them across all participating countries are required. Both these perspectives, that is, the notable differences in Canadian youth compared with youth in other countries and the patterns of health-risk behaviours common to youth across the countries, reinforce these recommendations.

In the following sections the main findings are summarized and strategies are suggested that might be used in program development. The relationships that exist among health-risk factors are also emphasized and common forces that underlie the development of these constellations of health-risk behaviours are suggested. To do this, an expanded conceptualization of the interrelationships between health-risk behaviours is presented.

B. Smoking, alcohol and drug use

There is a hard-core group of smokers in every country, and smoking in each country is linked to excessive alcohol use, that is, to having been drunk. Therefore, it appears that smoking behaviour exists in sub-groups of young people who are difficult to reach. The smoking habits of Canadians by age 15 are similar to the habits of most youth in European countries, with boys slightly less likely to smoke than girls. Girls have not been as influenced as boys by anti-smoking messages; many studies indicate more girls are now smoking. This increase in smoking behaviour in adolescent girls is a special concern because it

appears to be linked with other adjustment problems related to changing roles and expectations (King et al., 1988).

Education programs about the serious health implications of smoking are established in all of the study countries; yet, young people continue to smoke. It is suggested that the factors that precipitate smoking are not well understood and require further research.

A relationship between parents' smoking behaviour and children's smoking behaviour was also found: there is likely some role modelling present that influences adolescents' behaviour. Nevertheless, many young people smoke whose parents do not, and many adults are experiencing strains similar to their children's that contribute to their own smoking behaviours.

By age 15 over a quarter of Canadian youth drink alcohol at least once a week, and 60% have been drunk at least once. Early patterns of alcohol abuse are evident and clearly will relate to similar patterns in the future. It is fundamental that programs be established to discourage young people from this particularly hazardous behaviour.

Although much has been made of Canada's drug problem, evidence shows a decline in the use of most non-medical drugs (Smart et al. 1991). The large proportion of 15-year-olds who have been drunk indicates alcohol abuse is a greater problem and more effective programs are required to respond to this issue.

C. Physical activity

For the most part, Canadian youth compare favourably with those from other countries with regard to their level of physical activity. Young Canadians are particularly advantaged in their access to in-school and out-of-school teams. Typically, far more Canadian youth play on school and community teams and are involved in athletic clubs than students in the other survey countries. Given the programs in the schools and opportunities available in the community, one would expect young Canadians to be more physically fit than those in other countries, and this does appear to be the case. However, there are concerns associated with the downward trend from age 11 to age 15 in involvement in physical activity. If this trend is sustained into young adulthood it could lead to serious fitness problems. Only 40% of Canadian girls (60% of Canadian boys) expect to be involved in physical activity at age 20. This is simply not enough. Canadian youth tend to think their fitness levels are quite high, and the fact that this view occurs in an atmosphere where health and fitness are encouraged by the media and in school programs suggests that the programs have had the desired impact. The challenge now is to extend this attitude toward fitness throughout adulthood.

D. Leisure time

Comparing the time young Canadians across the years spend watching television shows that, if anything, there is a reduction in the amount of time Canadian youth spend in front of the television and in playing video games as they mature. Some of this is taken up in the increased amount of time youth spend watching movies on VCRs but, overall, Canadian youth tend to fall in the middle of other European countries in the amount of television they watch. This is remarkable considering how much more youth programming is offered by U.S. and Canadian television channels than by European ones.

E. Nutrition

The research questions used in the survey were not particularly well conceptualized to assess the health of respondents' nutritional lifestyles. However, some tentative conclusions can be drawn. With regard to the intake of fibre, Canada tends to fall in the middle of the European countries surveyed, although overall there is concern about the amount of fibre in the diets of people in most of these countries. Again, in comparison with other countries, young Canadians did not seem to consume more fatty foods. Canadians do not appear to eat chocolate bars and candy excessively but are in the higher bracket with regard to the consumption of sugar-based soft drinks.

The vast majority of Canadian youth clean their teeth at least once a day and most of these brush at least twice. This compares favourably with most European countries.

F. Ailments

It is difficult to explain why more young Canadians report headaches, backaches and stomach aches than youth in most of the other study countries. Canadian youth do tend to experience more stress in their relationships and this may be reflected in more psychosomatic ailments, not only those noted above but also with difficulty sleeping and general irritability.

Canadian youth (girls in particular) are most likely to take headache pills and are also in the highest groups in the use of stomach, cough and cold medications. Whether this finding reflects better diagnoses and availability of medication or greater strains that precipitate these ailments is difficult to determine. Nevertheless, the proportion of ailments and medications used to deal with them does appear to be high.

G. Social adjustment

Perhaps the most significant finding in this study is that, compared with young people from European countries, young Canadians are experiencing more strain in their relationships with their parents and even with each other. This is especially pronounced with girls and may be related to adjustment problems they are experiencing with career aspirations, body image and dealing with the traditional values associated with marriage and family. Although there is no question that these young women have intern-alized the notion of a career, they seem to lack the full support of their parents and their teachers with regard to the implications of these aspirations for their future. While young men do not show as much evidence of this type of strain, they appear unaware of their increasing responsibilities with regard to child rearing and homemaking.

Also of concern is that young Canadians tend to be more aggressive in their relationships with others. They are more likely to be bullied or to bully others than are those in European countries. Both at the federal and local levels, Canadian educators have been investigating the possible use of interventions designed to discourage bullying behaviour among children and to increase respect for and understanding of others.

There are some differences among the countries participating in this study in the proportion of young people held back in school for academic reasons. When we examine the countries that advanced almost all of their students with their peers we found less evidence of bullying behaviour. Certainly, these findings are preliminary but it may be that students who are held back are more likely to turn to bullying behaviour because of the status loss inherent in being held back from their regular classmates.

The strains evident between young people and their parents might be mediated by improving relationships in school and at home. Such initiatives would be designed to improve communication between parents and their children and to provide a greater understanding of the stress young people feel in today's rapidly changing society.

H. Relationships among health-risk factors

Numerous studies have shown that health-risk behaviours are linked. The smokers are also the drinkers and other substance abusers, and are less likely to be physically active and more likely to have poor diets. But health-risk behaviours are also tied to self-esteem, adjustment to school and relationships-with-parents problems. The young person who experiences academic problems in school and who has difficulty at home as a result tends to turn to more satisfying relationships, often with peers experiencing similar difficulties. This pattern contributes to the formation of peer groups alienated from school and home and to reaching out to each other for comfort and acceptance. These groups typically share anti-societal values or participate in behaviours that put them at risk. Interventions designed to meet the needs of these youth must take into account the importance peer group membership plays in their lives. If smoking is one of the requirements of group membership then it will be difficult to discourage young people from this behaviour. Something more structural in nature is needed to deal with this issue. Young people must feel more comfortable both at school and home. In both settings there has to be more acceptance and greater understanding of differences in achievement, and a variety of opportunities offered for success and the enhanced self-esteem that follows from it. The WHO/HBSC team of researchers is planning to investigate in much greater depth the role of the school in contributing to health-risk behaviour.

I. Developing theory to guide health promotion intervention

This study was not designed to produce a comprehensive theory of health-risk behaviours. Nevertheless, it did enable us to develop a tentative model that explains a number of relationships among significant factors. Comprehensive health programs that employ school and community resources and target complexes of health-risk factors are consistent with the findings in the study. However, more research and intervention development is required to understand the powerful group forces that exist among young people that precipitate health-risk behaviours.

Appendix A

Sampling Procedures

The Sample

The sampling plan was established by the WHO/HBSC committee and each country attempted to adhere to its requirements.

A. Canada

1. Sample size

Three age groups were targeted to simulate a longitudinal study. The ages for these groups were set at 11 years, six months, 13 years, six months and 15 years, six months with 90% of the respondents falling within a six-month range of the mean. The other 10% would be drawn from an additional six-month range to give a one-year span from the mean. It was anticipated that to achieve these results the survey would be administered early in the school year. A total of 1500 students was recommended for each age group. Unfortunately, various factors mitigated against the study being conducted until late spring.

The data for each country were assessed and cleaned by the Norwegian data centre, where the decision was taken to use the mean age of each actual group rather than adjust the data to use only those students whose age fell in the targeted age range at the time the survey was administered. As a result the data are based on responses from students older than was originally set in the sampling plan (see Table 1.1 in Chapter 1). To simplify presentation of the data, findings are reported by the original ages (11, 13, and 15) throughout this report.

To determine how to achieve the sample of 1500 at each of grades 6, 8, and 10, the following steps were implemented. The requirement of having 90% of the sample within six months on either side of the median age indicated a sample of 1350 meeting this age requirement. It was calculated that the additional 10%, or 150, would be the students in the classes surveyed outside the narrower age range. Return rates from the *Canada Youth and AIDS Study,* 1988 and the *Canada Health Attitudes and Behaviours Survey,* 1985 suggested an expected average return of 17 surveys per class surveyed, with between 60% and 70% of the ages falling within six months on either side of the median. The minimum of 60% was chosen as a worst case. The formula for the final sample was as follows:

> Number of classes to be sampled =
> desired sample size in one-year age range
> (1350)/
> expected return per class (17)/
> minimum proportion of class within the
> one-year age range (60%)
> = 1350/17/.6 = 132

The sample at each grade level, including the oversample, was determined to be 132 classes.

2. Regional representation

To gather the data in Canada on a national basis, a proportional representation had to be determined in each province and territory. As previously mentioned, to obtain a sufficient oversample to meet the required 1500 participants within the

Table A.1
Representative number of classes from each province and territory

Province	% of population	# classes chosen
British Columbia	11.4	14
Alberta	9.4	12
Saskatchewan	4.0	5
Manitoba	4.2	6
Ontario	35.9	47
Quebec	25.8	34
New Brunswick	2.8	4
Nova Scotia	3.4	5
Prince Edward Island	.5	1
Newfoundland	2.2	3
Yukon/Northwest Territories*		1

* Only one class was chosen at each grade level to represent the territories because of cost limitations.

required age ranges at each grade level it was decided that 132 classes at each level across the country would be surveyed. These were chosen by prorating the population in each province and territory (see Table A.1).

3. Sampling plan
To draw the Canadian sample, a two-stage cluster sampling design was used, with the first stage being the systematic selection of the schools from a master list and the second stage being the random selection of school classes at grades 6, 8 and 10.

To create the master sampling list of schools in each province, only those schools were included that had an enrolment of 30 or more students in Grade 10 as indicated in provincial school directories. If Grade 6 or 8 classes, or both, were not available in the selected schools with Grade 10, they were randomly selected from among other schools with grades 6 and 8 in the same jurisdictions. If either a Grade 6 or 8 class was available from the school with the selected Grade 10 class, it was included in the sample. The alternative method — constructing sampling lists for each of the three grade levels — was purposely rejected to minimize the time and expense required to conduct the survey. This eliminated the need to construct two additional lists and make contacts with more school jurisdictions and schools. The degree of precision of the three samples was not seriously jeopardized.

For each province, the schools were clustered on the list by the characteristics of the school jurisdiction; that is, by (1) language of instruction, (2) whether it was public or separate, (3) type of community served, for example, urban or rural, (4) location within the province, and (5) total student enrolment. Priority was given in the ordering of the schools to first, language of instruction; then, whether the school jurisdiction was public or separate; then, type of community.

Schools with enrolments over 2000 were listed twice in the master list with the intent that classes from very large schools would have similar chances of being selected as classes from smaller schools. In each province the number of schools on the school list was divided by the number of schools to be sampled from the province to determine **k**. A systematic sample of schools was taken by selecting every **k-th** school in a province's list from a randomly selected starting point between **1** and **k**. This produced a sample of the desired number of schools from each province.

As previously explained, in schools with Grade 10 but no Grade 6, Grade 8, or both, additional schools were randomly selected from other schools with those grades from the same school jurisdiction as the Grade 10 class.

The principals in each school selected to be in the sample were asked to provide a list of classes, the class teachers' names and class enrolments by gender at the grade levels required. The classes

were assigned consecutive numbers and, with the use of a table of random numbers, the class to be sampled at the designated grade level was identified. In some cases, time did not permit this procedure and principals were asked to choose the classes at the required levels on a random selection basis using a list of random numbers. In some of the small schools there was only one class at the required level.

B. Gender
An even division of male and female respondents was expected since students were surveyed in school classes selected at random. This equal division did not occur in very many instances. There were few 50:50 divisions of male and female respondents for any age level; however, most fell within a 48:52 range with the exception of all groups in Spain and the 15-year-old group in five other countries — Austria, Hungary, Poland, Scotland and Wales (see Table 1.3). All age groups in Canada were divided 48:52 with girls in the majority at ages 11 and 13, and boys in the majority at age 15.

C. Grade
For most countries the grade level corresponding to the desired age ranges are grades 6, 8 and 10. However, where the lower age of compulsory education is 7, the grade levels are the equivalent of the Canadian grades 5, 7 and 9.

Table A.2
Percentages of males and females in each age group

Country	11		13		15	
	M	F	M	F	M	F
Austria	51	49	50	50	55	45
Belgium	51	49	51	49	53	47
Canada	48	52	48	52	52	48
Finland	52	48	50	50	50	50
Hungary	48	52	49	51	41	59
Norway	49	51	51	49	49	51
Poland	48	52	48	52	54	46
Scotland	48	52	48	52	46	54
Spain	56	44	55	45	42	58
Sweden	50	50	51	49	52	48
Wales	50	50	50	50	48	52

Regression and Factor Analysis

Multiple regression analyses were used to estimate the influence of certain factors on 'smoking', 'liking school' and 'feeling like an outsider'. The results of the analyses are presented in summary form for a selected sample of countries in Chapter 7.

In each case, stepwise selection has been used with listwise deletion of missing values (only cases that have valid values for all variables named in the regression equation are included). A more detailed summary of this information appears in Tables B.1 to B.14 which list by country, age and gender the variables that fit into each regression equation. The standardized beta for each item is included and the summary statistics multiple R and R square. Each independent variable is listed so that it indicates the direction of the relationship to the dependent variable.

Confirmatory factor analyses were conducted by gender and age levels for a number of countries. These analyses were conducted to examine groups of variables that came together as factors. The results are summarily discussed in Chapter 7. Factor loadings of variables from the analyses for Canada, Scotland and Finland appear in Tables B.15 to B.17. In each case the method of extraction used is principal components analysis, missing values are deleted pairwise and the factor rotation method is varimax. Variables listed do not indicate their direction in contributing to the factor, but appear in their non-directional format.

Table B.1
Multiple regression on smoking, 15-year-olds—Austria

| | Standardized beta | |
Independent variables	M	F
been drunk	.43	.39
difficult to talk about problems with father	—	.18
easy to talk about problems with same sex friends	—	.16
is not involved in sports	—	.15
talk to parents infrequently	.15	—
have pocket money	.10	.14
drink wine	.11	—
father smokes	.09	—
spend a great deal of time with friends	.09	—
low academic achievement	—	.09
not afraid of other pupils	.08	—
Multiple R	.62	.60
R Square	.38	.37

Table B.2
Multiple regression on smoking, 15-year-olds—Belgium

Independent variables	Standardized beta	
	M	F
been drunk	.36	.33
drink liquor	.25	—
don't like school	—	.21
difficult to talk about problems with father	—	.16
often tired in the morning	.15	—
Multiple R	.53	.48
R Square	.28	.24

Table B.3
Multiple regression on smoking, 15-year-olds—Canada

Independent variables	Standardized beta	
	M	F
been drunk	.35	.39
drink liquor	.19	—
poor physical fitness	.14	—
don't expect to participate in sports at age 20	.14	.09
poorer parent relationships	—	.12
spend a great deal of time with friends	.08	.12
low health status	—	.11
talk to parents infrequently	—	.11
poor academic achievement	—	.10
not a member of a school club	.08	—
have pocket money	—	.08
don't like school	—	.07
Multiple R	.54	.60
R Square	.30	.36

Table B.4
Multiple regression on smoking, 15-year-olds—Finland

Independent variables	Standardized beta	
	M	F
been drunk	.34	.35
is not involved in sports	.21	.10
drink beer	.15	.19
spend a great deal of time with friends	—	.17
easy to make new friends	.13	—
drink soft drinks	.13	—
is irritable or bad tempered	—	.10
don't expect to participate in sports at age 20	—	.09
Multiple R	.58	.62
R Square	.34	.38

Table B.5
Multiple regression on smoking, 15-year-olds—Hungary

Independent variables	Standardized beta	
	M	F
been drunk	.44	.41
easy to talk about problems with opposite sex friends	—	.21
spend a great deal of time with friends	.17	—
is not involved in sports	.11	.17
drink liquor	.16	—
difficult to talk about problems with father	.15	—
mother drinks	—	.13
is irritable or bad tempered	.11	—
drink soft drinks	—	.11
Multiple R	.60	.54
R Square	.36	.29

Table B.6
Multiple regression on smoking, 15-year-olds—Scotland

Independent variables	Standardized beta	
	M	F
been drunk	.34	.32
parents disagree about how to spend leisure time	—	.19
is not involved in sports	.18	—
don't like school	—	.15
have not been bullied	.14	—
don't eat fruit	—	.13
often feel low	.13	—
easy to make new friends	—	.11
have bullied others	.11	—
often have headaches	—	.10
spend a great deal of time with friends	.10	—
often tired in the morning	.09	—
drink beer	—	.08
Multiple R	.54	.57
R Square	.29	.33

Table B.7
Multiple regression on liking school - Austria

Independent variables	Standardized beta					
	11-year-olds		13-year-olds		15-year-olds	
	M	F	M	F	M	F
Not tired in the morning	—	—	.11	.18	—	.15
Have not bullied other pupils	—	.18	—	—	—	—
Academic achievement	.24	.21	.14	.11	.17	.26
Have not been drunk	—	—	.23	—	.26	—
Are happy	—	—	.12	.17	—	.19
Don't eat sweets	—	—	.12	—	—	—
Have not been bullied	.12	.18	—	—	—	—
Eat whole wheat or rye bread	—	—	—	—	—	.10
Father doesn't smoke	—	—	—	.11	—	—
Talk to parents often	—	—	—	—	.11	—
Seldom feel like an outsider	—	.20	—	—	—	—
Easy to talk about problems with same sex friends	.18	—	.13	—	—	—
Not afraid of teachers	.15	—	—	—	—	—
Mother smokes	.18	—	—	—	—	—
Seldom drink cider	.17	—	—	.13	—	—
Spend few hours watching television	—	—	.11	—	—	—
Have more close friends	—	.19	—	—	.11	—
Spend more time at sports	—	.18	—	—	—	—
Don't smoke	—	.16	.24	.17	—	.11
Seldom drink beer	—	.20	—	—	—	—
Seldom drink wine	—	.17	—	—	—	—
Easy to talk about problems with opposite sex friends	—	—	.19	—	—	—
Spend less time with friends	—	—	—	.13	.10	—
Multiple R	.45	.54	.56	.44	.40	.44
R Square	.20	.30	.32	.20	.16	.19

Table B.8
Multiple regression on liking school - Canada

| | Standardized beta | | | | | |
| | 11-year-olds | | 13-year-olds | | 15-year-olds | |
Independent variables	M	F	M	F	M	F
Not tired in the morning	.15	.13	.15	.23	.14	.13
Have not bullied other pupils	.18	—	.08	—	—	.07
Academic achievement	.15	.17	.21	.21	.27	.22
Have not been drunk	.09	—	—	.15	.17	.10
Are happy	—	—	—	.16	.10	—
Member of a school club	.10	—	.08	.10	—	—
Seldom have a hard time saying no	.11	—	—	—	—	—
Don't eat sweets	.08	.10	—	—	—	—
Have not been bullied	—	—	.10	—	.09	—
Seldom irritable or bad tempered	.10	—	.09	—	—	—
Seldom feel low	.12	—	—	.10	—	—
Don't need to lose weight	—	—	—	.10	—	.08
Relationship with parents	.08	—	.10	—	—	—
Self-esteem	—	.17	—	—	—	.07
Easy to talk about problems with mother	—	—	.10	—	—	—
Talk to parents often	—	.13	—	—	—	.14
Good at sports	—	.08	—	—	—	—
Don't drink liquor	—	—	.12	—	—	.07
Seldom feel like an outsider	—	.08	—	—	—	—
Easy to talk about problems with opposite sex friends	—	—	—	.09	.12	—
Spend less time with friends	—	—	—	.08	—	.07
Easy to talk about problems with father	—	—	—	.08	—	—
Seldom drink wine	—	—	—	.07	—	—
Spend fewer hours watching television	—	—	—	.06	—	—
Have less pocket money	—	—	—	—	.08	—
Eat whole wheat (brown) bread	—	—	—	—	.07	—
Find it easy to make new friends	—	—	—	—	—	.11
Don't smoke	—	—	—	—	—	.08
Participate in sports	—	—	—	—	—	.07
Multiple R	.49	.42	.47	.53	.47	.55
R Square	.24	.17	.22	.28	22	.30

Table B.9
Multiple regression on liking school - Finland

Independent variables	Standardized beta					
	11-year-olds		13-year-olds		15-year-olds	
	M	F	M	F	M	F
Not tired in the morning	—	.11	.23	.21	.18	.15
Academic achievement	.21	.22	.16	.20	.22	.35
Have not been drunk	—	—	.27	.20	.15	—
Are happy	.18	.13	.14	.20	.14	.11
Member of a school club	—	.14	—	—	—	—
Don't eat sweets	—	—	—	.19	.09	—
Seldom irritable or bad tempered	—	.09	—	—	—	.11
Seldom drink wine	.15	—	—	.17	—	.11
Expect to participate in sports at age 20	.18	—	—	—	—	—
Eat whole wheat or rye bread	—	.11	—	—	—	—
Eat fruits	—	—	.15	.13	—	—
Have fewer close friends	—	—	.15	—	—	—
Make new friends easily	—	—	—	.15	—	—
Seldom drink beer	—	—	—	.14	—	—
Spend more time at sports	—	—	—	—	.13	.11
Seldom feel lonely	—	—	—	—	.13	—
Easy to talk about problems with father	—	—	—	—	—	.09
Multiple R	.41	.41	.56	.57	.46	.54
R Square	.17	.17	.32	.33	.22	.29

Table B.10
Multiple regression on liking school - Scotland

Independent variables	Standardized beta					
	11-year-olds		13-year-olds		15-year-olds	
	M	F	M	F	M	F
Not tired in the morning	—	—	.21	—	.17	.29
Academic achievement	.19	.11	.23	.15	.32	.17
Have not been drunk	—	—	—	.17	—	—
Eat fruits	—	.13	—	—	—	—
Seldom irritable or bad tempered	—	.15	—	—	—	—
Seldom feel low	—	.23	—	—	—	—
Talk to parents often	.16	.17	—	—	—	—
Find it easy to make new friends	—	—	—	—	—	.09
Don't drink liquor	—	—	—	—	—	.13
Seldom feel like an outsider	—	—	—	.16	—	—
Easy to talk about problems with father	.16	.18	—	—	—	—
Not afraid of other pupils	.17	—	—	—	—	—
Don't smoke	.14	.18	—	—	—	.16
Easy to talk about problems with same sex friends	.15	—	—	—	—	—
Spend fewer hours watching television	—	—	—	.14	—	—
Have more close friends	—	—	—	.13	—	.09
Seldom drink wine	—	—	—	.13	.22	.14
Parents agree about how to spend leisure time	—	—	.21	—	—	—
Spend more time at sports	—	—	.13	—	.11	—
Seldom drink beer	—	—	—	—	.20	—
Not afraid of teachers	—	.15	—	—	.10	—
Seldom drink cider	—	—	—	—	—	.11
Multiple R	.43	.53	.46	.39	.52	.52
R Square	.19	.28	.21	.15	.27	.27

Table B.11
Multiple regression on feeling like an outsider - Austria

| Independent variables | Standardized beta | | | | | |
| | 11-year-olds | | 13-year-olds | | 15-year-olds | |
	M	F	M	F	M	F
Have not bullied other pupils	—	—	—	.10	—	.14
Have been drunk	.15	—	—	—	—	—
Not happy	—	—	—	—	.15	.14
Have few close friends	—	—	—	—	.11	—
Have been bullied	.24	.23	.24	.17	.29	.30
Often feel low	—	—	—	.16	—	—
Difficult to talk about problems with mother	—	—	—	—	—	.12
Don't talk to parents often	—	—	—	—	.10	—
Don't drink liquor	—	—	—	—	.12	—
Don't make new friends easily	.19	.26	.18	.12	—	.10
Seldom eat whole wheat or rye bread	.16	—	—	—	—	—
Mother drinks	.13	.13	—	—	—	—
Afraid of other pupils	—	.13	—	.14	.13	—
Not very healthy	—	.14	—	—	—	—
Often irritable or bad tempered	—	.15	—	—	—	—
Often feel lonely	—	—	.24	.30	.16	.18
Afraid of teachers	—	—	.13	—	—	—
Mother smokes	—	—	.11	—	—	—
Parents disagree about how to spend leisure time	—	—	—	—	.14	—
Difficult to talk about problems with same sex friends	—	—	—	—	—	.11
Don't like school	—	.12	—	—	—	—
Multiple R	.46	.59	.51	.55	.54	.58
R Square	.21	.35	.26	.30	.30	.33

Table B.12
Multiple regression on feeling like an outsider - Canada

| Independent variables | Standardized beta | | | | | |
| | 11-year-olds | | 13-year-olds | | 15-year-olds | |
	M	F	M	F	M	F
Tired in the morning	—	—	.07	—	.08	.07
Have not bullied other pupils	—	—	—	.10	—	—
Have not been drunk	—	—	—	—	—	.11
Not happy	.11	—	—	—	—	.12
Often feel lonely	.23	.16	.18	.22	.14	.15
Often have a hard time saying no	—	—	—	.06	—	—
Have been bullied	.12	.20	.19	.12	.17	.13
Often feel low	.11	—	.13	.13	.11	.08
Need to lose weight	—	—	—	—	.08	—
Less positive relationship with parents	—	—	—	.11	—	—
Lower self-esteem	—	.17	.18	.14	.15	.16
Seldom talk to parents	—	—	—	.09	—	—
Not good at sports	.09	—	.16	—	—	.06
Don't drink liquor	—	—	—	—	.11	—
Don't make new friends easily	.17	.15	.15	.11	.11	.15
Smoking	.07	—	—	.13	—	—
Afraid of other pupils	—	.13	—	.07	.12	.11
Don't spend a great deal of time with friends	—	.09	—	.09	.09	—
Parents disagree about how to spend leisure time	—	.07	—	—	—	—
Difficult to talk about problems with opposite sex friends	—	.07	—	.10	.07	—
Not very healthy	—	—	.11	.10	—	—
Often get headaches	—	—	.07	—	—	—
Have few close friends	—	—	—	—	.09	—
Don't drink soft drinks	—	—	—	—	—	.08
Don't like school	—	—	—	—	—	.08
Multiple R	.54	.58	.59	.62	.62	.56
R Square	.29	.33	.35	.39	.38	.31

Table B.13
Multiple regression on feeling like an outsider - Hungary

| Independent variables | Standardized beta | | | | | |
| | 11-year-olds | | 13-year-olds | | 15-year-olds | |
	M	F	M	F	M	F
Have not been drunk	—	—	—	—	—	.18
Not happy	—	—	—	—	.17	—
Have been bullied	.12	—	—	—	—	—
Often irritable or bad tempered	—	.14	.25	—	—	.18
Often feel low	—	—	—	.20	—	—
Don't talk to parents often	.14	.20	—	—	—	—
Often feel lonely	.22	.40	.19	.20	.23	.17
Don't make new friends easily	.16	—	.11	—	—	.19
Often get headaches	.17	—	—	—	—	.13
Spend little time at sports	—	.11	—	—	—	—
Difficult to talk about problems with opposite sex friends	—	—	—	.20	—	—
Mother drinks	—	—	—	.15	—	—
Don't spend a great deal of time with friends	—	—	—	.15	—	—
Parents disagree about how to spend leisure time	—	—	—	.15	—	—
Afraid of other pupils	—	—	—	—	.22	—
Difficult to talk about problems with father	—	—	—	—	—	.11
Multiple R	.41	.54	.37	.48	.44	.43
R Square	.17	.29	.14	.23	.19	.18

Table B.14
Multiple regression on feeling like an outsider - Scotland

| Independant variables | Standardized beta | | | | | |
| | 11-year-olds | | 13-year-olds | | 15-year-olds | |
	M	F	M	F	M	F
Have not bullied other pupils	—	—	—	—	.13	—
Often feel lonely	.22	.27	.31	.40	.29	.37
Have been bullied	.27	.13	—	.12	.16	.17
Often irritable or bad tempered	—	.17	—	—	—	—
Often feel low	—	—	.14	—	—	.09
Don't drink cider	—	—	.14	—	—	—
Don't drink beer	.12	—	.18	—	—	—
Difficult to talk about problems with mother	—	—	.13	—	—	.09
Don't talk to parents often	—	.10	—	—	—	—
Don't make new friends easily	.17	—	.15	—	—	.11
Afraid of other pupils	.15	.18	.12	—	—	—
Difficult to talk about problems with same sex friends	—	.15	—	.14	—	—
Afraid of teachers	—	—	—	.15	.16	—
Don't spend a great deal of time with friends	—	—	—	—	—	.10
Multiple R	.57	.57	.56	.56	.43	.56
R Square	.32	.32	.31	.31	.19	.32

Table B.15a
Factor analysis of selected variables for Canada - Age 11

| Variable name | Factor loadings | | | | | |
| | Factor 1 | | Factor 2 | | Factor 3 | |
	M	F	M	F	M	F
Academic achievement	.44	—	—	—	—	—
Drinking beer	—	—	.44	.55	—	—
Drinking wine	—	—	—	.44	—	—
Drinking liquor	—	—	.46	.47	—	—
Times been drunk	—	—	.52	.54	—	—
Drink soft drinks	—	—	.42	—	—	—
Eat sweets	—	—	.42	—	—	—
Reported health	.53	.49	—	—	—	—
Happiness	.64	.64	—	—	—	—
Ever feel lonely	.51	.51	—	—	.44	—
How often feel low	.56	.58	—	—	.41	—
How often irritable or bad tempered	.44	.42	—	—	—	—
Tired in the morning	.46	.50	—	—	—	—
Feel like an outsider	.52	.49	—	—	—	—
Talk to parents often	.41	.51	—	—	—	—
Parents agree about how to spend leisure time	.51	.51	—	—	—	—
Easy to make new friends	.47	.46	—	.41	—	—
Easy to talk about problems with father	.50	.51	—	—	—	—
Easy to talk about problems with mother	.45	.48	—	—	—	—
Easy to talk about problems with opposite sex friends	—	—	.44	.41	—	—
Amount of time spent with friends	—	—	.43	—	—	—
Expect to participate in sports at age 20	.40	—	—	—	—	.40
Good at sports	.48	—	.44	.45	—	—
Physical fitness	.55	.50	—	—	—	—
Sports - times per week	—	—	—	—	—	.47
Sports - hours per week	—	—	—	—	—	.51
Self-esteem	.67	.69	—	—	—	—
Relationship with parents	.69	.68	—	—	—	—

Table B.15b
Factor analysis of selected variables for Canada - Age 13

Variable name	Factor 1		Factor 2		Factor 3	
	M	F	M	F	M	F
Academic achievement	—	.43	—	—	—	—
Liking school	.40	.42	—	—	—	—
Smoking	—	—	.43	.40	—	—
Drinking beer	—	—	.65	.55	—	—
Drinking wine	—	—	.41	—	—	—
Drinking liquor	—	—	.60	.50	—	—
Times been drunk	—	—	.66	.59	—	—
Reported health	.53	.48	—	—	—	—
Happiness	.65	.67	—	—	—	—
Ever feel lonely	.41	.51	—	—	.43	—
How often get headaches	—	.41	—	—	—	—
How often feel low	.52	.59	—	—	—	—
How often irritable or bad tempered	—	.42	—	—	—	—
Tired in the morning	.43	.47	—	—	—	—
Feel like an outsider	.46	.44	—	—	—	.40
Talk to parents often	.44	.55	—	—	—	—
Parents agree about how to spend leisure time	—	.54	—	—	—	—
Easy to make new friends	.40	—	—	.46	—	—
Easy to talk about problems with father	.48	.48	—	—	—	—
Easy to talk about problems with mother	.43	.52	—	—	—	—
Amount of time spent with friends	—	—	—	.50	—	—
Member of a sports club	—	—	—	—	.40	—
Expect to participate in sports at age 20	.45	—	—	—	.48	—
Good at sports	.48	.42	—	.46	—	—
Physical fitness	.61	.53	—	—	—	—
Sports - times per week	—	—	—	—	—	.46
Sports - hours per week	—	—	—	—	.41	.52
Self-esteem	.59	.65	—	—	—	—
Relationship with parents	.56	.68	—	—	—	—
Easy to talk about problems with opposite sex friends	—	—	—	.52	—	—

Table B.15c
Factor analysis of selected variables for Canada - Age 15

| | Factor loadings | | | | | |
| | Factor 1 | | Factor 2 | | Factor 3 | |
Variable name	M	F	M	F	M	F
Academic achievement	—	.48	—	—	—	—
Liking school	—	.50	—	—	—	—
Smoking	—	—	.52	—	—	—
Drinking beer	—	—	.74	.46	—	—
Drinking liquor	—	—	.68	.49	—	—
Times been drunk	—	—	.76	.57	—	—
Reported health	.56	.50	—	—	—	—
Happiness	.59	.60	—	—	—	—
Ever feel lonely	.46	.46	—	—	—	.47
How often feel low	.52	.56	—	—	—	—
How often irritable or bad tempered	—	.45	—	—	—	—
Tired in the morning	—	.47	—	—	—	—
Feel like an outsider	.49	—	—	—	—	.45
Talk to parents often	.44	.57	—	—	—	—
Parents agree about how to spend leisure time	.50	.54	—	—	—	—
Easy to make new friends	.40	—	—	—	—	—
Easy to talk about problems with father	.48	.49	—	—	—	—
Easy to talk about problems with mother	.48	.55	—	—	—	—
Amount of time spent with friends	—	—	.45	.44	—	—
Member of a sports club	—	—	—	.43	—	—
Member of a school club	—	—	—	.44	—	—
Expect to participate in sports at age 20	.51	.47	—	—	.44	—
Good at sports	.57	—	—	.50	.41	—
Physical fitness	.61	.53	—	.46	.43	—
Sports - times per week	.47	—	—	.48	.44	—
Sports - hours per week	.43	—	—	.53	.48	—
Self-esteem	.57	.61	—	—	—	—
Relationship with parents	.58	.67	—	—	—	—

Table B.16a
Factor analysis of selected variables for Finland - Age 11

Variable name	Factor 1		Factor 2		Factor 3	
	M	F	M	F	M	F
Liking school	—	.40	—	—	—	—
Smoking	—	—	.49	.49	—	—
Drinking beer	—	—	.52	—	—	—
Drinking wine	—	—	.61	—	—	—
Drinking liquor	—	—	.57	.48	—	—
Drinking cider	—	—	.63	.50	—	—
Times been drunk	—	—	.54	.44	—	—
Reported health	.45	.49	—	—	—	—
Happiness	.53	.54	—	—	—	—
Ever feel lonely	.48	.44	—	—	—	—
How often feel low	—	.46	—	—	—	—
How often irritable or bad tempered	—	.43	—	.40	—	—
Tired in the morning	—	.45	—	—	—	—
Easy to make new friends	.59	.51	—	—	—	—
Easy to talk about problems with father	.48	.48	—	—	—	—
Easy to talk about problems with mother	.51	.45	—	—	—	—
Drink soft drinks	—	—	.55	—	—	—
Eat sweets	—	—	.43	—	—	—
Member of a sports club	.42	—	—	—	—	—
Expect to participate in sports at age 20	.59	.51	—	—	—	—
Good at sports	.62	.56	—	—	—	—
Physical fitness	.64	.61	—	—	—	—
Sports - times per week	.54	.50	—	.43	—	—
Sports -hours per week	.58	.54	—	.41	—	—

Table B.16b
Factor analysis of selected variables for Finland - Age 13

Variable name	Factor 1		Factor 2		Factor 3	
	M	F	M	F	M	F
Academic achievement	.41	—	—	—	—	—
Liking school	.53	.50	—	—	—	—
Smoking	.53	.51	—	—	—	—
Drinking beer	.55	.58	.42	.46	—	—
Drinking wine	—	.45	.48	.44	—	—
Drinking liquor	.44	.58	.41	—	—	—
Drinking cider	.40	.53	.41	.43	—	—
Times been drunk	.59	.54	.47	.52	—	—
Drink soft drinks	—	—	.44	—	—	—
Reported health	.44	—	—	—	—	—
Happiness	.52	—	—	—	—	—
Ever feel lonely	—	—	—	.47	.53	—
How often feel low	.48	—	—	—	.46	.49
How often irritable or bad tempered	.47	—	—	—	—	.42
Tired in the morning	.49	.40	—	—	—	—
Easy to make new friends	—	—	—	.57	—	—
Easy to talk about problems with father	.47	.41	—	—	.46	—
Easy to talk about problems with mother	.45	—	—	—	.41	—
Amount of time spent with friends	—	—	—	.51	—	—
Member of a sports club	—	—	.50	—	—	—
Expect to participate in sports at age 20	.50	—	.46	—	—	—
Good at sports	—	—	.58	—	—	—
Physical fitness	.48	.47	.49	.47	—	—
Sports - times per week	.46	—	.47	.43	—	.50
Sports - hours per week	.46	.46	.50	—	—	.53

Table B.16c
Factor analysis of selected variables for Finland - Age 15

Variable name	Factor loadings					
	Factor 1		Factor 2		Factor 3	
	M	F	M	F	M	F
Academic achievement	—	.42	—	—	—	—
Liking school	.47	.55	—	—	—	—
Pocket money	—	—	.44	.45	—	—
Smoking	.54	.47	—	.47	—	—
Drinking beer	.52	.42	.47	.50	—	—
Drinking liquor	.49	—	—	—	—	—
Times been drunk	.58	.41	.53	.65	—	—
Reported health	—	.46	—	—	—	—
Happiness	.41	.46	—	—	—	.47
Ever feel lonely	—	.41	—	—	.51	.48
How often feel low	.41	.50	—	—	.52	.51
How often irritable or bad tempered	.42	.46	—	—	—	—
Tired in the morning	—	.47	—	—	—	—
Easy to make new friends	—	—	.49	.45	.44	—
Easy to talk about problems with father	—	.46	—	—	.46	—
Easy to talk about problems with mother	—	.43	—	—	—	—
Amount of time spent with friends	—	—	.45	.62	—	—
Member of a sports club	—	—	.44	—	—	.44
Expect to participate in sports at age 20	.46	.52	.46	—	—	.41
Good at sports	—	.44	.60	—	—	—
Physical fitness	.44	.54	.54	—	—	—
Sports - times per week	.48	.55	.54	—	—	.50
Sports - hours per week	.47	.54	.57	—	—	.49

Table B.17a
Factor analysis of selected variables for Scotland - Age 11

Variable name	Factor 1 M	Factor 1 F	Factor 2 M	Factor 2 F	Factor 3 M	Factor 3 F
Father's occupation	—	—	—	—	.52	.46
Pocket money	—	—	.44	.52	—	—
Liking school	—	.51	—	—	—	—
Smoking	—	—	—	—	—	—
Drinking beer	.49	—	—	.46	—	.40
Drinking wine	.40	—	—	.41	—	.44
Drinking liquor	.44	—	.41	.46	—	.40
Drinking cider	.52	—	—	.48	—	.42
Times been drunk	.53	—	.42	.50	—	—
Sports - hours per week	—	—	—	—	—	.42
Drink soft drinks	—	—	.45	.42	—	—
Eat sweets	—	—	—	.41	—	.44
Eat whole wheat or rye bread	—	—	—	—	.44	.42
Ever feel lonely	.58	.51	—	—	—	—
Time watching television	—	—	—	—	—	.41
How often feel low	.47	—	—	—	—	—
Talk to parents often	—	.48	—	—	—	—
How often irritable or bad tempered	.43	.43	—	—	—	—
Parents agree about how to spend leisure time	—	.53	—	—	—	—
Tired in the morning	.40	.48	—	—	—	—
Easy to talk about problems with opposite sex friends	—	—	—	.41	—	—
Feel like an outsider	.43	.47	—	—	—	—
Have been bullied	—	.49	—	—	—	—
Easy to make new friends	—	.48	.48	—	—	—
Easy to talk about problems with father	—	.53	—	—	—	—
Easy to talk about problems with same sex friends	—	—	.50	—	—	—
Easy to talk about problems with mother	—	.51	—	—	—	—
Afraid of teachers	—	.42	—	—	—	—
Afraid of other pupils	—	.45	—	—	—	—
Amount of time spent with friends	—	—	.46	.46	—	—

Table B.17b
Factor analysis of selected variables for Scotland - Age 13

Variable name	Factor 1 M	Factor 1 F	Factor 2 M	Factor 2 F	Factor 3 M	Factor 3 F
Father's occupation	—	—	—	—	.43	.41
Academic achievement	—	.41	—	—	—	—
Liking school	.53	.44	—	—	—	—
Pocket money	—	—	.43	—	—	—
Smoking	.45	.55	—	—	—	—
Drinking beer	.59	.46	—	—	—	—
Drinking wine	—	.45	—	—	.48	—
Drinking liquor	.49	.59	—	—	—	—
Drinking cider	.58	.62	—	—	—	—
Times been drunk	.62	.66	—	—	—	—
Drink soft drinks	.42	—	—	—	—	.41
Eat sweets	.42	—	—	—	—	—
Eat whole wheat or rye bread	—	—	—	—	.41	.42
Ever feel lonely	—	—	.55	.62	—	—
How often feel low	—	—	—	—	—	—
How often irritable or bad tempered	.42	—	—	—	—	—
Tired in the morning	.57	—	—	—	—	—
Sports - times per week	—	—	—	—	—	.43
Sports - hours per week	—	—	—	—	—	.46
Afraid of other pupils	—	—	.41	—	—	—
Feel like an outsider	—	—	.54	.60	—	—
Have been bullied	—	—	.41	.46	—	—
Talk to parents often	.41	—	—	—	—	—
Parents agree about how to spend leisure time	.42	.43	—	—	—	—
Easy to make new friends	—	—	.60	.50	—	—
Easy to talk about problems with father	—	—	—	—	—	—
Easy to talk about problems with mother	—	—	—	.41	—	—
Easy to talk about problems with same sex friends	—	—	.54	.46	—	—
Easy to talk about problems with opposite sex friends	—	—	.55	.46	—	—
Amount of time spent with friends	—	—	.52	.45	—	
Number of close friends	—	—	.44	—	—	—

Factor analysis of selected variables for Scotland - Age 15

Variable name	Factor 1		Factor loadings Factor 2		Factor 3	
	M	F	M	F	M	F
Father's occupation	—	—	—	—	.55	.49
Academic achievement	—	.41	—	—	—	—
Liking school	—	.49	—	—	—	—
Pocket money	.47	—	—	—	—	—
Smoking	.48	.58	—	—	—	—
Drinking beer	.66	—	—	—	—	—
Drinking wine	—	—	—	—	.52	.40
Drinking liquor	.60	.54	—	—	—	—
Drinking cider	.54	.44	—	—	—	—
Times been drunk	.74	.63	—	—	—	—
Sports - hour per week	—	—	—	—	—	.40
Drink soft drinks	—	—	—	—	.43	—
Eat sweets	—	.40	—	—	—	—
Reported health	—	—	.42	—	—	—
Ever feel lonely	—	—	.42	.51	—	—
How often feel low	—	—	.51	—	—	.43
How often irritable or bad tempered	—	—	.43	—	—	—
Tired in the morning	—	.43	—	—	—	—
Time watching television	—	—	—	—	.43	.40
Feel like an outsider	—	—	—	.51	—	.43
Talk to parents often	—	.43	.43	—	—	—
Parent agree about how to spend leisure time	—	.48	.46	—	—	—
Easy to make new friends	—	—	—	.55	—	—
Easy to talk about problems with father	—	—	—	.42	—	—
Easy to talk about problems with mother	—	—	—	.44	—	—
Easy to talk about problems with same sex friends	—	—	.40	.52	—	—
Easy to talk about problems with opposite sex friends	.46	—	—	.54	—	—
Amount of time spent with friends	.56	.40	—	—	—	—

Tables

Table 1a
How often students smoke tobacco, by gender (Age 11)

	I do not smoke		Every day		At least once a week, but not every day		Less than once a week	
Country	M	F	M	F	M	F	M	F
Austria	97%	99%	0%	0%	1%	0%	2%	1%
Belgium	96	99	3	1	1	0	1	0
Canada	93	95	1	1	2	1	4	3
Finland	94	97	1	0	1	1	4	2
Hungary	90	98	1	1	2	0	7	2
Norway	97	98	1	0	0	0	2	1
Poland	90	98	1	0	3	0	6	1
Scotland	96	95	1	1	1	2	2	2
Spain	95	97	0	0	1	1	4	3
Sweden	95	98	1	0	1	1	3	1
Wales	94	95	1	0	1	2	3	3

Table 1b
How often students smoke tobacco, by gender (Age 13)

	I do not smoke		Every day		At least once a week, but not every day		Less than once a week	
Country	M	F	M	F	M	F	M	F
Austria	89%	92%	3%	1%	2%	3%	6%	5%
Belgium	88	93	4	1	3	4	5	3
Canada	86	80	5	9	3	5	6	6
Finland	78	79	13	8	4	5	5	8
Hungary	79	89	5	3	6	2	10	6
Norway	91	89	2	4	2	2	5	5
Poland	85	97	2	0	3	1	10	2
Scotland	88	86	5	4	3	4	4	6
Spain	82	88	4	1	3	4	11	7
Sweden	90	91	3	3	2	2	5	4
Wales	89	80	5	6	3	5	4	9

Table 1c
How often students smoke tobacco, by gender (Age 15)

	I do not smoke		Every day		At least once a week, but not every day		Less than once a week	
Country	M	F	M	F	M	F	M	F
Austria	70%	73%	15%	12%	8%	8%	6%	6%
Belgium	80	77	11	13	4	4	5	6
Canada	77	71	13	18	4	5	5	6
Finland	63	61	28	25	5	7	4	7
Hungary	61	71	25	14	6	6	8	9
Norway	71	68	17	16	4	7	8	9
Poland	67	84	14	6	6	4	11	6
Scotland	80	77	12	13	4	5	4	5
Spain	73	65	12	19	6	8	9	8
Sweden	76	71	10	14	5	6	9	9
Wales	80	71	11	16	3	6	5	7

Table 2a
Father's use of tobacco, by gender (Age 11)

	Every day		Time to time		Stopped		Never	
Country	M	F	M	F	M	F	M	F
Austria	25%	28%	19%	19%	19%	22%	37%	32%
Belgium	36	30	15	16	24	27	25	27
Spain	38	36	22	23	19	20	21	21

Table 2b
Father's use of tobacco, by gender (Age 13)

	Every day		Time to time		Stopped		Never	
Country	M	F	M	F	M	F	M	F
Austria	32%	33%	13%	15%	23%	24%	32%	28%
Belgium	33	34	14	10	29	29	25	27
Canada	31	35	9	6	30	32	30	27
Spain	43	45	16	17	23	21	17	17

Table 2c
Father's use of tobacco, by gender (Age 15)

	Every day		Time to time		Stopped		Never	
Country	M	F	M	F	M	F	M	F
Austria	34%	42%	11%	10%	23%	26%	32%	22%
Belgium	36	41	10	12	29	27	25	20
Canada	33	33	6	5	33	33	28	29
Spain	45	40	11	15	23	21	20	24

Table 3a
Mother's use of tobacco, by gender (Age 11)

	Every day		Time to time		Stopped		Never	
Country	M	F	M	F	M	F	M	F
Austria	16%	21%	16%	15%	11%	16%	56%	48%
Belgium	20	19	14	14	12	15	54	52
Spain	13	18	21	17	8	10	58	55

Table 3b
Mother's use of tobacco, by gender (Age 13)

	Every day		Time to time		Stopped		Never	
Country	M	F	M	F	M	F	M	F
Austria	26%	22%	11%	14%	18%	17%	46%	47%
Belgium	20	26	10	10	18	16	52	49
Canada	24	27	6	6	24	25	46	42
Spain	14	17	17	12	7	8	61	62

Table 3c
Mother's use of tobacco, by gender (Age 15)

	Every day		Time to time		Stopped		Never	
Country	M	F	M	F	M	F	M	F
Austria	25%	28%	12%	11%	16%	17%	47%	44%
Belgium	23	31	9	8	16	16	52	45
Canada	25	32	3	5	24	22	48	46
Spain	10	12	12	9	9	10	68	69

Table 4a
Have tasted an alcoholic drink, by gender (Age 11)

	Yes		No		Don't know	
Country	M	F	M	F	M	F
Austria	74%	69%	26%	31%	0%	0%
Belgium	72	66	24	29	4	5
Canada	76	70	21	27	3	3
Finland	65	46	31	49	4	5
Hungary	61	49	37	48	2	3
Norway	35	22	52	67	13	11
Poland	73	63	24	33	3	4
Scotland	80	70	17	26	3	4
Spain	78	64	22	36	0	0
Sweden	72	54	24	37	4	9
Wales	82	75	15	20	3	4

Table 4b
Have tasted an alcoholic drink, by gender (Age 13)

	Yes		No		Don't know	
Country	M	F	M	F	M	F
Austria	88%	88%	12%	12%	0%	0%
Belgium	84	82	16	16	1	2
Canada	89	88	11	11	1	1
Finland	85	79	14	19	2	2
Hungary	78	75	21	24	1	1
Norway	57	51	35	42	8	7
Poland	82	67	15	29	2	3
Scotland	92	90	7	9	1	1
Spain	86	82	14	18	0	0
Sweden	82	73	15	21	4	5
Wales	93	92	7	6	1	1

Table 4c
Have tasted an alcoholic drink, by gender (Age 15)

	Yes		No		Don't know	
Country	M	F	M	F	M	F
Austria	96%	96%	4%	4%	0%	0%
Belgium	91	88	8	12	1	1
Canada	94	94	6	6	0	0
Finland	91	96	9	3	0	0
Hungary	88	92	11	7	1	1
Norway	84	80	14	18	2	2
Poland	88	85	10	14	2	1
Scotland	97	97	3	3	0	0
Spain	96	92	4	8	0	0
Sweden	93	91	6	8	1	1
Wales	97	98	2	2	1	0

Table 5a
How often students drink beer, by gender (Age 11)

Country	Every day		Every week		Every month		Less than once a month		Never	
	M	F	M	F	M	F	M	F	M	F
Austria	1%	1%	3%	1%	5%	4%	25%	20%	66%	74%
Belgium	4	1	6	3	9	5	28	25	53	66
Canada	2	0	5	2	7	4	28	25	58	69
Finland	0	0	3	0	4	1	14	7	79	92
Hungary	1	0	2	0	3	1	21	10	73	89
Poland	1	0	2	0	5	2	31	17	61	81
Scotland	1	0	4	2	8	4	32	21	55	73
Spain	2	0	4	1	10	4	24	19	60	76
Sweden	1	0	5	1	8	3	29	16	58	79
Wales	3	1	8	2	17	9	28	21	44	67

Table 5b
How often students drink beer, by gender (Age 13)

Country	Every day		Every week		Every month		Less than once a month		Never	
	M	F	M	F	M	F	M	F	M	F
Austria	3%	1%	9%	2%	8%	3%	33%	22%	48%	72%
Belgium	2	2	12	7	12	9	32	25	42	57
Canada	1	1	11	8	17	14	30	30	41	48
Finland	0	1	4	3	12	6	24	21	60	69
Hungary	1	0	2	1	2	1	31	13	64	85
Poland	1	0	3	0	8	1	42	21	46	77
Scotland	1	0	10	4	16	7	4	2	70	86
Spain	2	0	9	3	12	10	35	28	42	59
Sweden	1	0	4	4	11	7	32	18	52	72
Wales	3	1	13	8	21	14	32	23	32	55

Table 5c
How often students drink beer, by gender (Age 15)

Country	Every day		Every week		Every month		Less than once a month		Never	
	M	F	M	F	M	F	M	F	M	F
Austria	4%	0%	25%	9%	14%	8%	21%	27%	36%	56%
Belgium	6	2	28	18	15	16	25	26	25	38
Canada	4	1	26	18	19	20	27	32	24	29
Finland	0	0	8	4	26	23	36	31	30	42
Hungary	2	0	13	3	5	2	40	23	40	72
Poland	1	0	7	2	17	4	44	30	31	64
Scotland	0	0	24	5	22	9	4	4	49	81
Spain	5	1	31	20	22	18	25	31	18	31
Sweden	0	0	12	8	23	17	33	34	32	41
Wales	6	2	37	18	22	18	19	23	16	40

Table 6a
How often students drink wine by gender (Age 11)

Country	Every day		Every week		Every month		Less than once a month		Never	
	M	F	M	F	M	F	M	F	M	F
Austria	0%	0%	1%	0%	3%	1%	13%	11%	83%	88%
Belgium	1	0	6	3	11	4	33	33	49	60
Canada	1	0	2	1	7	3	30	29	60	67
Finland	0	0	1	0	3	1	11	7	85	92
Hungary	1	0	1	0	2	0	74	77	22	22
Poland	0	0	1	0	1	0	19	16	78	84
Scotland	1	0	4	2	6	5	38	41	51	51
Spain	1	0	3	1	11	6	38	34	46	59
Sweden	0	0	1	1	2	1	17	7	80	91
Wales	2	1	6	4	11	10	22	28	59	57

Table 6b
How often students drink wine by gender (Age 13)

Country	Every day		Every week		Every month		Less than once a month		Never	
	M	F	M	F	M	F	M	F	M	F
Austria	0%	0%	6%	2%	7%	5%	22%	26%	65%	67%
Belgium	1	1	3	3	10	9	39	35	39	53
Canada	1	1	3	3	10	9	35	38	51	50
Finland	0	0	0	2	6	7	22	19	72	72
Hungary	0	0	2	1	2	1	76	84	19	14
Poland	0	0	1	0	4	0	30	24	65	75
Scotland	1	0	6	9	12	9	3	5	78	77
Spain	1	0	3	1	14	12	48	47	34	40
Sweden	0	0	0	1	4	3	24	18	72	78
Wales	2	1	7	9	12	18	28	34	51	38

Table 6c
How often students drink wine, by gender (Age 15)

Country	Every day		Every week		Every month		Less than once a month		Never	
	M	F	M	F	M	F	M	F	M	F
Austria	2%	0%	12%	9%	14%	11%	25%	34%	48%	46%
Belgium	3	0	10	5	17	9	35	42	36	44
Canada	2	1	4	4	12	12	37	46	45	37
Finland	0	0	1	1	9	11	42	44	48	44
Hungary	0	0	6	1	4	2	74	86	16	11
Poland	0	0	3	1	13	6	43	44	42	48
Scotland	0	0	11	13	16	17	4	5	69	65
Spain	1	1	8	6	22	20	51	54	18	19
Sweden	0	0	2	4	13	9	34	39	51	48
Wales	1	2	11	20	18	26	28	32	42	20

Table 7a
How often students drink liquor (Age 11)

Country	Every day		Every week		Every month		Less than once a month		Never	
	M	F	M	F	M	F	M	F	M	F
Austria	0%	0%	1%	0%	2%	1%	14%	14%	84%	85%
Belgium	1	0	1	0	5	1	15	10	78	88
Canada	1	0	1	1	3	3	15	11	79	85
Finland	1	0	1	0	1	1	9	5	88	94
Hungary	0	0	0	0	2	0	9	7	89	93
Scotland	1	0	1	1	3	3	13	11	81	86
Spain	0	0	1	0	4	0	10	5	85	95
Sweden	0	0	0	0	1	0	10	3	89	97
Wales	2	0	2	1	5	2	9	8	83	89

Table 7b
How often students drink liquor (Age 13)

Country	Every day		Every week		Every month		Less than once a month		Never	
	M	F	M	F	M	F	M	F	M	F
Austria	1%	0%	3%	2%	6%	6%	21%	27%	69%	64%
Belgium	0	0	2	1	5	3	16	11	77	85
Canada	1	1	6	4	10	11	23	26	60	58
Finland	0	0	0	2	8	8	21	20	71	70
Hungary	1	0	1	0	1	0	20	15	77	85
Scotland	1	0	5	5	8	9	2	2	84	84
Spain	1	0	3	3	9	6	19	15	68	77
Sweden	1	0	1	0	3	4	13	9	82	87
Wales	1	1	3	3	7	7	17	14	73	75

Table 7c
How often students drink liquor (Age 15)

Country	Every day		Every week		Every month		Less than once a month		Never	
	M	F	M	F	M	F	M	F	M	F
Austria	1%	1%	7%	4%	13%	13%	29%	35%	50%	47%
Belgium	1	0	4	1	8	7	28	21	59	71
Canada	2	0	13	11	20	19	30	35	35	35
Finland	0	0	2	2	25	13	39	50	35	35
Hungary	1	0	7	1	5	2	37	36	50	60
Scotland	0	0	10	12	18	17	3	3	68	68
Spain	1	0	21	15	19	20	29	23	30	42
Sweden	0	0	4	3	15	12	34	35	47	49
Wales	2	1	9	13	16	16	21	21	52	49

Table 8a
How often students drink alcoholic beverages (Age 11)

Country	Every day		Every week		Every month		Less than once a month		Never	
	M	F	M	F	M	F	M	F	M	F
Austria	2%	2%	4%	4%	11%	7%	31%	29%	52%	58%
Belgium	4	1	10	5	14	9	38	44	34	41
Canada	2	1	6	2	10	5	36	36	45	56
Finland	1	0	6	1	10	5	29	24	54	70
Hungary	2	0	3	1	3	1	42	39	50	59
Poland	1	0	2	0	5	2	63	57	29	41
Scotland	2	1	7	3	9	6	38	36	44	54
Spain	3	1	6	2	19	15	44	43	27	40
Sweden	2	2	4	4	11	7	31	29	52	58
Wales	4	1	12	6	21	14	32	37	31	42

Table 8b
How often students drink alcoholic beverages (Age 13)

Country	Every day		Every week		Every month		Less than once a month		Never	
	M	F	M	F	M	F	M	F	M	F
Austria	7%	1%	10%	6%	14%	13%	39%	42%	31%	38%
Belgium	3	3	15	10	18	13	42	46	22	28
Canada	1	1	13	10	20	19	35	38	31	32
Finland	1	1	8	7	21	18	40	39	29	35
Hungary	2	0	4	2	4	2	61	63	30	33
Poland	1	0	4	1	10	1	63	57	22	41
Scotland	2	1	15	14	20	15	4	5	59	65
Spain	3	0	11	7	22	20	45	50	19	23
Sweden	7	1	10	6	14	13	39	42	31	38
Wales	4	2	16	14	24	23	37	36	19	25

Table 8c
How often students drink alcoholic beverages (Age 15)

Country	Every day		Every week		Every month		Less than once a month		Never	
	M	F	M	F	M	F	M	F	M	F
Austria	7%	2%	30%	16%	17%	19%	28%	48%	18%	15%
Belgium	8	3	29	21	21	20	29	37	13	19
Canada	5	1	28	23	20	24	29	37	18	15
Finland	1	0	11	7	35	37	36	42	17	14
Hungary	4	0	16	4	7	5	54	77	19	13
Poland	1	0	9	3	21	9	52	65	17	23
Scotland	1	1	31	25	27	23	4	6	37	46
Spain	5	1	37	28	24	29	25	30	9	12
Sweden	7	2	30	16	17	19	28	48	18	15
Wales	6	4	41	31	24	29	20	27	9	9

Table 9a
How often students have been really drunk (Age 11)

Country	Never		Once		2 - 3 times		4 - 10 times		More than 10 times	
	M	F	M	F	M	F	M	F	M	F
Austria	84%	87%	12%	9%	3%	3%	0%	0%	1%	1%
Belgium	76	87	16	11	7	1	1	0	1	0
Canada	83	91	10	7	4	2	1	0	2	0
Finland	92	97	5	2	2	1	1	0	0	0
Hungary	87	96	10	3	3	1	0	0	0	0
Poland	86	95	11	4	2	0	1	0	1	0
Scotland	83	91	12	6	3	3	1	0	1	0
Spain	86	92	11	6	2	1	0	0	0	0
Sweden	94	97	4	2	1	1	1	0	0	0
Wales	68	87	17	9	9	3	4	1	3	0

Table 9b
How often students have been really drunk (Age 13)

Country	Never		Once		2 - 3 times		4 - 10 times		More than 10 times	
	M	F	M	F	M	F	M	F	M	F
Austria	69%	75%	16%	16%	9%	7%	3%	2%	3%	0%
Belgium	70	78	19	15	8	6	2	1	1	0
Canada	65	66	12	14	11	11	6	6	6	3
Finland	68	77	10	8	11	7	6	6	5	2
Hungary	80	90	13	8	5	1	1	0	1	0
Poland	78	93	16	7	5	0	1	0	1	0
Scotland	61	69	20	17	10	7	5	5	5	2
Spain	74	83	15	11	7	4	2	1	2	1
Sweden	85	91	8	6	3	3	2	0	2	0
Wales	53	56	21	21	16	13	7	7	3	3

Table 9c
How often students have been really drunk (Age 15)

Country	Never		Once		2 - 3 times		4 - 10 times		More than 10 times	
	M	F	M	F	M	F	M	F	M	F
Austria	47%	54%	15%	22%	20%	16%	10%	5%	8%	4%
Belgium	54	59	21	24	14	13	6	3	4	1
Canada	40	39	12	16	16	18	12	14	20	13
Finland	33	38	11	13	15	14	18	18	23	17
Hungary	46	71	14	15	23	11	9	2	8	1
Poland	58	76	16	15	16	6	7	2	3	1
Scotland	38	45	16	20	20	18	12	10	13	7
Spain	49	60	21	15	15	13	8	6	7	6
Sweden	52	55	10	14	16	16	12	8	10	7
Wales	26	30	16	20	23	24	15	16	20	10

Table 10a
Father's use of alcohol (Age 11)

| | Every day | | Time to time | | Stopped | | Never | |
Country	M	F	M	F	M	F	M	F
Austria	15%	15%	69%	71%	6%	5%	10%	9%
Hungary	19	17	70	73	6	4	5	6
Spain	15	8	63	71	6	4	16	17

Table 10b
Father's use of alcohol (Age 13)

| | Every day | | Time to time | | Stopped | | Never | |
Country	M	F	M	F	M	F	M	F
Austria	17%	15%	71%	74%	7%	5%	5%	5%
Canada	14	10	64	71	10	7	12	12
Hungary	19	16	71	74	5	5	5	5
Spain	20	11	63	66	4	5	13	18

Table 10c
Father's use of alcohol (Age 15)

| | Every day | | Time to time | | Stopped | | Never | |
Country	M	F	M	F	M	F	M	F
Austria	22%	20%	65%	69%	7%	7%	6%	4%
Canada	13	15	64	64	9	10	13	11
Hungary	18	20	69	71	5	5	8	5
Spain	18	13	61	62	7	4	13	21

Table 11a
Mother's use of alcohol (Age 11)

| | Every day | | Time to time | | Stopped | | Never | |
Country	M	F	M	F	M	F	M	F
Austria	4%	3%	61%	69%	4%	4%	31%	24%
Hungary	4	4	70	71	1	1	25	24
Spain	3	2	42	49	4	2	50	47

Table 11b
Mother's use of alcohol (Age 13)

| | Every day | | Time to time | | Stopped | | Never | |
Country	M	F	M	F	M	F	M	F
Austria	5%	6%	66%	74%	4%	3%	24%	17%
Canada	4	3	60	66	8	5	28	26
Hungary	3	3	69	73	1	1	28	23
Spain	3	3	45	42	2	2	50	53

Table 11c
Mother's use of alcohol (Age 15)

| | Every day | | Time to time | | Stopped | | Never | |
Country	M	F	M	F	M	F	M	F
Austria	5%	5%	70%	74%	5%	3%	20%	18%
Canada	4	5	60	65	7	5	29	25
Hungary	2	2	59	72	1	1	38	25
Spain	3	3	40	42	3	3	54	51

Table 12a
How often Canadian students have used drugs (Age 13)

Drugs	Three times or more		Once or twice		Never	
	M	F	M	F	M	F
Hashish/marijuana (e.g., hash, grass)	5%	4%	6%	6%	89%	90%
Solvents (e.g., glue sniffing)	2	2	4	4	94	94
Cocaine (e.g., crack)	1	1	1	1	98	99
Heroin/opium/morphine	1	1	1	1	98	99
Amphetamines (e.g., uppers, speed)	2	1	2	1	97	98
LSD (e.g., acid)	2	1	3	2	95	97
Medical drugs to get stoned (e.g., valium or seconal)	2	1	3	3	95	96

Table 12b
How often Canadian students have used drugs (Age 15)

Drugs	Three times or more		Once or twice		Never	
	M	F	M	F	M	F
Hashish/marijuana (e.g., hash, grass)	16%	13%	10%	11%	74%	76%
Solvents (e.g., glue sniffing)	2	1	5	4	93	95
Cocaine (e.g., crack)	2	1	2	2	96	97
Heroin/opium/morphine	2	1	1	1	96	99
Amphetamines (e.g., uppers, speed)	3	2	4	4	93	94
LSD (e.g., acid)	5	2	5	4	90	94
Medical drugs to get stoned (e.g., valium or seconal)	3	3	4	5	93	92

Table 13a
How often students exercise vigorously out of school (Age 11)

	Every day		4 - 6 times a week		2 - 3 times a week		Once a week		Once a month		Less than once a month		Never	
	M	F	M	F	M	F	M	F	M	F	M	F	M	F
Austria	47%	33%	24%	20%	18%	27%	5%	11%	1%	1%	4%	7%	2%	1%
Belgium	27	13	18	12	34	36	14	23	2	5	1	3	4	8
Canada	48	27	22	25	16	26	6	13	2	3	2	3	4	3
Finland	24	15	25	19	27	33	16	23	4	4	2	4	2	2
Hungary	21	10	24	13	33	40	13	20	2	4	3	5	4	9
Norway	19	9	20	15	35	45	17	21	1	2	2	2	5	5
Poland	40	24	23	21	22	34	9	11	2	3	3	2	1	5
Scotland	30	18	27	19	25	37	11	15	2	4	2	2	4	4
Spain	26	10	20	8	30	33	13	24	3	6	3	7	6	12
Sweden	17	8	24	13	32	38	17	23	2	3	3	4	5	10
Wales	42	24	25	21	18	32	10	15	1	3	1	2	3	3

Table 13b
How often students exercise vigorously out of school (Age 13)

	Every day		4 - 6 times a week		2 - 3 times a week		Once a week		Once a month		Less than once a month		Never	
	M	F	M	F	M	F	M	F	M	F	M	F	M	F
Austria	47%	24%	23%	24%	17%	31%	7%	12%	1%	2%	4%	5%	1%	1%
Belgium	24	10	23	14	31	38	16	26	1	3	2	2	3	7
Canada	41	17	30	23	15	31	9	18	1	5	1	4	2	3
Finland	21	15	22	17	30	27	16	25	4	7	5	7	1	2
Hungary	24	11	21	11	37	33	12	25	2	7	3	6	1	7
Norway	14	6	26	20	36	43	14	21	3	3	3	3	4	4
Poland	29	14	24	15	27	36	11	21	3	6	4	5	2	3
Scotland	31	18	24	21	30	35	10	18	2	2	1	2	3	3
Spain	17	7	20	9	31	27	16	21	4	9	6	10	7	17
Sweden	15	4	25	18	37	43	15	22	2	4	3	4	3	5
Wales	40	11	27	19	20	36	7	21	2	5	1	3	3	5

Table 13c
How often students exercise vigorously out of school (Age 15)

	Every day		4 - 6 times a week		2 - 3 times a week		Once a week		Once a month		Less than once a month		Never	
	M	F	M	F	M	F	M	F	M	F	M	F	M	F
Austria	34%	19%	25%	17%	28%	30%	8%	19%	1%	3%	3%	8%	1%	3%
Belgium	21	8	22	10	32	28	14	28	5	5	2	8	3	13
Canada	33	12	29	19	21	28	10	24	3	9	2	6	2	2
Finland	16	10	21	13	29	33	17	25	9	8	7	9	2	1
Hungary	17	9	22	8	33	29	17	27	4	10	4	9	3	8
Norway	16	7	26	21	30	40	12	17	5	4	5	5	6	6
Poland	20	9	22	9	32	31	15	25	5	10	4	11	2	5
Scotland	27	8	30	14	28	41	9	25	3	4	1	4	1	4
Spain	10	3	21	6	32	18	19	20	5	13	7	13	7	27
Sweden	10	4	28	17	38	37	11	23	4	6	3	7	5	6
Wales	33	8	28	14	24	32	9	27	2	6	1	6	2	6

Table 14a
How many hours per week students exercise vigorously out of school (Age 11)

	None		About 1/2 hour		About 1 hour		About 2 - 3 hours		About 4 - 6 hours		7 hours or more	
Country	M	F	M	F	M	F	M	F	M	F	M	F
Austria	4%	4%	6%	13%	9%	15%	31%	32%	23%	21%	27%	14%
Belgium	5	12	13	14	19	27	24	28	22	12	19	7
Canada	4	6	14	22	20	25	25	26	14	11	22	10
Finland	4	5	16	18	16	24	27	29	18	14	18	9
Hungary	2	3	8	12	17	25	34	33	20	17	19	10
Norway	7	9	15	15	22	26	28	31	18	14	10	5
Poland	4	6	10	15	24	30	30	29	15	12	16	7
Scotland	5	8	23	25	23	28	24	22	17	12	8	6
Spain	11	22	19	28	25	26	25	18	10	4	8	2
Sweden	12	17	15	16	20	28	25	26	18	9	10	4
Wales	4	6	9	17	23	29	36	32	14	9	14	6

Table 14b
How many hours per week students exercise vigorously out of school (Age 13)

	None		About 1/2 hour		About 1 hour		About 2 - 3 hours		About 4 - 6 hours		7 hours or more	
Country	M	F	M	F	M	F	M	F	M	F	M	F
Austria	1%	2%	5%	10%	8%	11%	27%	37%	23%	23%	36%	17%
Belgium	5	13	9	16	13	19	27	25	28	19	19	7
Canada	3	6	10	19	18	23	25	25	18	14	26	13
Finland	3	6	16	22	16	21	26	26	23	18	16	7
Hungary	1	4	6	13	13	24	32	34	23	15	25	10
Norway	7	8	9	10	13	19	30	34	24	23	16	6
Poland	4	5	11	17	20	28	32	32	17	11	15	7
Scotland	5	7	17	22	16	23	24	24	24	15	15	9
Spain	11	28	15	21	19	25	28	16	16	6	11	4
Sweden	7	9	11	9	18	22	27	39	26	17	12	5
Wales	4	9	6	12	17	30	34	33	19	11	20	5

Table 14c
How many hours per week students exercise vigorously out of school (Age 15)

	None		About 1/2 hour		About 1 hour		About 2 - 3 hours		About 4 - 6 hours		7 hours or more	
Country	M	F	M	F	M	F	M	F	M	F	M	F
Austria	3%	7%	4%	9%	8%	15%	26%	33%	25%	23%	34%	13%
Belgium	5	22	7	15	9	19	31	22	25	14	23	8
Canada	4	9	9	17	12	22	26	26	21	17	28	9
Finland	9	9	17	16	17	24	22	26	18	17	18	7
Hungary	2	3	5	12	13	25	28	32	27	20	25	8
Norway	14	10	9	8	12	17	21	31	24	23	20	11
Poland	6	12	12	22	21	30	31	24	14	7	16	4
Scotland	4	7	11	21	13	20	26	30	28	15	18	6
Spain	13	40	9	16	16	20	28	15	20	8	14	1
Sweden	9	12	9	11	13	21	29	31	24	18	16	7
Wales	5	12	6	15	17	28	30	31	21	11	21	4

Table 15a
Father encourages student to participate in sports or other physical activities (Age 11)

	Often		Sometimes		Never		Don't know		Don't have	
Country	M	F	M	F	M	F	M	F	M	F
Canada	46%	31%	36%	44%	11%	16%	3%	5%	4%	4%
Finland	40	27	48	55	8	13	*	*	4	4
Poland	26	21	37	45	24	23	7	7	6	4

*'Don't know' was not a response choice.

Table 15b
Father encourages student to participate in sports or other physical activities (Age 13)

	Often		Sometimes		Never		Don't know		Don't have	
Country	M	F	M	F	M	F	M	F	M	F
Canada	44%	28%	35%	44%	14%	19%	2%	4%	4%	4%
Finland	33	24	50	52	12	19	*	*	5	5
Poland	20	19	41	43	28	25	7	8	5	5

*'Don't know' was not a response choice.

Table 15c
Father encourages student to participate in sports or other physical activities (Age 15)

	Often		Sometimes		Never		Don't know		Don't have	
Country	M	F	M	F	M	F	M	F	M	F
Canada	30%	23%	42%	39%	20%	31%	3%	2%	5%	5%
Finland	25	22	54	46	16	27	*	*	5	5
Poland	15	13	41	40	30	30	8	8	6	8

*'Don't know' was not a response choice.

Table 16a
Mother encourages student to participate in sports or other physical activities (Age 11)

	Often		Sometimes		Never		Don't know		Don't have	
Country	M	F	M	F	M	F	M	F	M	F
Canada	42%	40%	40%	43%	12%	12%	4%	4%	2%	1%
Finland	35	34	56	57	7	8	*	*	2	1
Poland	14	27	46	45	28	21	8	6	2	1

*'Don't know' was not a response choice.

Table 16b
Mother encourages student to participate in sports or other physical activities (Age 13)

	Often		Sometimes		Never		Don't know		Don't have	
Country	M	F	M	F	M	F	M	F	M	F
Canada	39%	33%	40%	48%	18%	16%	2%	2%	1%	1%
Finland	30	29	57	58	11	12	*	*	2	0
Poland	13	22	46	48	29	23	9	6	2	2

*'Don't know' was not a response choice.

Table 16c
Mother encourages student to participate in sports or other physical activities (Age 15)

	Often		Sometimes		Never		Don't know		Don't have	
Country	M	F	M	F	M	F	M	F	M	F
Canada	29%	29%	45%	47%	22%	22%	3%	1%	1%	1%
Finland	23	27	58	54	17	18	*	*	2	1
Poland	11	15	42	53	34	24	11	7	2	1

*'Don't know' was not a response choice.

Table 17a
How often father participates in sports or other physical activities (Age 11)

	Every week		Occasionally		Never		Don't know		Don't have	
Country	**M**	**F**	**M**	**F**	**M**	**F**	**M**	**F**	**M**	**F**
Canada	25%	22%	40%	42%	21%	23%	9%	10%	5%	4%
Finland	47	50	26	26	11	10	13	11	3	3
Poland	13	13	18	20	45	46	18	17	6	4
Spain	16	11	34	29	37	39	9	19	4	2
Wales	28	26	15	16	41	37	13	17	3	4

Table 17b
How often father participates in sports or other physical activities (Age 13)

	Every week		Occasionally		Never		Don't know		Don't have	
Country	**M**	**F**	**M**	**F**	**M**	**F**	**M**	**F**	**M**	**F**
Canada	26%	25%	38%	34%	25%	30%	7%	7%	5%	4%
Finland	41	48	32	22	16	16	7	9	4	4
Poland	10	10	18	21	50	49	17	15	5	5
Spain	14	16	24	33	49	42	8	7	4	2
Wales	30	27	17	17	40	41	10	13	3	2

Table 17c
How often father participates in sports or other physical activities (Age 15)

	Every week		Occasionally		Never		Don't know		Don't have	
Country	**M**	**F**	**M**	**F**	**M**	**F**	**M**	**F**	**M**	**F**
Canada	18%	23%	35%	35%	35%	33%	6%	4%	6%	5%
Finland	43	46	28	22	17	20	8	10	4	3
Poland	7	9	15	16	60	54	14	13	4	8
Spain	10	14	20	25	60	55	7	2	3	4
Wales	26	24	19	19	45	47	7	7	3	3

Table 18a
How often mother participates in sports or other physical activities (Age 11)

Country	Every week M	F	Occasionally M	F	Never M	F	Don't know M	F	Don't have M	F
Canada	18%	20%	38%	43%	31%	26%	11%	10%	2%	1%
Finland	48	58	28	26	13	9	10	7	1	1
Poland	7	9	13	18	59	56	19	16	2	1
Spain	7	10	24	23	59	50	9	17	1	1
Wales	19	19	13	17	53	48	14	15	1	1

Table 18b
How often mother participates in sports or other physical activities (Age 13)

Country	Every week M	F	Occasionally M	F	Never M	F	Don't know M	F	Don't have M	F
Canada	17%	19%	39%	39%	36%	36%	7%	5%	2%	1%
Finland	47	53	34	30	13	12	6	4	1	1
Poland	4	7	13	17	65	60	16	14	2	2
Spain	9	15	17	26	67	54	7	3	1	2
Wales	17	21	18	18	54	50	10	10	1	1

Table 18c
How often mother participates in sports or other physical activities (Age 15)

Country	Every week M	F	Occasionally M	F	Never M	F	Don't know M	F	Don't have M	F
Canada	13%	22%	33%	35%	47%	40%	6%	3%	2%	1%
Finland	46	48	29	32	19	17	4	3	1	1
Poland	2	5	9	16	75	69	13	9	1	1
Spain	8	10	14	17	72	69	5	3	1	2
Wales	15	19	18	20	60	56	6	4	1	1

Table 19a
How often best friend participates in sports or other physical activities (Age 11)

Country	Every week		Occasionally		Never		Don't know		Don't have	
	M	F	M	F	M	F	M	F	M	F
Canada	58%	46%	23%	30%	4%	4%	11%	16%	3%	3%
Finland	60	60	14	14	4	3	20	21	2	2
Poland	48	29	17	15	8	10	24	37	3	9
Spain	57	37	26	32	4	7	11	24	2	1
Wales	60	47	8	11	7	10	23	29	2	3

Table 19b
How often best friend participates in sports or other physical activities (Age 13)

Country	Every week		Occasionally		Never		Don't know		Don't have	
	M	F	M	F	M	F	M	F	M	F
Canada	65%	43%	20%	37%	4%	7%	8%	9%	2%	3%
Finland	54	53	15	20	4	6	25	19	2	2
Poland	54	33	14	16	6	9	21	31	4	11
Spain	66	49	21	29	3	8	8	14	2	0
Wales	64	45	9	16	8	13	17	23	2	2

Table 19c
How often best friend participates in sports or other physical activities (Age 15)

Country	Every week		Occasionally		Never		Don't know		Don't have	
	M	F	M	F	M	F	M	F	M	F
Canada	63%	41%	24%	38%	5%	12%	6%	6%	2%	3%
Finland	53	56	18	23	7	8	20	11	2	2
Poland	51	36	16	16	7	10	22	29	3	8
Spain	60	35	28	35	6	20	5	8	1	2
Wales	61	39	14	23	10	21	14	16	1	1

Table 20a
Student expectations of participation in sports
or other physical activities at age 20 (Age 11)

| | Definitely yes | | Probably yes | | Probably not | | Definitely not | |
Country	M	F	M	F	M	F	M	F
Belgium	72%	50%	20%	37%	6%	6%	3%	7%
Canada	58	41	35	52	6	7	1	1
Finland	39	34	48	57	12	8	1	0
Poland	36	23	47	54	12	18	5	5
Spain	45	35	44	50	9	8	2	7
Wales	47	32	43	52	8	15	2	1

Table 20b
Student expectations of participation in sports
or other physical activities at age 20 (Age 13)

| | Definitely yes | | Probably yes | | Probably not | | Definitely not | |
Country	M	F	M	F	M	F	M	F
Belgium	65%	50%	26%	36%	8%	10%	1%	4%
Canada	60	44	34	48	5	7	1	0
Finland	35	32	48	57	17	12	0	0
Poland	28	20	51	57	18	20	2	2
Spain	49	30	41	53	8	15	2	2
Wales	49	29	38	49	10	19	3	3

Table 20c
Student expectations of participation in sports
or other physical activities at age 20 (Age 15)

| | Definitely yes | | Probably yes | | Probably not | | Definitely not | |
Country	M	F	M	F	M	F	M	F
Belgium	65%	46%	27%	34%	6%	15%	2%	5%
Canada	62	43	29	46	8	10	1	1
Finland	34	33	51	56	14	11	1	0
Poland	29	17	52	54	17	27	2	2
Spain	48	28	37	48	10	20	4	4
Wales	58	32	33	46	7	20	2	2

Table 21a
Student perceptions of their sports ability (Age 11)

	Among the best		Good		Average		Below average	
Country	M	F	M	F	M	F	M	F
Canada	41%	19%	38%	44%	16%	33%	5%	5%
Finland	17	9	35	30	40	53	8	8
Poland	22	17	54	53	22	27	2	2
Spain	30	12	41	47	27	36	2	5

Table 21b
Student perceptions of their sports ability (Age 13)

	Among the best		Good		Average		Below average	
Country	M	F	M	F	M	F	M	F
Canada	40%	18%	36%	36%	20%	39%	4%	8%
Finland	12	7	36	25	45	61	7	7
Poland	16	10	48	53	30	33	6	5
Spain	27	9	40	31	30	53	3	7

Table 21c
Student perceptions of their sports ability (Age 15)

	Among the best		Good		Average		Below average	
Country	M	F	M	F	M	F	M	F
Canada	32%	13%	40%	35%	23%	44%	5%	8%
Finland	12	6	37	31	44	55	7	8
Poland	10	5	43	34	39	48	7	13
Spain	18	5	41	26	32	55	10	14

Table 22a
Student perceptions of their fitness (Age 11)

	Very fit		Fit		Somewhat fit		Not fit	
Country	M	F	M	F	M	F	M	F
Canada	37%	23%	46%	55%	14%	20%	3%	2%
Finland	18	10	48	52	31	36	3	2
Poland	33	26	49	51	17	21	1	1
Wales	22	12	45	44	25	36	8	9

Table 22b
Student perceptions of their fitness (Age 13)

	Very fit		Fit		Somewhat fit		Not fit	
Country	M	F	M	F	M	F	M	F
Canada	34%	13%	48%	54%	16%	30%	1%	4%
Finland	13	8	50	43	34	47	3	2
Poland	22	19	52	51	21	26	4	4
Wales	17	6	46	37	28	43	9	4

Table 22c
Student perceptions of their fitness (Age 15)

	Very fit		Fit		Somewhat fit		Not fit	
Country	M	F	M	F	M	F	M	F
Canada	29%	11%	50%	47%	17%	38%	4%	5%
Finland	12	5	45	37	39	52	4	6
Poland	14	7	50	43	31	41	5	9
Wales	18	6	45	31	28	47	9	16

Table 23a
What students think of their physical education classes (Age 11)

Country	Like very much		Like them		Like nor dislike		Dislike them		Dislike very much		Do not attend	
	M	F	M	F	M	F	M	F	M	F	M	F
Canada	43%	38%	32%	38%	15%	19%	4%	2%	5%	2%	1%	1%
Finland	40	30	41	44	15	23	2	2	1	1	0	0
Poland	68	61	24	29	5	5	1	2	1	1	1	1
Spain	39	40	31	35	20	19	3	3	6	3	1	0
Wales	58	50	25	28	11	17	3	3	2	2	1	0

Table 23b
What students think of their physical education classes (Age 13)

Country	Like very much		Like them		Like nor dislike		Dislike them		Dislike very much		Do not attend	
	M	F	M	F	M	F	M	F	M	F	M	F
Canada	38%	24%	38%	38%	16%	28%	4%	4%	3%	4%	1%	1%
Finland	28	13	42	42	25	32	3	10	2	3	0	0
Poland	53	46	34	40	9	9	2	4	1	1	2	0
Spain	21	16	36	28	31	40	4	5	5	7	3	3
Wales	51	37	27	29	14	22	4	5	3	5	1	1

Table 23c
What students think of their physical education classes (Age 15)

Country	Like very much		Like them		Like nor dislike		Dislike them		Dislike very much		Do not attend	
	M	F	M	F	M	F	M	F	M	F	M	F
Canada	29%	24%	35%	35%	17%	20%	4%	6%	5%	3%	10%	12%
Finland	26	13	45	38	22	38	4	7	2	3	1	1
Poland	32	25	42	45	18	14	5	8	1	2	2	6
Spain	19	10	25	33	37	41	7	5	12	10	3	2
Wales	45	29	30	30	14	27	3	6	3	3	5	5

Table 24a
Importance to student of some reasons for liking sports or physical activity (Age 11)

Item	Response	Canada		Poland	
		M	F	M	F
To have fun	Very important	81%	83%	22%	25%
	Fairly important	17	15	52	59
	Not important	2	1	26	16
To be good at the activity	Very important	48	36	46	40
	Fairly important	37	47	35	38
	Not important	15	17	19	21
To win	Very important	23	9	45	43
	Fairly important	29	26	38	34
	Not important	48	65	17	24
To make new friends	Very important	56	51	45	37
	Fairly important	33	41	44	46
	Not important	10	9	11	17
To improve my health	Very important	76	76	78	84
	Fairly important	19	21	20	15
	Not important	5	3	2	1
To see my friends	Very important	54	48	28	22
	Fairly important	34	38	58	55
	Not important	12	15	14	23
To get in good shape	Very important	80	76	70	70
	Fairly important	16	21	27	26
	Not important	4	3	2	4
To look good	Very important	41	43	49	69
	Fairly important	30	30	40	26
	Not important	29	27	11	5
To enjoy the feeling of using my body	Very important	61	53	53	60
	Fairly important	30	38	39	36
	Not important	9	9	8	4
To be like a sports star	Very important	31	12	33	35
	Fairly important	25	21	38	29
	Not important	44	66	39	36
To please my parents	Very important	31	24	62	67
	Fairly important	27	29	30	26
	Not important	42	47	8	7

Table 24b
Importance to student of some reasons for liking sports or physical activity (Age 13)

Item	Response	Canada		Poland	
		M	F	M	F
To have fun	Very important	82%	82%	17%	20%
	Fairly important	16	16	53	63
	Not important	2	2	30	17
To be good at the activity	Very important	53	36	36	34
	Fairly important	36	45	40	40
	Not important	11	18	23	27
To win	Very important	28	10	39	34
	Fairly important	34	32	35	35
	Not important	38	57	26	31
To make new friends	Very important	50	48	32	36
	Fairly important	38	44	49	50
	Not important	12	9	19	15
To improve my health	Very important	71	75	76	83
	Fairly important	24	21	21	16
	Not important	5	4	3	1
To see my friends	Very important	56	55	24	22
	Fairly important	36	35	59	60
	Not important	7	10	17	18
To get in good shape	Very important	75	76	67	69
	Fairly important	22	21	30	29
	Not important	3	3	3	2
To look good	Very important	46	48	44	67
	Fairly important	32	27	41	29
	Not important	22	26	15	4
To enjoy the feeling of using my body	Very important	56	43	44	52
	Fairly important	33	39	46	41
	Not important	11	18	9	7
To be like a sports star	Very important	30	8	21	18
	Fairly important	24	17	28	26
	Not important	46	75	51	56
To please my parents	Very important	23	10	37	39
	Fairly important	27	25	41	43
	Not important	50	64	22	18

Table 24c
Importance to student of some reasons for liking sports or physical activity (Age 15)

Item	Response	Canada		Poland	
		M	F	M	F
To have fun	Very important	81%	83%	20%	28%
	Fairly important	16	15	55	61
	Not important	3	1	25	11
To be good at the activity	Very important	50	31	28	25
	Fairly important	38	49	42	43
	Not important	12	20	30	32
To win	Very important	30	9	30	21
	Fairly important	41	34	42	38
	Not important	29	57	28	41
To make new friends	Very important	40	49	30	35
	Fairly important	45	44	52	47
	Not important	14	7	18	18
To improve my health	Very important	69	76	79	83
	Fairly important	25	21	19	16
	Not important	6	3	2	1
To see my friends	Very important	56	54	23	23
	Fairly important	35	38	61	60
	Not important	9	8	16	17
To get in good shape	Very important	73	79	69	73
	Fairly important	23	20	28	25
	Not important	4	1	3	2
To look good	Very important	47	48	47	72
	Fairly important	34	29	43	26
	Not important	19	23	10	2
To enjoy the feeling of using my body	Very important	49	47	48	53
	Fairly important	38	40	42	40
	Not important	13	13	10	7
To be like a sports star	Very important	24	6	13	8
	Fairly important	24	15	27	24
	Not important	52	79	60	67
To please my parents	Very important	11	9	23	20
	Fairly important	23	20	40	45
	Not important	66	71	37	36

Table 25a
Hours a day students watch television (Age 11)

Country	Not at all		Less than 1/2 hour		1/2 - 1 hour		2 - 3 hours		4 hours		More than 4 hours	
	M	F	M	F	M	F	M	F	M	F	M	F
Austria	4%	5%	19%	20%	32%	37%	29%	27%	10%	7%	7%	4%
Belgium	3	1	9	11	30	30	35	38	12	11	11	10
Canada	2	1	8	9	25	29	35	35	13	12	17	14
Finland	2	2	3	5	22	34	44	45	15	7	15	6
Hungary	1	1	1	3	11	16	44	47	23	20	20	13
Norway	2	1	10	18	35	45	36	28	8	5	9	3
Poland	1	1	3	7	14	23	39	43	19	14	24	13
Spain	2	2	4	8	33	38	39	37	13	9	8	6
Sweden	1	0	9	14	30	39	38	34	10	8	13	5
Wales	2	1	4	3	20	20	37	39	12	13	24	24

Table 25b
Hours a day students watch television (Age 13)

Country	Not at all		Less than 1/2 hour		1/2 - 1 hour		2 - 3 hours		4 hours		More than 4 hours	
	M	F	M	F	M	F	M	F	M	F	M	F
Austria	3%	2%	7%	8%	30%	31%	37%	41%	12%	11%	10%	7%
Belgium	3	4	9	6	30	30	34	34	13	14	11	12
Canada	1	2	5	7	24	30	44	40	13	11	13	10
Finland	3	4	2	4	21	32	51	47	13	7	9	6
Hungary	0	0	2	1	10	12	51	57	22	21	14	9
Norway	1	1	6	13	33	45	44	33	11	5	5	3
Poland	1	1	3	5	14	23	41	44	19	15	22	14
Spain	1	1	3	5	26	34	47	43	15	12	8	5
Sweden	0	2	3	5	29	43	40	35	13	7	15	9
Wales	0	1	2	2	16	14	42	43	15	16	24	25

Table 25c
Hours a day students watch television (Age 15)

Country	Not at all		Less than 1/2 hour		1/2 - 1 hour		2 - 3 hours		4 hours		More than 4 hours	
	M	F	M	F	M	F	M	F	M	F	M	F
Austria	2%	3%	4%	8%	26%	30%	39%	45%	17%	7%	12%	7%
Belgium	3	3	8	7	28	26	37	38	12	14	12	13
Canada	2	3	7	9	28	38	40	35	12	9	11	6
Finland	2	3	5	9	24	41	54	40	9	4	6	3
Hungary	1	3	4	7	20	23	53	50	14	12	8	5
Norway	1	4	10	19	35	40	36	31	10	4	8	2
Poland	1	2	5	9	20	32	46	38	16	10	13	9
Spain	2	2	5	6	28	31	47	47	13	10	6	4
Sweden	1	1	6	11	35	43	40	32	10	7	9	5
Wales	1	1	3	2	16	18	46	47	13	14	21	19

Table 26a
Hours a week students watch VCR movies (Age 11)

	Not at all		Less than 1 hour		1 - 3 hours		4 - 6 hours		7 - 9 hours		10+ hours	
Country	M	F	M	F	M	F	M	F	M	F	M	F
Austria	44%	47%	20%	26%	23%	21%	7%	4%	3%	1%	2%	1%
Belgium	26	33	23	24	21	14	25	27	2	0	2	2
Canada	15	20	18	20	38	45	18	9	4	4	7	2
Finland	18	25	11	22	40	38	17	11	8	3	6	1
Hungary	41	52	11	12	24	23	11	8	8	3	5	2
Norway	29	38	26	33	31	22	9	5	2	1	3	1
Poland	43	52	14	13	21	20	22	14	0	0	0	0
Scotland	15	20	20	28	42	39	14	9	3	2	5	2
Spain	32	37	15	18	36	33	10	9	4	2	2	1
Sweden	21	31	22	28	33	30	13	8	6	2	5	1
Wales	16	19	16	24	45	42	16	9	3	4	4	2

Table 26b
Hours a week students watch VCR movies (Age 13)

	Not at all		Less than 1 hour		1 - 3 hours		4 - 6 hours		7 - 9 hours		10+ hours	
Country	M	F	M	F	M	F	M	F	M	F	M	F
Austria	35%	44%	17%	23%	29%	21%	13%	8%	3%	2%	3%	2%
Belgium	25	28	23	22	20	19	25	27	3	2	4	2
Canada	12	20	17	18	44	42	19	14	4	4	4	3
Finland	15	21	12	20	37	38	21	14	8	4	7	2
Hungary	39	52	11	10	27	26	14	7	5	3	4	1
Norway	28	33	25	31	30	26	11	8	3	1	3	1
Poland	36	59	14	12	21	18	28	12	0	0	0	0
Scotland	11	13	17	23	42	46	19	11	6	4	4	3
Spain	28	33	18	18	35	36	13	9	4	3	2	1
Sweden	14	20	18	26	38	38	17	10	7	3	6	3
Wales	11	14	17	17	45	47	17	14	5	5	5	3

Table 26c
Hours a week students watch VCR movies (Age 15)

	Not at all		Less than 1 hour		1 - 3 hours		4 - 6 hours		7 - 9 hours		10+ hours	
Country	M	F	M	F	M	F	M	F	M	F	M	F
Austria	33%	42%	17%	22%	30%	26%	14%	8%	3%	2%	3%	1%
Belgium	24	23	21	24	18	22	30	25	4	3	3	3
Canada	14	18	19	18	42	46	17	14	4	3	3	2
Finland	9	22	13	17	44	46	24	12	5	2	5	1
Hungary	32	50	13	10	33	28	12	8	5	3	5	1
Norway	18	31	27	29	32	30	15	8	5	2	3	0
Poland	35	58	17	12	23	18	24	13	0	0	0	0
Scotland	13	14	16	22	45	46	19	12	4	3	3	3
Spain	33	41	13	17	38	31	13	9	3	1	0	1
Sweden	9	16	19	28	42	39	21	12	5	3	4	2
Wales	11	14	18	22	47	45	16	12	4	4	4	3

Table 27a
Hours a week students play computer games (Age 11)

Country	Not at all		Less than 1 hour		1 - 3 hours		4 - 6 hours		7 - 9 hours		10+ hours	
	M	F	M	F	M	F	M	F	M	F	M	F
Austria	53%	76%	22%	16%	13%	7%	9%	1%	2%	0%	2%	0%
Belgium	43	62	25	26	20	10	7	1	3	0	3	1
Canada	14	31	29	38	26	20	12	6	8	2	11	3
Finland	18	62	21	23	30	9	17	3	8	1	6	1
Hungary	52	74	11	10	24	12	8	3	3	0	2	1
Norway	38	70	23	19	21	8	11	2	3	0	3	0
Poland	56	78	17	13	13	7	7	2	3	0	4	0
Scotland	21	49	22	30	31	16	13	4	6	1	8	1
Spain	40	60	29	27	22	10	6	2	2	1	1	0
Sweden	21	31	22	28	33	30	13	8	6	2	5	1
Wales	21	48	24	31	30	16	13	3	5	1	7	1

Table 27b
Hours a week students play computer games (Age 13)

Country	Not at all		Less than 1 hour		1 - 3 hours		4 - 6 hours		7 - 9 hours		10+ hours	
	M	F	M	F	M	F	M	F	M	F	M	F
Austria	39%	73%	21%	16%	21%	7%	10%	2%	2%	1%	7%	0%
Belgium	43	67	25	20	20	10	6	2	3	0	3	1
Canada	14	45	30	35	29	14	13	3	5	1	9	1
Finland	24	66	22	21	22	9	15	2	8	1	9	1
Hungary	49	72	10	7	28	19	6	1	3	0	4	0
Norway	34	76	27	16	18	6	11	1	5	0	4	0
Poland	59	86	16	9	13	4	5	1	4	0	3	0
Scotland	27	60	23	24	25	12	12	3	5	0	8	1
Spain	34	66	33	24	20	8	9	1	3	1	2	0
Sweden	14	20	18	26	38	38	17	10	7	3	6	3
Wales	27	61	25	25	26	12	12	2	5	0	5	0

Table 27c
Hours a week students play computer games (Age 15)

Country	Not at all		Less than 1 hour		1 - 3 hours		4 - 6 hours		7 - 9 hours		10+ hours	
	M	F	M	F	M	F	M	F	M	F	M	F
Austria	39%	75%	19%	11%	20%	13%	10%	1%	5%	0%	7%	0%
Belgium	46	76	23	13	15	8	9	2	2	1	5	0
Canada	23	60	34	27	23	8	10	3	4	1	6	1
Finland	46	80	25	16	17	4	5	0	3	0	4	0
Hungary	62	72	9	7	19	20	5	1	2	0	3	0
Norway	48	86	24	11	14	3	7	0	2	0	5	0
Poland	57	88	20	6	14	5	4	1	2	0	3	0
Scotland	43	80	24	15	15	4	12	1	3	0	2	0
Spain	39	71	37	19	15	9	6	1	1	0	2	0
Sweden	10	16	19	28	41	39	21	12	5	3	4	2
Wales	50	80	24	14	16	42	62	2	2	0	2	0

Table 28a
How often students eat fruit (Age 11)

Country	More than once/day		Once/day		At least once/week		Seldom		Never	
	M	F	M	F	M	F	M	F	M	F
Austria	34%	43%	42%	41%	17%	10%	4%	2%	3%	4%
Belgium	56	65	29	24	8	7	5	3	2	1
Canada	39	44	38	40	16	13	5	2	2	1
Finland	29	29	33	42	29	25	6	3	3	1
Hungary	33	35	47	48	15	12	4	5	1	0
Norway	28	32	29	31	33	30	8	6	2	1
Poland	54	65	31	25	11	7	3	3	1	0
Scotland	24	26	31	38	26	24	11	7	7	6
Spain	52	53	33	31	11	9	2	4	3	3
Sweden	39	46	42	36	15	13	4	3	1	2
Wales	24	27	30	34	38	34	4	3	4	2

Table 28b
How often students eat fruit (Age 13)

Country	More than once/day		Once/day		At least once/week		Seldom		Never	
	M	F	M	F	M	F	M	F	M	F
Austria	34%	44%	43%	40%	18%	11%	4%	3%	2%	2%
Belgium	55	65	32	24	9	6	3	3	1	2
Canada	37	41	38	37	20	18	3	3	2	1
Finland	22	27	39	39	32	30	4	3	2	1
Hungary	34	32	49	51	14	14	3	3	0	0
Norway	20	27	32	32	39	37	8	3	1	1
Poland	50	57	29	28	15	11	4	3	2	0
Scotland	17	26	32	38	36	27	7	4	8	5
Spain	44	55	35	31	14	10	4	3	2	1
Sweden	32	39	41	41	22	18	3	2	1	1
Wales	23	26	30	32	40	37	3	3	3	2

Table 28c
How often students eat fruit (Age 15)

Country	More than once/day		Once/day		At least once/week		Seldom		Never	
	M	F	M	F	M	F	M	F	M	F
Austria	20%	33%	44%	45%	27%	15%	7%	5%	2%	2%
Belgium	53	54	32	30	9	11	4	5	2	0
Canada	32	38	38	38	24	21	5	3	1	1
Finland	13	29	35	40	44	28	6	3	3	0
Hungary	21	28	53	48	21	20	4	3	0	0
Norway	13	19	28	29	48	46	10	5	1	1
Poland	40	50	32	30	23	18	3	2	1	0
Scotland	16	26	28	33	37	32	12	6	7	2
Spain	47	54	32	26	13	13	6	6	2	2
Sweden	25	39	39	39	31	19	4	3	1	0
Wales	21	25	28	35	44	35	5	4	2	1

Table 29a
How often respondents eat raw vegetables (Age 11)

Country	More than once/day		Once/day		At least once/week		Seldom		Never	
	M	F	M	F	M	F	M	F	M	F
Austria	15%	16%	34%	37%	30%	26%	16%	15%	5%	6%
Belgium	17	21	36	37	19	21	13	13	15	8
Canada	24	25	28	34	26	25	17	11	5	4
Finland	12	13	41	42	29	32	16	12	2	1
Hungary	10	12	33	33	32	34	22	18	3	3
Norway	10	9	17	20	34	39	32	28	7	4
Poland	10	11	18	25	26	25	31	28	15	11
Scotland	5	6	13	17	26	32	27	26	29	19
Spain	14	14	26	23	40	46	13	12	8	5
Sweden	9	8	30	37	28	27	26	20	8	7

Table 29b
How often respondents eat raw vegetables (Age 13)

Country	More than once/day		Once/day		At least once/week		Seldom		Never	
	M	F	M	F	M	F	M	F	M	F
Austria	12%	14%	36%	36%	36%	54%	53%	11%	3%	4%
Belgium	19	18	38	44	21	20	15	12	7	6
Canada	18	22	30	32	30	30	17	13	5	2
Finland	11	13	38	34	38	44	12	9	1	0
Hungary	10	12	35	39	36	35	16	12	3	2
Norway	6	7	17	16	44	50	30	24	4	3
Poland	9	11	17	23	30	31	37	30	7	5
Scotland	5	10	17	18	30	37	25	24	22	11
Spain	7	9	23	25	51	51	14	12	4	3
Sweden	8	8	29	35	37	36	21	17	5	4

Table 29c
How often respondents eat raw vegetables (Age 15)

Country	More than once/day		Once/day		At least once/week		Seldom		Never	
	M	F	M	F	M	F	M	F	M	F
Austria	6%	9%	33%	34%	42%	41%	16%	12%	3%	3%
Belgium	21	20	45	44	18	23	11	8	5	5
Canada	17	19	32	33	30	32	17	13	4	3
Finland	6	10	35	45	43	36	13	8	3	1
Hungary	8	11	28	32	44	41	18	14	2	2
Norway	3	5	14	15	44	48	34	30	5	2
Poland	5	7	14	17	31	31	43	39	7	6
Scotland	4	8	12	20	35	39	30	22	19	11
Spain	7	12	23	28	58	44	7	13	5	3
Sweden	8	10	27	32	36	40	23	16	6	2

Table 30a
How often students eat whole wheat/rye bread (Age 11)

	More than once/day		Once/day		At least once/week		Seldom		Never	
Country	M	F	M	F	M	F	M	F	M	F
Austria	14%	11%	23%	24%	19%	23%	25%	28%	19%	14%
Belgium	38	40	24	26	10	10	13	14	15	10
Canada	25	21	25	24	16	15	21	27	12	13
Finland	13	15	30	31	32	35	16	14	10	5
Hungary	53	51	34	35	3	3	6	6	4	5
Norway	53	53	16	16	14	15	12	12	6	5
Poland	22	22	12	10	16	17	36	37	15	15
Scotland	22	19	27	28	18	19	20	20	13	14
Spain	18	13	11	11	11	11	24	25	36	40
Sweden	12	9	17	12	20	18	33	44	18	17
Wales	10	11	15	16	38	36	13	15	24	23

Table 30b
How often students eat whole wheat/rye bread (Age 13)

	More than once/day		Once/day		At least once/week		Seldom		Never	
Country	M	F	M	F	M	F	M	F	M	F
Austria	10%	8%	22%	22%	24%	27%	30%	30%	14%	13%
Belgium	37	40	25	21	10	12	15	15	12	12
Canada	22	19	23	24	19	17	24	28	12	13
Finland	18	12	37	35	30	41	11	11	4	1
Hungary	60	54	30	36	2	2	6	5	2	3
Norway	52	53	17	16	18	21	11	8	2	2
Poland	21	16	8	8	16	18	40	42	15	16
Scotland	20	22	27	27	21	20	20	20	11	11
Spain	13	14	10	9	12	11	34	30	31	36
Sweden	11	7	20	16	27	28	31	40	11	9
Wales	12	9	14	19	38	38	16	17	21	17

Table 30c
How often students eat whole wheat/rye bread (Age 15)

	More than once/day		Once/day		At least once/week		Seldom		Never	
Country	M	F	M	F	M	F	M	F	M	F
Austria	5%	8%	15%	19%	25%	27%	38%	35%	17%	12%
Belgium	36	35	21	23	12	10	18	19	13	13
Canada	20	16	19	21	19	20	31	29	11	14
Finland	14	19	39	39	35	32	9	9	3	1
Hungary	59	48	34	39	2	3	3	7	2	3
Norway	55	51	15	17	18	19	9	11	3	2
Poland	17	13	8	6	18	17	45	46	12	18
Scotland	23	26	28	29	19	20	20	17	10	8
Spain	11	12	9	9	12	11	30	33	38	35
Sweden	7	8	14	16	32	30	37	36	10	10
Wales	13	11	15	20	39	37	17	18	17	14

Table 31a
How often students drink low fat milk (Age 11)

Country	More than once/day		Once/day		At least once/week		Seldom		Never	
	M	F	M	F	M	F	M	F	M	F
Canada	52%	52%	15%	15%	7%	7%	12%	11%	14%	15%
Finland	63	66	21	18	3	4	4	3	8	9
Norway	65	66	10	12	3	5	8	8	13	9
Scotland	28	25	16	14	8	9	18	20	30	32
Sweden	30	27	16	16	11	10	22	26	21	21
Wales	25	22	11	11	14	17	6	9	44	41

Table 31b
How often students drink low fat milk (Age 13)

Country	More than once/day		Once/day		At least once/week		Seldom		Never	
	M	F	M	F	M	F	M	F	M	F
Canada	57%	52%	16%	16%	5%	6%	11%	11%	12%	15%
Finland	64	64	18	17	6	7	5	3	8	9
Norway	69	64	10	15	4	6	6	9	11	6
Scotland	33	29	14	14	9	8	17	21	27	28
Sweden	32	29	12	17	11	11	24	26	21	18
Wales	25	22	11	11	14	17	6	9	44	41

Table 31c
How often students drink low fat milk (Age 15)

Country	More than once/day		Once/day		At least once/week		Seldom		Never	
	M	F	M	F	M	F	M	F	M	F
Canada	54%	49%	14%	16%	5%	8%	14%	13%	13%	14%
Finland	63	61	22	17	4	4	4	4	8	14
Norway	66	66	7	12	5	7	8	8	14	8
Scotland	32	35	11	11	10	9	21	20	27	25
Sweden	28	35	10	13	11	11	26	25	25	17
Wales	27	30	9	10	14	14	8	9	42	37

Table 32a
How often students drink whole milk (homogenized) (Age 11)

Country	More than once/day		Once/day		At least once/week		Seldom		Never	
	M	F	M	F	M	F	M	F	M	F
Canada	27%	22%	10%	11%	8%	7%	21%	22%	35%	38%
Finland	6	5	5	5	7	7	25	21	57	62
Norway	22	16	8	6	5	5	26	28	39	46
Scotland	38	31	20	19	9	9	14	16	19	25
Sweden	57	51	23	21	9	9	7	11	3	8
Wales	28	29	17	14	21	21	4	6	30	30

Table 32b
How often students drink whole milk (homogenized) (Age 13)

Country	More than once/day		Once/day		At least once/week		Seldom		Never	
	M	F	M	F	M	F	M	F	M	F
Canada	22%	19%	12%	10%	7%	7%	23%	22%	36%	42%
Finland	10	4	7	4	9	5	21	19	53	68
Norway	19	13	7	5	5	4	25	25	44	53
Scotland	39	31	14	17	8	9	14	14	24	29
Sweden	63	53	18	21	9	9	7	12	3	6
Wales	38	28	12	14	18	19	6	7	26	32

Table 32c
How often students drink whole milk (homogenized) (Age 15)

Country	More than once/day		Once/day		At least once/week		Seldom		Never	
	M	F	M	F	M	F	M	F	M	F
Canada	27%	15%	10%	8%	8%	7%	26%	24%	29%	46%
Finland	10	5	6	3	10	5	18	12	56	75
Norway	21	10	4	4	6	5	23	26	46	55
Scotland	42	25	17	17	8	10	14	16	19	32
Sweden	71	48	14	22	6	12	6	11	3	7
Wales	40	29	12	11	15	15	7	8	26	37

Table 33a
How often students eat candy/chocolate bars (Age 11)

Country	More than once/day		Once/day		At least once/week		Seldom		Never	
	M	F	M	F	M	F	M	F	M	F
Austria	9%	7%	18%	18%	33%	30%	33%	41%	7%	4%
Belgium	27	25	45	43	14	17	11	12	4	3
Canada	12	8	16	14	47	49	23	28	2	1
Finland	8	4	15	13	64	70	13	12	1	1
Hungary	9	7	28	27	34	32	27	32	2	1
Norway	5	5	7	4	63	66	22	22	3	2
Poland	24	25	30	34	24	23	20	18	2	1
Scotland	29	23	33	32	31	34	6	8	1	3
Spain	25	27	21	22	32	34	17	15	5	2
Sweden	7	4	13	10	64	68	14	14	2	3
Wales	16	16	22	26	52	50	6	5	4	3

Table 33b
How often students eat candy/chocolate bars (Age 13)

Country	More than once/day		Once/day		At least once/week		Seldom		Never	
	M	F	M	F	M	F	M	F	M	F
Austria	10%	7%	27%	27%	34%	34%	26%	29%	3%	4%
Belgium	22	26	46	43	16	17	13	12	3	2
Canada	10	6	20	16	47	50	21	26	2	2
Finland	9	7	21	25	63	60	7	6	0	1
Hungary	8	7	30	28	35	36	25	28	2	1
Norway	6	5	9	8	66	73	17	12	2	2
Poland	28	27	30	33	27	25	14	14	1	1
Scotland	34	30	35	35	24	29	5	5	2	1
Spain	18	28	21	17	41	35	18	17	2	3
Sweden	11	9	21	18	53	58	12	8	3	7
Wales	21	15	25	25	48	52	4	6	2	2

Table 33c
How often students eat candy/chocolate bars (Age 15)

Country	More than once/day		Once/day		At least once/week		Seldom		Never	
	M	F	M	F	M	F	M	F	M	F
Austria	9%	7%	29%	26%	37%	39%	24%	25%	2%	3%
Belgium	27	31	47	38	15	16	9	12	2	4
Canada	9	5	19	13	48	50	22	30	2	2
Finland	8	10	23	20	58	60	10	9	1	1
Hungary	5	5	28	29	34	37	31	27	2	2
Norway	9	7	13	10	59	65	17	16	2	2
Poland	21	23	27	26	32	32	19	18	1	1
Scotland	28	17	35	36	26	34	9	10	2	3
Spain	16	21	19	23	41	38	21	16	3	2
Sweden	9	5	18	17	56	59	13	17	3	3
Wales	19	16	26	21	47	53	7	8	2	2

Table 34a
How often students eat potato chips/crisps (Age 11)

Country	More than once/day		Once/day		At least once/week		Seldom		Never	
	M	F	M	F	M	F	M	F	M	F
Austria	6%	5%	8%	4%	21%	21%	56%	58%	9%	11%
Canada	8	4	14	11	45	49	31	35	2	1
Finland	1	0	3	1	26	15	64	79	6	5
Hungary	3	2	8	6	56	58	32	32	2	2
Norway	2	1	4	0	51	46	41	50	3	3
Poland	4	4	8	8	26	28	51	52	10	8
Scotland	22	21	45	47	23	20	8	10	2	2
Spain	9	8	11	8	33	35	36	41	11	8
Sweden	1	0	2	1	23	15	70	78	4	6

Table 34b
How often students eat potato chips/crisps (Age 13)

Country	More than once/day		Once/day		At least once/week		Seldom		Never	
	M	F	M	F	M	F	M	F	M	F
Austria	4%	3%	5%	6%	28%	23%	57%	62%	6%	6%
Canada	6	4	14	13	52	47	25	33	2	2
Finland	1	0	2	1	29	18	66	76	2	4
Hungary	2	2	9	6	61	61	26	30	2	1
Norway	1	0	2	1	51	49	43	47	3	3
Poland	3	2	5	6	23	25	60	61	9	6
Scotland	22	19	38	46	28	25	10	9	2	1
Spain	4	3	7	7	44	43	41	41	4	6
Sweden	0	0	1	1	28	23	68	70	3	4

Table 34c
How often students eat potato chips/crisps (Age 15)

Country	More than once/day		Once/day		At least once/week		Seldom		Never	
	M	F	M	F	M	F	M	F	M	F
Austria	2%	2%	5%	3%	36%	22%	51%	64%	7%	9%
Canada	4	2	14	8	50	46	29	40	3	3
Finland	0	0	1	0	29	17	67	79	3	4
Hungary	2	1	8	6	64	65	25	28	1	1
Norway	1	0	2	1	54	47	41	49	2	3
Poland	1	1	4	3	17	19	67	68	11	9
Scotland	19	13	30	40	36	34	13	10	2	2
Spain	2	2	5	5	44	45	44	44	5	4
Sweden	0	0	1	0	31	22	66	74	2	4

Table 35a
How often students eat french fries (Age 11)

Country	More than once/day		Once/day		At least once/week		Seldom		Never	
	M	F	M	F	M	F	M	F	M	F
Austria	5%	3%	4%	3%	30%	22%	55%	66%	6%	6%
Belgium	4	3	51	47	31	39	11	10	3	1
Canada	6	2	7	5	53	50	33	43	2	1
Finland	2	1	7	4	29	22	52	65	10	8
Hungary	1	0	1	1	6	4	35	40	57	55
Norway	1	0	0	0	10	8	78	81	11	11
Poland	6	3	8	6	37	37	45	50	3	4
Scotland	8	7	19	15	52	49	17	24	4	5
Spain	15	11	22	18	49	57	10	11	4	3
Sweden	1	1	3	0	39	29	54	65	3	5
Wales	9	7	15	12	64	66	7	10	6	5

Table 35b
How often students eat french fries (Age 13)

Country	More than once/day		Once/day		At least once/week		Seldom		Never	
	M	F	M	F	M	F	M	F	M	F
Austria	3%	2%	4%	3%	31%	24%	58%	68%	4%	3%
Belgium	3	2	51	48	36	42	9	7	2	1
Canada	4	2	6	5	58	56	31	36	1	1
Finland	1	0	3	1	29	21	62	70	5	8
Hungary	0	0	2	1	7	5	41	43	50	51
Norway	1	0	0	0	9	8	83	86	7	6
Poland	3	2	5	3	36	39	54	54	3	3
Scotland	10	7	22	19	51	52	12	20	4	3
Spain	7	7	21	21	62	61	6	8	3	2
Sweden	1	0	2	1	38	29	56	64	3	6
Wales	9	3	12	9	67	71	8	13	4	4

Table 35c
How often students eat french fries (Age 15)

Country	More than once/day		Once/day		At least once/week		Seldom		Never	
	M	F	M	F	M	F	M	F	M	F
Austria	1%	1%	3%	1%	35%	21%	59%	69%	3%	8%
Belgium	3	2	56	48	33	37	7	10	1	3
Canada	3	1	10	6	56	53	29	38	2	2
Finland	0	0	2	1	29	20	64	72	5	7
Hungary	0	0	1	1	7	8	44	49	48	42
Norway	1	0	0	0	12	8	82	85	5	7
Poland	1	1	4	3	37	33	55	61	3	2
Scotland	10	4	23	14	50	52	16	25	1	5
Spain	8	4	18	20	67	65	6	9	1	2
Sweden	1	0	2	0	32	23	61	70	4	7
Wales	5	2	11	6	74	68	8	18	2	6

Table 36a
How often students eat hamburgers/hot dogs/sausages (Age 11)

Country	More than once/day		Once/day		At least once/week		Seldom		Never	
	M	F	M	F	M	F	M	F	M	F
Austria	5%	2%	3%	2%	17%	14%	56%	63%	19%	19%
Belgium	2	1	15	8	29	28	36	43	18	21
Canada	4	2	6	4	61	55	28	38	1	1
Finland	1	0	2	0	21	9	68	80	8	10
Hungary	1	0	2	1	19	12	70	79	8	9
Norway	1	0	1	1	23	17	71	78	5	4
Poland	3	1	5	4	20	20	59	64	13	11
Scotland	4	3	11	8	53	47	27	33	5	10
Spain	7	5	9	14	52	50	24	25	8	7
Sweden	1	1	1	1	33	20	63	75	3	4
Wales	6	3	11	7	54	53	20	25	9	12

Table 36b
How often students eat hamburgers/hot dogs/sausages (Age 13)

Country	More than once/day		Once/day		At least once/week		Seldom		Never	
	M	F	M	F	M	F	M	F	M	F
Austria	3%	2%	3%	2%	23%	15%	60%	68%	12%	14%
Belgium	1	1	13	9	28	29	39	47	19	14
Canada	3	1	5	2	64	59	27	35	1	2
Finland	1	0	2	1	21	12	72	80	4	7
Hungary	1	1	3	1	24	14	66	77	5	7
Norway	0	0	1	0	20	19	75	79	4	2
Poland	2	1	3	2	21	19	65	71	9	8
Scotland	7	2	12	7	57	52	20	29	5	10
Spain	3	2	7	7	67	62	21	24	2	5
Sweden	0	0	1	1	36	25	61	69	2	5
Wales	3	1	8	4	57	49	23	29	9	17

Table 36c
How often students eat hamburgers/hot dogs/sausages (Age 15)

Country	More than once/day		Once/day		At least once/week		Seldom		Never	
	M	F	M	F	M	F	M	F	M	F
Austria	1%	1%	4%	1%	29%	17%	57%	64%	10%	17%
Belgium	3	0	16	12	34	31	35	41	12	14
Canada	2	0	6	3	67	54	24	39	1	3
Finland	0	0	2	1	29	17	65	77	4	5
Hungary	1	0	5	3	28	20	60	70	6	7
Norway	0	0	1	1	25	18	72	78	2	3
Poland	1	1	3	2	28	19	62	72	6	7
Scotland	4	1	12	5	60	44	20	36	4	14
Spain	2	1	7	6	59	55	25	32	6	5
Sweden	1	0	1	0	39	28	58	68	1	4
Wales	2	0	4	2	63	42	24	37	7	18

Table 37a
How often students drink soft drinks such as cola or other drinks with sugar (Age 11)

Country	More than once/day		Once/day		At least once/week		Seldom		Never	
	M	F	M	F	M	F	M	F	M	F
Austria	12%	12%	15%	13%	30%	20%	40%	50%	3%	5%
Belgium	46	46	28	26	11	12	11	12	4	4
Canada	22	16	25	22	37	44	14	16	2	3
Finland	5	1	10	3	58	51	25	43	2	2
Hungary	11	7	26	18	36	33	25	40	2	2
Norway	5	3	7	4	60	59	26	33	2	2
Poland	12	8	18	14	38	38	30	39	3	2
Scotland	39	31	20	19	27	31	10	16	4	4
Spain	20	14	13	13	43	41	19	24	6	8
Sweden	6	3	10	5	60	54	20	34	4	4
Wales	33	35	18	18	39	37	4	6	5	4

Table 37b
How often students drink soft drinks such as cola or other drinks with sugar (Age 13)

Country	More than once/day		Once/day		At least once/week		Seldom		Never	
	M	F	M	F	M	F	M	F	M	F
Austria	15%	13%	18%	20%	36%	29%	29%	25%	2%	3%
Belgium	52	48	24	24	10	10	10	13	4	5
Canada	28	19	28	25	35	41	7	13	2	2
Finland	6	3	12	5	64	51	18	40	0	1
Hungary	14	7	30	25	33	35	21	32	1	1
Norway	4	3	5	3	70	71	20	22	1	0
Poland	11	8	18	11	45	40	24	40	2	1
Scotland	40	32	30	27	22	31	6	8	2	2
Spain	16	13	14	13	53	45	13	25	4	4
Sweden	8	4	11	4	65	64	14	23	2	5
Wales	35	32	20	22	39	38	4	6	2	2

Table 37c
How often students drink soft drinks such as cola or other drinks with sugar (Age 15)

Country	More than once/day		Once/day		At least once/week		Seldom		Never	
	M	F	M	F	M	F	M	F	M	F
Austria	18%	15%	27%	20%	35%	29%	17%	33%	2%	3%
Belgium	59	49	24	25	8	10	5	11	3	5
Canada	31	19	32	26	29	40	7	13	1	3
Finland	5	1	16	6	58	49	21	41	0	2
Hungary	13	8	37	26	30	32	19	32	1	2
Norway	9	5	13	7	66	68	11	19	1	1
Poland	11	8	19	11	43	36	26	43	1	2
Scotland	42	29	27	26	23	30	7	12	1	3
Spain	12	12	18	12	50	52	17	21	3	3
Sweden	8	2	15	7	63	59	12	29	2	3
Wales	34	29	22	23	36	38	4	8	3	3

Table 38a
How often students drink coffee (Age 11)

Country	More than once/day		Once/day		At least once/week		Seldom		Never	
	M	F	M	F	M	F	M	F	M	F
Austria	3%	1%	16%	9%	9%	9%	25%	25%	47%	56%
Belgium	26	22	20	18	6	7	11	18	37	35
Canada	2	1	4	3	9	6	24	23	60	67
Finland	10	4	10	4	12	10	23	21	45	61
Hungary	0	0	1	1	2	1	18	15	79	84
Norway	1	0	1	0	2	1	11	7	85	91
Poland	1	0	1	1	6	4	29	25	62	70
Scotland	11	9	9	10	15	10	18	18	47	53
Spain	6	3	8	8	10	10	25	24	51	55
Sweden	2	1	3	2	10	3	28	23	57	71
Wales	12	11	12	13	20	20	9	9	47	47

Table 38b
How often students drink coffee (Age 13)

Country	More than once/day		Once/day		At least once/week		Seldom		Never	
	M	F	M	F	M	F	M	F	M	F
Austria	3%	1%	22%	19%	10%	12%	24%	31%	40%	38%
Belgium	35	25	19	17	7	3	8	16	31	39
Canada	3	2	5	2	9	9	28	29	55	58
Finland	18	11	11	8	14	12	20	19	37	50
Hungary	0	0	1	2	6	2	24	26	69	70
Norway	1	0	1	1	3	1	11	6	84	92
Poland	1	0	2	1	10	8	32	37	55	53
Scotland	19	13	9	12	16	14	17	17	39	44
Spain	5	3	11	8	16	15	29	32	39	42
Sweden	3	1	6	2	9	7	26	24	56	66
Wales	19	16	12	13	20	19	9	12	40	40

Table 38c
How often students drink coffee (Age 15)

Country	More than once/day		Once/day		At least once/week		Seldom		Never	
	M	F	M	F	M	F	M	F	M	F
Austria	6%	5%	29%	27%	14%	15%	21%	23%	30%	30%
Belgium	33	34	15	18	7	4	10	16	34	28
Canada	4	4	7	6	13	11	27	25	49	54
Finland	26	19	13	11	16	17	17	14	28	40
Hungary	1	2	3	5	4	6	26	35	66	52
Norway	4	2	2	1	7	5	18	12	69	80
Poland	1	1	3	3	15	21	41	48	39	27
Scotland	23	25	9	11	12	12	18	12	39	40
Spain	11	9	17	16	19	18	28	27	26	30
Sweden	9	5	6	5	15	11	25	23	46	56
Wales	29	25	11	11	20	20	9	10	32	34

Table 39a
How often students eat peanuts (Age 11)

Country	More than once/day		Once/day		At least once/week		Seldom		Never	
	M	F	M	F	M	F	M	F	M	F
Austria	4%	3%	8%	4%	12%	9%	62%	67%	14%	18%
Canada	3	2	5	3	22	18	54	59	16	18
Finland	1	1	5	1	8	10	58	61	28	27
Hungary	2	1	3	3	14	11	76	81	5	5
Norway	1	0	2	1	15	11	66	71	16	17
Spain	11	7	13	10	36	37	33	38	6	8
Sweden	3	1	1	1	19	10	63	73	14	15

Table 39b
How often students eat peanuts (Age 13)

Country	More than once/day		Once/day		At least once/week		Seldom		Never	
	M	F	M	F	M	F	M	F	M	F
Austria	2%	2%	2%	2%	15%	9%	68%	72%	13%	16%
Canada	3	1	5	2	20	15	56	63	17	19
Finland	1	0	2	1	10	7	66	67	20	25
Hungary	0	0	2	1	17	10	78	85	3	4
Norway	0	0	1	0	14	8	69	73	16	19
Spain	6	5	12	11	50	39	29	40	3	5
Sweden	1	0	2	1	20	13	68	71	9	15

Table 39c
How often students eat peanuts (Age 15)

Country	More than once/day		Once/day		At least once/week		Seldom		Never	
	M	F	M	F	M	F	M	F	M	F
Austria	2%	1%	3%	1%	12%	8%	72%	66%	11%	24%
Canada	2	0	3	2	19	11	63	69	13	18
Finland	0	0	0	1	10	4	62	61	28	34
Hungary	1	0	2	1	12	8	79	85	6	7
Norway	1	0	1	0	12	5	72	72	14	23
Spain	8	4	9	8	50	44	29	39	4	5
Sweden	1	0	1	0	14	6	74	75	10	18

Table 40a
How often students brush their teeth (Age 11)

Country	More than once/day		Once/day		At least once/week not daily		Seldom		Never	
	M	F	M	F	M	F	M	F	M	F
Austria	65%	74%	19%	16%	5%	3%	3%	1%	8%	6%
Belgium	31	39	45	45	15	12	6	4	3	0
Canada	51	68	32	24	11	6	4	1	2	1
Finland	21	43	59	47	15	8	5	1	1	0
Hungary	34	52	47	40	10	6	6	2	3	0
Poland	37	61	41	31	15	6	6	2	1	0
Scotland	52	67	33	25	10	5	4	2	1	1
Spain	26	42	39	35	14	9	18	13	3	1
Sweden	77	84	21	14	2	2	1	0	0	0
Wales	52	66	38	30	7	3	2	1	1	0

Table 40b
How often students brush their teeth (Age 13)

Country	More than once/day		Once/day		At least once/week not daily		Seldom		Never	
	M	F	M	F	M	F	M	F	M	F
Austria	64%	75%	21%	18%	5%	3%	2%	1%	9%	3%
Belgium	36	56	44	37	12	6	4	1	4	0
Canada	52	76	34	20	9	3	3	1	2	0
Finland	24	50	52	42	17	6	6	2	1	0
Hungary	39	66	44	29	10	3	6	2	1	0
Poland	32	60	43	32	15	5	8	2	2	1
Scotland	51	73	35	24	9	2	3	1	2	0
Spain	23	45	36	38	20	9	19	8	2	0
Sweden	79	87	17	12	3	1	0	0	0	0
Wales	50	71	37	25	9	3	1	1	2	0

Table 40c
How often students brush their teeth (Age 15)

Country	More than once/day		Once/day		At least once/week not daily		Seldom		Never	
	M	F	M	F	M	F	M	F	M	F
Austria	57%	81%	29%	15%	6%	2%	1%	0%	7%	2%
Belgium	30	56	49	38	14	5	5	1	2	0
Canada	54	78	35	19	6	2	2	1	2	0
Finland	22	58	59	38	12	4	6	0	1	0
Hungary	44	79	44	19	6	1	5	1	1	0
Poland	30	69	43	27	16	3	8	1	3	0
Scotland	49	78	37	19	9	2	4	1	1	0
Spain	24	48	39	36	16	9	17	5	4	1
Sweden	77	93	21	6	2	1	0	0	0	0
Wales	57	80	35	18	6	2	1	0	1	0

Table 41a
How often students use dental floss (Age 11)

	Daily		Weekly		Seldom/Never	
Country	M	F	M	F	M	F
Austria	12%	11%	8%	7%	80%	82%
Canada	12	20	22	26	66	54
Finland	3	6	9	12	88	82
Norway	11	20	16	15	73	65
Scotland	7	9	13	15	80	76
Spain	12	12	7	6	81	82
Sweden	6	6	13	13	81	81
Wales	11	10	10	13	79	77

Table 41b
How often students use dental floss (Age 13)

	Daily		Weekly		Seldom/Never	
Country	M	F	M	F	M	F
Austria	5%	5%	8%	7%	87%	88%
Canada	11	19	20	23	69	58
Finland	5	6	10	16	85	78
Norway	9	15	15	22	76	63
Scotland	8	11	15	16	77	72
Spain	6	10	6	8	88	82
Sweden	6	6	15	19	79	75
Wales	6	8	10	13	83	79

Table 41c
How often students use dental floss (Age 15)

	Daily		Weekly		Seldom/Never	
Country	M	F	M	F	M	F
Austria	5%	3%	5%	7%	90%	90%
Canada	9	15	18	25	73	60
Finland	2	6	10	19	88	75
Norway	8	17	15	19	77	64
Scotland	6	8	10	13	84	79
Spain	13	14	12	13	75	73
Sweden	4	9	15	25	81	66
Wales	4	6	9	13	87	81

Table 42a
How often students have had a headache in the last six months (Age 11)

	Often		Sometimes		Seldom		Never	
Country	M	F	M	F	M	F	M	F
Austria*	6%	14%	9%	11%	30%	32%	55%	43%
Belgium	14	17	31	37	36	35	19	12
Canada	15	18	28	32	39	37	18	13
Finland	1	3	13	16	41	44	45	36
Hungary	3	2	6	8	50	50	41	40
Norway	8	10	24	32	39	36	29	22
Poland	7	13	18	25	46	43	29	19
Scotland	13	19	29	37	42	34	16	10
Spain	8	13	35	39	44	40	13	8
Sweden	12	17	32	35	37	38	19	10
Wales	15	23	32	32	32	32	21	13

Austrian codes were different: "Often" = "Almost every day" and "Weekly"; "Sometimes" = "Nearly every week"; "Seldom" = "Once a month"; "Never" = "Almost never".

Table 42b
How often students have had a headache in the last six months (Age 13)

	Often		Sometimes		Seldom		Never	
Country	M	F	M	F	M	F	M	F
Austria*	5%	14%	8%	14%	37%	37%	50%	35%
Belgium	13	18	33	35	36	32	18	14
Canada	12	25	28	32	43	32	17	11
Finland	1	3	9	18	46	49	44	30
Hungary	2	5	8	9	43	45	47	41
Norway	6	12	24	35	43	36	26	17
Poland	6	13	18	30	48	41	28	16
Scotland	16	22	37	43	35	28	13	8
Spain	5	8	24	35	57	47	14	10
Sweden	10	15	32	39	42	35	16	11
Wales	13	24	29	37	37	29	21	10

Austrian codes were different: "Often" = "Almost every day" and "Weekly"; "Sometimes" = "Nearly every week"; "Seldom" = "Once a month"; "Never" = "Almost never".

Table 42c
How often students have had a headache in the last six months (Age 15)

	Often		Sometimes		Seldom		Never	
Country	M	F	M	F	M	F	M	F
Austria*	5%	15%	10%	13%	37%	39%	48%	33%
Belgium	10	24	29	36	38	30	23	9
Canada	11	29	28	34	44	31	17	6
Finland	1	3	10	20	49	48	40	29
Hungary	3	5	7	10	47	48	43	37
Norway	6	16	24	34	41	35	29	15
Poland	4	19	19	31	50	38	27	13
Scotland	15	28	31	43	42	24	13	5
Spain	4	12	26	37	56	41	14	10
Sweden	7	21	30	42	44	30	18	7
Wales	11	30	33	36	35	26	21	8

Austrian codes were different: "Often" = "Almost every day" and "Weekly"; "Sometimes" = "Nearly every week"; "Seldom" = "Once a month"; "Never" = "Almost never".

Table 43a
How often students have had a stomach ache in the last six months (Age 11)

	Often		Sometimes		Seldom		Never	
Country	M	F	M	F	M	F	M	F
Austria*	4%	8%	4%	11%	27%	23%	65%	58%
Canada	9	14	25	33	43	41	23	12
Finland	1	1	7	13	34	42	59	44
Norway	6	11	26	36	41	33	27	20
Poland	4	11	17	26	46	44	32	18
Scotland	8	16	28	38	44	33	20	13
Spain	8	15	37	38	44	38	12	9
Sweden	6	12	30	34	46	42	18	12
Wales	9	17	30	35	37	31	24	17

*Austrian codes were different: "Often" = "Almost every day" and "Weekly"; "Sometimes" = "Nearly every week"; "Seldom" = "Once a month"; "Never" = "Almost never".

Table 43b
How often students have had a stomach ache in the last six months (Age 13)

	Often		Sometimes		Seldom		Never	
Country	M	F	M	F	M	F	M	F
Austria*	3%	8%	4%	8%	26%	34%	67%	51%
Canada	5	17	24	37	48	36	23	11
Finland	1	1	5	12	41	53	53	35
Norway	3	11	23	36	45	38	29	15
Poland	4	11	17	31	46	46	34	12
Scotland	7	16	30	41	42	34	21	9
Spain	3	9	28	45	52	38	17	8
Sweden	4	11	26	42	49	37	21	10
Wales	5	16	26	40	42	32	27	12

*Austrian codes were different: "Often" = "Almost every day" and "Weekly"; "Sometimes" = "Nearly every week"; "Seldom" = "Once a month"; "Never" = "Almost never".

Table 43c
How often students have had a stomach ache in the last six months (Age 15)

	Often		Sometimes		Seldom		Never	
Country	M	F	M	F	M	F	M	F
Austria	2%	5%	5%	8%	25%	32%	68%	55%
Canada	6	17	20	39	48	35	25	9
Finland	0	1	5	9	40	63	55	27
Norway	2	9	19	43	44	36	35	12
Poland	2	11	15	35	49	42	34	12
Scotland	3	15	27	46	52	32	18	7
Spain	3	9	24	50	53	34	20	7
Sweden	3	11	25	44	53	39	19	6
Wales	5	16	22	44	43	32	30	9

*Austrian codes were different: "Often" = "Almost every day" and "Weekly"; "Sometimes" = "Nearly every week"; "Seldom" = "Once a month"; "Never" = "Almost never".

Table 44a
How often students have had a backache in the last six months (Age 11)

Country	Often		Sometimes		Seldom		Never	
	M	F	M	F	M	F	M	F
Austria*	3%	3%	5%	4%	9%	14%	83%	79%
Belgium	7	7	14	16	25	26	54	51
Canada	8	8	13	13	26	27	52	52
Finland	1	2	4	2	14	19	81	77
Hungary	4	5	6	9	26	26	65	60
Norway	3	4	8	10	21	21	68	65
Poland	2	3	4	8	16	22	77	67
Scotland	4	5	7	10	27	29	62	56
Spain	4	8	15	17	29	28	52	47
Wales	5	8	13	13	25	24	58	55

*Austrian codes were different: "Often" = "Almost every day" and "Weekly"; "Sometimes" = "Nearly every week"; "Seldom" = "Once a month"; "Never" = "Almost never".

Table 44b
How often students have had a backache in the last six months (Age 13)

Country	Often		Sometimes		Seldom		Never	
	M	F	M	F	M	F	M	F
Austria*	5%	8%	6%	7%	20%	25%	68%	60%
Belgium	8	13	17	25	22	23	53	39
Canada	12	14	16	20	27	31	45	35
Finland	1	1	6	6	22	25	71	68
Hungary	4	8	8	14	29	27	59	50
Norway	5	10	14	18	22	26	59	46
Poland	2	4	9	9	22	29	66	59
Scotland	6	8	15	18	32	35	47	39
Spain	5	9	22	23	32	35	41	33
Wales	6	9	17	21	27	28	50	41

*Austrian codes were different: "Often" = "Almost every day" and "Weekly"; "Sometimes" = "Nearly every week"; "Seldom" = "Once a month"; "Never" = "Almost never".

Table 44c
How often students have had a backache in the last six months (Age 15)

Country	Often		Sometimes		Seldom		Never	
	M	F	M	F	M	F	M	F
Austria*	8%	8%	10%	9%	27%	33%	55%	51%
Belgium	9	22	20	25	28	25	43	28
Canada	12	16	23	26	31	28	34	30
Finland	2	3	8	7	26	29	64	62
Hungary	6	14	10	15	30	31	54	40
Norway	10	13	23	23	27	26	40	38
Poland	2	5	10	14	29	31	58	50
Scotland	9	10	21	22	29	33	41	35
Spain	7	12	26	27	34	35	33	27
Wales	8	13	22	28	28	27	42	32

*Austrian codes were different: "Often" = "Almost every day" and "Weekly"; "Sometimes" = "Nearly every week"; "Seldom" = "Once a month"; "Never" = "Almost never".

Table 45a
How often students have felt low (depressed) in the last six months (Age 11)

Country	Often		Sometimes		Seldom		Never	
	M	F	M	F	M	F	M	F
Austria*	3%	5%	3%	4%	13%	22%	81%	69%
Belgium	7	8	19	17	28	29	46	45
Canada	10	11	19	21	30	31	41	37
Finland	2	3	9	14	36	38	53	45
Hungary	12	14	20	20	44	47	24	18
Norway	4	8	20	26	37	33	39	33
Poland	2	6	13	18	34	36	51	40
Scotland	11	13	28	31	33	32	27	24
Spain	4	5	20	26	31	33	45	37
Wales	10	13	22	28	27	26	41	33

*Austrian codes were different: "Often" = "Almost every day" and "Weekly"; "Sometimes" = "Nearly every week"; "Seldom" = "Once a month"; "Never" = "Almost never".

Table 45b
How often students have felt low (depressed) in the last six months (Age 13)

Country	Often		Sometimes		Seldom		Never	
	M	F	M	F	M	F	M	F
Austria*	1%	5%	3%	6%	17%	25%	78%	64%
Belgium	10	10	21	26	29	25	40	39
Canada	8	18	18	26	33	34	41	23
Finland	3	3	9	13	38	44	50	40
Hungary	10	22	27	28	42	38	21	12
Norway	4	10	19	30	39	40	38	21
Poland	3	7	18	22	34	36	45	35
Scotland	12	18	32	38	31	32	25	12
Spain	4	6	23	30	40	39	32	25
Wales	9	16	23	32	29	29	39	22

*Austrian codes were different: "Often" = "Almost every day" and "Weekly"; "Sometimes" = "Nearly every week"; "Seldom" = "Once a month"; "Never" = "Almost never".

Table 45c
How often students have felt low (depressed) in the last six months (Age 15)

Country	Often		Sometimes		Seldom		Never	
	M	F	M	F	M	F	M	F
Austria*	2%	4%	4%	5%	22%	29%	72%	62%
Belgium	10	21	29	33	30	24	31	22
Canada	9	22	21	32	37	30	33	16
Finland	4	4	8	17	38	43	50	35
Hungary	18	33	30	33	35	28	17	6
Norway	5	10	24	34	38	38	33	18
Poland	4	14	17	27	41	38	38	21
Scotland	11	24	36	47	36	22	17	7
Spain	7	14	32	38	39	36	22	12
Wales	9	22	27	39	31	26	33	13

*Austrian codes were different: "Often" = "Almost every day" and "Weekly"; "Sometimes" = "Nearly every week"; "Seldom" = "Once a month"; "Never" = "Almost never".

Table 46a
How often students have had a bad temper in the last six months (Age 11)

Country	Often		Sometimes		Seldom		Never	
	M	F	M	F	M	F	M	F
Austria*	11%	11%	12%	12%	25%	36%	52%	41%
Canada	23	16	31	34	30	33	16	17
Finland	7	8	25	34	48	43	20	15
Hungary	9	10	15	14	35	34	41	42
Norway	10	15	40	45	34	27	16	13
Poland	11	14	32	34	40	37	17	15
Scotland	20	24	37	39	29	23	14	14
Spain	21	19	49	50	20	23	9	8
Sweden	15	14	44	48	34	31	7	7
Wales	21	25	33	36	23	22	23	17

*Austrian codes were different: "Often" = "Almost every day" and "Weekly"; "Sometimes" = "Nearly every week"; "Seldom" = "Once a month"; "Never" = "Almost never".

Table 46b
How often students have had a bad temper in the last six months (Age 13)

Country	Often		Sometimes		Seldom		Never	
	M	F	M	F	M	F	M	F
Austria*	8%	10%	16%	19%	38%	37%	38%	34%
Canada	21	22	33	34	30	32	16	12
Finland	6	7	25	33	48	46	21	14
Hungary	14	17	21	26	36	36	29	21
Norway	12	20	45	50	32	24	11	6
Poland	13	20	39	44	36	29	13	7
Scotland	26	26	37	45	26	24	11	5
Spain	17	18	52	50	24	27	7	6
Sweden	13	19	43	48	37	29	7	4
Wales	19	27	36	40	25	24	20	10

*Austrian codes were different: "Often" = "Almost every day" and "Weekly"; "Sometimes" = "Nearly every week"; "Seldom" = "Once a month"; "Never" = "Almost never".

Table 46c
How often students have had a bad temper in the last six months (Age 15)

Country	Often		Sometimes		Seldom		Never	
	M	F	M	F	M	F	M	F
Austria*	11%	12%	18%	20%	34%	42%	37%	25%
Canada	20	23	38	39	32	30	11	8
Finland	4	8	23	31	55	52	18	9
Hungary	19	31	27	31	33	28	22	10
Norway	11	17	47	53	30	26	11	4
Poland	12	26	46	45	35	26	7	3
Scotland	22	28	42	48	26	21	10	3
Spain	12	19	51	50	30	27	7	4
Sweden	13	20	48	55	31	22	8	3
Wales	17	26	41	44	26	23	16	8

*Austrian codes were different: "Often" = "Almost every day" and "Weekly"; "Sometimes" = "Nearly every week"; "Seldom" = "Once a month"; "Never" = "Almost never".

Table 47a
How often students have felt nervous in the last six months (Age 11)

Country	Often		Sometimes		Seldom		Never	
	M	F	M	F	M	F	M	F
Austria*	9%	14%	9%	8%	25%	28%	57%	51%
Belgium	22	18	29	28	23	27	26	27
Canada	14	15	30	32	37	39	19	14
Finland	6	4	19	20	41	38	34	38
Hungary	15	19	22	18	38	43	25	20
Norway	3	6	16	22	33	32	48	40
Poland	17	24	31	33	36	31	16	12
Scotland	13	15	37	40	30	29	20	16
Spain	25	24	40	45	21	20	14	11
Sweden	6	11	33	38	42	39	19	12
Wales	10	16	31	32	28	28	31	24

*Austrian codes were different: "Often" = "Almost every day" and "Weekly"; "Sometimes" = "Nearly every week"; "Seldom" = "Once a month"; "Never" = "Almost never".

Table 47b
How often students have felt nervous in the last six months (Age 13)

Country	Often		Sometimes		Seldom		Never	
	M	F	M	F	M	F	M	F
Austria*	8%	11%	10%	15%	29%	26%	53%	47%
Belgium	19	25	27	23	24	22	30	30
Canada	11	19	32	34	36	36	21	11
Finland	4	3	20	19	39	39	38	39
Hungary	19	27	25	26	34	33	22	14
Norway	2	6	14	19	35	36	49	39
Poland	18	30	37	40	35	24	10	6
Scotland	11	18	37	37	34	32	19	13
Spain	22	31	41	42	26	20	11	7
Sweden	6	6	35	42	40	40	19	12
Wales	8	12	28	35	31	32	33	21

*Austrian codes were different: "Often" = "Almost every day" and "Weekly"; "Sometimes" = "Nearly every week"; "Seldom" = "Once a month"; "Never" = "Almost never".

Table 47c
How often students have felt nervous in the last six months (Age 15)

Country	Often		Sometimes		Seldom		Never	
	M	F	M	F	M	F	M	F
Austria*	10%	11%	14%	17%	29%	31%	47%	41%
Belgium	17	34	28	29	24	19	30	18
Canada	13	21	35	35	34	36	19	8
Finland	4	4	21	18	44	46	31	32
Hungary	24	42	27	26	33	25	16	7
Norway	2	4	11	16	34	34	54	46
Poland	20	40	40	42	33	16	6	3
Scotland	11	17	36	41	38	32	15	10
Spain	20	36	41	42	27	17	12	5
Sweden	6	10	34	41	43	39	16	10
Wales	8	15	29	35	36	32	27	18

*Austrian codes were different: "Often" = "Almost every day" and "Weekly"; "Sometimes" = "Nearly every week"; "Seldom" = "Once a month"; "Never" = "Almost never".

Table 48a
How often students have had difficulties in getting to sleep in the last six months (Age 11)

Country	Often		Sometimes		Seldom		Never	
	M	F	M	F	M	F	M	F
Austria*	10%	17%	8%	7%	18%	21%	64%	55%
Belgium	13	10	17	19	22	20	48	50
Canada	15	18	18	21	25	26	41	35
Finland	9	6	13	16	22	30	56	48
Hungary	9	10	14	13	30	32	47	45
Norway	10	12	19	22	26	28	45	38
Poland	10	11	10	15	25	28	55	47
Scotland	19	24	22	22	22	23	37	31
Spain	9	8	17	21	27	24	47	47
Sweden	16	15	27	33	35	32	22	21
Wales	14	18	20	21	21	20	45	41

*Austrian codes were different: "Often" = "Almost every day" and "Weekly"; "Sometimes" = "Nearly every week"; "Seldom" = "Once a month"; "Never" = "Almost never".

Table 48b
How often students have had difficulties in getting to sleep in the last six months (Age 13)

Country	Often		Sometimes		Seldom		Never	
	M	F	M	F	M	F	M	F
Austria*	11%	14%	5%	10%	20%	21%	64%	55%
Belgium	9	12	14	16	22	22	55	50
Canada	14	17	19	23	26	28	42	32
Finland	4	6	12	14	32	26	52	54
Hungary	7	13	14	16	30	32	49	39
Norway	6	10	15	21	31	32	48	37
Poland	7	8	12	14	28	30	53	48
Scotland	15	15	25	25	26	29	35	31
Spain	8	8	17	18	33	33	42	41
Sweden	11	10	29	31	32	39	28	20
Wales	11	15	18	20	24	29	47	36

*Austrian codes were different: "Often" = "Almost every day" and "Weekly"; "Sometimes" = "Nearly every week"; "Seldom" = "Once a month"; "Never" = "Almost never".

Table 48c
How often students have had difficulties in getting to sleep in the last six months (Age 15)

Country	Often		Sometimes		Seldom		Never	
	M	F	M	F	M	F	M	F
Austria*	11%	11%	9%	10%	21%	23%	60%	55%
Belgium	7	15	15	20	27	25	50	40
Canada	13	20	21	23	30	31	36	26
Finland	5	5	13	16	31	27	50	52
Hungary	9	16	16	19	30	30	45	35
Norway	6	11	18	19	28	32	48	37
Poland	5	11	13	18	33	30	49	41
Scotland	11	19	22	25	33	31	34	25
Spain	9	9	16	20	36	35	39	36
Sweden	12	13	25	29	36	35	27	22
Wales	10	18	20	23	23	25	47	33

*Austrian codes were different: "Often" = "Almost every day" and "Weekly"; "Sometimes" = "Nearly every week"; "Seldom" = "Once a month"; "Never" = "Almost never".

Table 49a
How often students have felt dizzy in the last six months (Age 11)

Country	Often		Sometimes		Seldom		Never	
	M	F	M	F	M	F	M	F
Austria*	3%	6%	3%	6%	13%	13%	82%	75%
Belgium	6	6	11	12	19	25	64	58
Canada	6	7	12	13	27	27	55	53
Finland	1	3	3	5	16	16	80	76
Hungary	4	7	10	10	30	33	56	50
Norway	4	4	13	14	28	32	56	50
Poland	2	5	8	10	20	25	70	60
Scotland	8	10	18	19	29	27	45	44
Spain	5	6	20	25	36	35	39	34
Sweden	5	5	15	15	35	34	45	46
Wales	8	9	15	15	23	22	54	54

*Austrian codes were different: "Often" = "Almost every day" and "Weekly"; "Sometimes" = "Nearly every week"; "Seldom" = "Once a month"; "Never" = "Almost never".

Table 49b
How often students have felt dizzy in the last six months (Age 13)

Country	Often		Sometimes		Seldom		Never	
	M	F	M	F	M	F	M	F
Austria*	4%	10%	4%	6%	16%	22%	76%	62%
Belgium	4	8	8	15	18	17	70	60
Canada	7	12	12	15	28	30	53	43
Finland	1	3	4	12	16	19	79	67
Hungary	3	10	10	14	27	30	60	46
Norway	2	6	11	15	28	28	59	50
Poland	3	4	6	12	21	28	70	56
Scotland	10	10	15	17	30	30	45	43
Spain	4	4	14	20	39	41	43	35
Sweden	3	7	12	16	35	34	50	43
Wales	7	9	14	18	24	23	56	51

*Austrian codes were different: "Often" = "Almost every day" and "Weekly"; "Sometimes" = "Nearly every week"; "Seldom" = "Once a month"; "Never" = "Almost never".

Table 49c
How often students have felt dizzy in the last six months (Age 15)

Country	Often		Sometimes		Seldom		Never	
	M	F	M	F	M	F	M	F
Austria*	4%	8%	7%	9%	17%	24%	72%	58%
Belgium	7	11	9	16	20	26	64	47
Canada	6	10	13	20	30	32	51	38
Finland	4	3	8	8	20	21	68	68
Hungary	4	13	8	16	27	33	61	39
Norway	4	6	12	16	28	31	56	47
Poland	2	6	9	16	25	28	64	50
Scotland	8	9	18	21	26	28	48	42
Spain	2	5	15	18	42	41	41	36
Sweden	5	8	13	17	35	35	47	40
Wales	6	9	13	18	24	23	57	50

*Austrian codes were different: "Often" = "Almost every day" and "Weekly"; "Sometimes" = "Nearly every week"; "Seldom" = "Once a month"; "Never" = "Almost never".

Table 50a
How often students feel tired in the morning (Age 11)

Country	Seldom/Never		Once in a while		1 - 3 times/week		4 or more times/week	
	M	F	M	F	M	F	M	F
Austria	22%	22%	37%	40%	16%	16%	24%	22%
Belgium	31	29	45	52	10	8	14	11
Canada	22	18	41	55	18	16	19	12
Finland	26	31	37	33	25	25	12	11
Hungary	19	21	17	16	27	27	37	36
Poland	44	43	39	47	10	7	7	3
Scotland	27	26	40	48	13	11	20	15
Spain	33	30	54	62	4	3	9	5
Sweden	23	25	49	52	9	9	19	13
Wales	27	28	47	53	10	9	16	11

Table 50b
How often students feel tired in the morning (Age 13)

Country	Seldom/Never		Once in a while		1 - 3 times/week		4 or more times/week	
	M	F	M	F	M	F	M	F
Austria	16%	13%	40%	44%	17%	16%	27%	27%
Belgium	26	20	48	56	11	11	15	12
Canada	16	12	41	47	21	23	22	18
Finland	15	14	36	34	26	30	23	22
Hungary	18	20	16	18	31	36	35	26
Poland	44	44	41	46	9	6	6	4
Scotland	17	14	38	46	20	22	25	18
Spain	31	27	53	64	7	5	9	4
Sweden	20	16	46	53	14	14	21	17
Wales	25	18	48	55	14	15	13	12

Table 50c
How often students feel tired in the morning (Age 15)

Country	Seldom/Never		Once in a while		1 - 3 times/week		4 or more times/week	
	M	F	M	F	M	F	M	F
Austria	11%	10%	31%	43%	19%	21%	40%	26%
Belgium	22	18	48	49	15	17	15	16
Canada	9	7	36	37	25	35	30	22
Finland	7	7	30	34	32	32	31	27
Hungary	22	28	20	23	33	33	25	16
Poland	36	33	45	50	14	12	6	5
Scotland	9	9	42	41	19	27	30	23
Spain	25	19	55	65	10	8	10	8
Sweden	13	12	34	43	18	16	35	30
Wales	18	13	45	49	17	19	20	18

Table 51a
How often students talk to their parents about ideas and things
that interest them (Age 11)

Country	Very often		Quite often		Sometimes		Rarely	
	M	F	M	F	M	F	M	F
Austria	28%	26%	35%	38%	25%	23%	12%	13%
Canada	39	36	29	29	24	27	8	8
Hungary	15	17	53	46	28	34	4	3
Norway	22	22	50	50	23	23	5	4
Scotland	30	31	46	48	16	15	8	7

Table 51b
How often students talk to their parents about ideas and things
that interest them (Age 13)

Country	Very often		Quite often		Sometimes		Rarely	
	M	F	M	F	M	F	M	F
Austria	25%	25%	44%	38%	22%	26%	10%	11%
Canada	27	28	29	27	30	28	14	17
Hungary	17	18	50	51	29	28	4	3
Norway	17	21	52	51	26	24	5	4
Poland	16	23	53	49	25	23	6	5
Scotland	27	27	48	47	19	21	6	5

Table 51c
How often students talk to their parents about ideas and things
that interest them (Age 15)

Country	Very often		Quite often		Sometimes		Rarely	
	M	F	M	F	M	F	M	F
Austria	15%	24%	42%	38%	32%	28%	10%	10%
Canada	24	28	29	26	34	31	13	16
Hungary	7	20	49	45	39	30	5	5
Norway	16	26	50	47	28	24	7	3
Poland	12	19	50	49	31	26	7	6
Scotland	20	27	49	47	25	20	6	6

Table 52a
Students' ability to talk with their father about things that bother them (Age 11)

Country	Very easy		Easy		Difficult		Very difficult		Don't have that person	
	M	F	M	F	M	F	M	F	M	F
Austria	28%	21%	36%	37%	20%	23%	7%	13%	9%	6%
Belgium	40	34	40	40	12	17	6	6	2	3
Canada	26	16	37	33	26	33	8	14	4	4
Finland	23	16	47	44	24	30	3	6	3	4
Hungary	24	16	49	39	21	29	6	10	1	6
Norway	31	24	41	41	19	25	8	9	2	1
Scotland	22	16	46	36	22	30	7	13	3	5
Spain	44	28	33	42	14	21	6	7	3	2

Table 52b
Students' ability to talk with their father about things that bother them (Age 13)

Country	Very easy		Easy		Difficult		Very difficult		Don't have that person	
	M	F	M	F	M	F	M	F	M	F
Austria	21%	13%	41%	34%	21%	29%	8%	17%	9%	7%
Belgium	25	12	36	36	25	30	10	19	4	3
Canada	17	11	39	30	27	33	12	22	5	4
Finland	17	10	49	36	25	39	5	10	4	5
Hungary	23	11	48	39	18	32	7	12	4	6
Norway	20	13	46	40	23	30	9	14	1	3
Poland	15	10	42	39	27	31	11	15	5	5
Scotland	18	11	43	33	25	34	10	16	4	6
Spain	30	18	37	35	21	32	8	13	4	2

Table 52c
Students' ability to talk with their father about things that bother them (Age 15)

Country	Very easy		Easy		Difficult		Very difficult		Don't have that person	
	M	F	M	F	M	F	M	F	M	F
Austria	39%	27%	26%	35%	10%	19%	9%	8%	16%	11%
Belgium	24	10	32	27	26	31	15	28	3	4
Canada	14	7	34	29	31	37	16	22	5	5
Finland	9	6	49	34	31	37	7	19	4	4
Hungary	12	11	51	33	23	30	9	19	5	7
Norway	14	10	39	34	31	38	14	16	3	2
Poland	6	6	41	32	34	36	13	17	6	8
Scotland	13	10	42	33	28	34	13	17	4	6
Spain	22	8	36	36	30	36	10	16	2	4

Table 53a
Students' ability to talk with their mother about things that bother them (Age 11)

	Very easy		Easy		Difficult		Very difficult		Don't have that person	
Country	M	F	M	F	M	F	M	F	M	F
Austria	38%	37%	39%	43%	12%	11%	5%	6%	7%	3%
Belgium	51	56	40	33	7	8	2	2	0	1
Canada	36	43	38	35	19	16	6	5	1	1
Finland	30	37	49	45	16	15	3	1	1	2
Hungary	30	39	52	47	15	12	3	1	0	1
Norway	40	44	43	40	13	13	4	3	0	0
Scotland	36	44	44	37	15	13	4	4	1	1
Spain	56	57	27	30	12	9	4	3	1	1

Table 53b
Students' ability to talk with their mother about things that bother them (Age 13)

	Very easy		Easy		Difficult		Very difficult		Don't have that person	
Country	M	F	M	F	M	F	M	F	M	F
Austria	34%	34%	43%	41%	14%	15%	4%	7%	5%	3%
Belgium	39	38	40	39	14	15	5	7	2	1
Canada	27	31	40	39	22	20	9	10	2	1
Finland	24	27	54	51	18	18	3	4	1	0
Hungary	25	36	55	45	16	14	3	5	1	1
Norway	31	35	48	46	16	16	4	3	1	0
Poland	24	39	51	44	18	11	5	4	2	1
Scotland	29	39	46	42	18	13	6	5	2	1
Spain	47	41	37	43	12	12	3	4	1	0

Table 53c
Students' ability to talk with their mother about things that bother them (Age 15)

	Very easy		Easy		Difficult		Very difficult		Don't have that person	
Country	M	F	M	F	M	F	M	F	M	F
Austria	26%	37%	49%	39%	14%	16%	6%	5%	5%	2%
Belgium	33	37	41	38	17	14	8	9	1	2
Canada	25	31	40	36	24	22	10	10	1	1
Finland	14	26	56	46	24	23	5	5	1	1
Hungary	19	32	54	47	21	16	4	3	2	2
Norway	21	31	47	44	23	19	8	5	1	1
Poland	18	28	52	47	23	18	7	6	1	1
Scotland	26	35	47	42	19	17	7	5	1	1
Spain	36	35	39	39	17	19	6	6	1	1

Table 54a
Students' ability to talk with their brother(s) about things that bother them (Age 11)

	Very easy		Easy		Difficult		Very difficult		Don't have that person	
Country	M	F	M	F	M	F	M	F	M	F
Austria	21%	10%	21%	18%	9%	19%	13%	18%	36%	36%
Belgium	38	25	27	29	10	15	8	11	17	20
Canada	17	8	16	17	15	23	13	15	39	37
Hungary	14	5	27	21	14	18	7	11	39	44
Norway	11	5	18	16	11	16	8	10	52	52
Scotland	19	8	20	18	16	19	17	23	28	32
Spain	45	28	23	29	8	12	3	6	21	25

Table 54b
Students' ability to talk with their brother(s) about things that bother them (Age 13)

	Very easy		Easy		Difficult		Very difficult		Don't have that person	
Country	M	F	M	F	M	F	M	F	M	F
Austria	18%	9%	19%	22%	13%	16%	13%	16%	38%	37%
Belgium	23	14	29	25	17	21	17	24	14	16
Canada	17	11	21	19	14	20	10	13	38	37
Hungary	17	7	21	25	15	16	3	8	44	43
Norway	8	4	15	14	13	13	11	8	53	59
Poland	20	8	23	24	12	17	6	12	39	39
Scotland	21	12	22	19	11	17	16	19	30	33
Spain	36	31	29	26	8	16	4	5	23	22

Table 54c
Students' ability to talk with their brother(s) about things that bother them (Age 15)

	Very easy		Easy		Difficult		Very difficult		Don't have that person	
Country	M	F	M	F	M	F	M	F	M	F
Austria	20%	12%	22%	22%	9%	17%	10%	16%	39%	34%
Belgium	29	13	27	19	13	22	16	26	15	20
Canada	17	13	25	23	15	19	8	10	35	35
Hungary	20	9	30	25	7	14	7	6	36	46
Norway	8	6	19	13	14	12	6	8	53	61
Poland	17	11	27	23	11	14	7	10	38	42
Scotland	21	13	20	22	16	21	14	15	29	29
Spain	35	28	30	29	10	17	4	5	21	21

Table 55a
Students' ability to talk with their sister(s) about things that bother them (Age 11)

Country	Very easy		Easy		Difficult		Very difficult		Don't have that person	
	M	F	M	F	M	F	M	F	M	F
Austria	18%	17%	24%	27%	10%	11%	11%	10%	37%	35%
Belgium	30	34	27	27	16	11	11	9	16	19
Canada	14	16	15	23	15	14	14	8	42	39
Hungary	13	13	25	28	11	8	7	5	44	45
Norway	10	12	16	18	10	7	9	6	56	57
Scotland	19	19	23	22	17	12	15	11	26	36
Spain	36	37	21	24	7	6	7	2	29	31

Table 55b
Students' ability to talk with their sister(s) about things that bother them (Age 13)

Country	Very easy		Easy		Difficult		Very difficult		Don't have that person	
	M	F	M	F	M	F	M	F	M	F
Austria	16%	20%	15%	23%	12%	8%	14%	8%	43%	42%
Belgium	20	24	25	28	19	17	19	18	17	13
Canada	14	18	20	22	15	14	12	7	39	39
Hungary	13	21	27	24	10	8	8	3	41	45
Norway	8	14	16	17	10	8	9	2	57	60
Poland	15	18	25	23	12	9	7	6	41	43
Scotland	17	22	21	22	14	12	17	8	31	36
Spain	35	39	25	26	9	7	7	3	24	26

Table 55c
Students' ability to talk with their sister(s) about things that bother them (Age 15)

Country	Very easy		Easy		Difficult		Very difficult		Don't have that person	
	M	F	M	F	M	F	M	F	M	F
Austria	14%	21%	21%	20%	13%	8%	11%	8%	42%	43%
Belgium	20	24	29	21	16	17	19	17	16	20
Canada	13	22	21	21	16	12	11	6	39	38
Hungary	12	22	31	24	12	7	6	4	39	44
Norway	11	18	15	18	12	7	5	2	57	56
Poland	11	15	27	26	10	10	9	4	42	45
Scotland	14	21	21	23	14	11	16	9	35	35
Spain	27	37	30	24	11	7	3	4	29	28

Table 56a
**How often students agree with their parents
about how they spend their free time (Age 11)**

Country	Always		Most of the time		Sometimes		Rarely or never	
	M	F	M	F	M	F	M	F
Austria	30%	24%	60%	63%	10%	10%	1%	2%
Belgium	31	31	55	57	10	10	4	2
Canada	20	20	46	48	21	21	13	11
Hungary	32	34	56	52	9	12	3	2
Norway	15	13	62	64	20	21	3	2
Scotland	15	16	59	55	20	20	6	9

Table 56b
**How often students agree with their parents
about how they spend their free time (Age 13)**

Country	Always		Most of the time		Sometimes		Rarely or never	
	M	F	M	F	M	F	M	F
Austria	27%	25%	61%	59%	11%	13%	2%	3%
Belgium	26	26	58	56	12	12	4	6
Canada	17	14	48	47	22	24	13	16
Hungary	25	26	60	57	13	12	2	5
Norway	9	8	63	65	25	22	3	5
Poland	25	30	52	46	20	22	3	2
Scotland	10	11	59	60	21	20	10	9

Table 56c
**How often students agree with their parents
about how they spend their free time (Age 15)**

Country	Always		Most of the time		Sometimes		Rarely or never	
	M	F	M	F	M	F	M	F
Austria	31%	28%	59%	59%	8%	12%	1%	2%
Belgium	22	18	62	55	12	17	4	10
Canada	15	12	44	45	25	24	16	19
Hungary	21	20	59	61	17	14	3	5
Norway	8	7	57	64	28	22	7	7
Poland	14	18	58	56	24	22	4	4
Scotland	10	10	58	61	23	20	9	10

Table 57a
CANADA ONLY
How students feel about themselves (Age 11)

	Yes		No		Don't Know	
Item	M	F	M	F	M	F
I have trouble making decisions.	29%	37%	57%	47%	14%	17%
I like myself.	81	77	9	8	10	15
I am often sorry for the things I do.	57	58	31	29	12	13
I have confidence in myself.	74	66	12	15	14	19
I often wish I were someone else.	34	42	57	49	9	9
I would change how I look if I could.	36	47	55	44	9	9
My parents understand me.	66	63	17	19	17	18
What my parents think of me is important.	80	81	9	6	11	13
There are times when I would like to leave home.	43	42	52	50	6	8
My parents expect too much of me.	28	24	62	66	10	10
I have a happy home life.	76	75	12	11	12	14
My parents trust me.	74	79	12	8	14	12
I have a lot of arguments with my parents.	26	22	66	70	8	9
I need to lose weight.	25	37	69	54	6	9
I need to gain weight.	17	9	77	86	6	5
I often have a hard time saying 'no'.	28	32	63	56	9	12

Table 57b
CANADA ONLY
How students feel about themselves (Age 13)

	Yes		No		Don't Know	
Item	M	F	M	F	M	F
I have trouble making decisions.	24%	39%	63%	47%	13%	14%
I like myself.	82	68	7	13	11	19
I am often sorry for the things I do.	50	49	36	37	14	14
I have confidence in myself.	74	54	11	22	15	24
I often wish I were someone else.	29	45	62	44	9	11
I would change how I look if I could.	39	58	50	31	11	11
My parents understand me.	56	46	24	32	19	22
What my parents think of me is important.	75	73	13	14	12	13
There are times when I would like to leave home.	41	51	52	43	7	6
My parents expect too much of me.	32	34	57	56	12	10
I have a happy home life.	72	64	13	18	15	19
My parents trust me.	74	66	14	16	12	17
I have a lot of arguments with my parents.	27	33	63	58	10	9
I need to lose weight.	20	42	74	51	6	7
I need to gain weight.	21	11	73	85	6	4
I often have a hard time saying 'no'.	25	33	65	57	10	10

Table 57c
CANADA ONLY
How students feel about themselves (Age 15)

Item	Yes		No		Don't Know	
	M	F	M	F	M	F
I have trouble making decisions	24%	42%	64%	47%	12%	11%
I like myself	81	68	7	15	12	17
I am often sorry for the things I do	45	49	42	37	13	14
I have confidence in myself	69	48	14	27	17	24
I often wish I were someone else	26	41	65	50	9	9
I would change how I look if I could	41	55	46	34	13	11
My parents understand me	51	45	29	36	20	19
What my parents think of me is important	72	74	17	15	11	11
There are times when I would like to leave home	44	55	50	40	6	5
My parents expect too much of me.	34	34	56	55	9	11
I have a happy home life.	70	64	16	19	15	17
My parents trust me.	68	62	17	21	15	17
I have a lot of arguments with my parents.	30	35	63	59	7	6
I need to lose weight.	19	48	77	45	4	7
I need to gain weight.	25	7	69	90	6	3
I often have a hard time saying 'no'.	32	37	60	53	8	10

Table 58a
Reactions to being picked on (Age 11)

		Austria		Belgium		Canada		Hungary		Scotland	
		M	F	M	F	M	F	M	F	M	F
Fight	Yes	33%	13%	47%	12%	45%	15%	31%	18%	39%	17%
	No	67	87	53	88	55	85	69	82	61	83
Shout at others	Yes	34	27	47	32	50	44	7	9	42	40
	No	66	73	53	68	50	56	93	91	58	60
Do nothing and wait until they calm down	Yes	42	49	45	50	46	54	28	20	41	44
	No	58	51	55	50	54	46	72	80	59	56
Look for someone to help me	Yes	40	48	49	45	38	46	1	2	31	36
	No	60	52	51	55	62	54	99	98	69	64
Try to get away	Yes	53	60	24	27	52	56	22	20	46	50
	No	47	40	76	73	48	44	78	80	54	50
Go to a teacher	Yes	19	19	31	34	28	38	1	1	21	24
	No	81	81	69	66	72	62	99	99	79	76
Go to my parents	Yes	22	30	25	36	34	50	0	2	28	46
	No	78	70	75	64	66	50	100	98	72	54
Go to other adults	Yes	8	7	10	12	16	22	0	0	7	11
	No	92	93	90	88	84	78	100	100	93	89
Nothing, can't do anything anyway	Yes	25	30	28	28	30	32	3	3	28	27
	No	75	70	72	72	70	68	97	97	72	73

Table 58b
Reactions to being picked on (Age 13)

		Austria		Belgium		Canada		Hungary		Poland		Scotland	
		M	F	M	F	M	F	M	F	M	F	M	F
Fight	Yes	34%	12%	54%	28%	49%	18%	41%	24%	42%	11%	41%	15%
	No	66	88	46	72	51	82	59	76	58	89	59	85
Shout at others	Yes	40	33	42	51	54	49	5	6	8	7	45	46
	No	60	67	58	49	46	51	95	94	92	93	55	54
Do nothing and wait until they calm down	Yes	46	56	63	65	48	54	30	22	32	26	42	48
	No	54	44	37	35	52	46	70	78	68	74	58	52
Look for someone to help me	Yes	37	45	43	51	29	37	1	3	24	13	24	38
	No	63	55	57	49	71	63	99	97	76	87	76	62
Try to get away	Yes	56	63	31	25	41	50	13	21	17	10	44	50
	No	44	37	69	75	59	50	87	79	83	90	56	50
Go to a teacher	Yes	6	4	17	16	12	14	1	0	2	3	9	11
	No	94	96	83	84	88	86	99	100	98	97	91	89
Go to my parents	Yes	12	15	16	32	19	33	0	0	3	5	18	34
	No	88	85	84	68	81	67	100	100	97	95	82	66
Go to other adults	Yes	3	1	6	12	10	14	0	0	3	2	9	8
	No	97	99	94	88	90	86	100	100	97	98	91	92
Nothing, can't do anything anyway	Yes	26	38	40	37	31	38	4	4	23	18	29	33
	No	74	62	60	63	69	62	96	96	77	82	71	67

Table 58c
Reactions to being picked on (Age 15)

		Austria		Belgium		Canada		Hungary		Poland		Scotland	
		M	F	M	F	M	F	M	F	M	F	M	F
Fight	Yes	24%	15%	50%	35%	43%	17%	41%	31%	36%	9%	36%	14%
	No	76	85	50	65	57	83	59	69	64	91	64	86
Shout at others	Yes	40	36	29	50	54	52	4	4	7	8	52	49
	No	60	64	71	50	46	48	96	96	93	92	48	51
Do nothing and wait until	Yes	50	57	69	72	46	56	29	24	43	26	45	53
they calm down	No	50	43	31	28	54	44	71	76	57	74	55	47
Look for someone to help me	Yes	25	36	34	50	23	34	1	1	25	13	20	31
	No	75	64	66	50	77	66	99	99	75	87	80	69
Try to get away	Yes	48	59	20	25	34	44	11	14	16	8	36	48
	No	52	41	80	75	66	56	89	86	84	92	64	52
Go to a teacher	Yes	2	3	6	8	6	6	0	0	1	1	3	8
	No	98	97	94	92	94	94	100	100	99	99	97	92
Go to my parents	Yes	4	13	7	28	11	26	0	0	2	4	9	30
	No	96	87	93	72	89	74	100	100	98	96	91	70
Go to other adults	Yes	1	2	9	8	6	10	0	1	5	2	4	8
	No	99	98	91	92	94	90	100	99	95	98	96	92
Nothing, can't do anything anyway	Yes	31	37	39	50	36	43	6	4	27	21	31	31
	No	69	63	61	50	64	57	94	96	73	79	69	69

Table 59a
How easy it is for students to make new friends (Age 11)

Country	Very easy		Easy		Difficult		Very difficult	
	M	F	M	F	M	F	M	F
Austria	29%	24%	50%	54%	15%	16%	5%	6%
Belgium	34	28	51	50	12	20	3	2
Canada	24	25	53	54	19	17	5	4
Finland	15	12	67	68	16	19	2	1
Hungary	20	25	55	53	21	20	4	2
Norway	22	22	61	58	15	17	2	4
Scotland	17	18	64	59	16	18	3	5

Table 59b
How easy it is for students to make new friends (Age 13)

Country	Very easy		Easy		Difficult		Very difficult	
	M	F	M	F	M	F	M	F
Austria	27%	24%	56%	62%	14%	13%	3%	1%
Belgium	28	27	53	52	16	17	2	4
Canada	25	26	58	55	15	17	2	2
Finland	12	12	72	70	15	16	1	2
Hungary	17	22	66	57	15	19	2	2
Norway	20	19	64	63	15	16	2	2
Poland	16	16	63	63	18	17	3	4
Scotland	14	18	66	63	19	17	1	2

Table 59c
How easy it is for students to make new friends (Age 15)

Country	Very easy		Easy		Difficult		Very difficult	
	M	F	M	F	M	F	M	F
Austria	22%	24%	60%	58%	17%	16%	2%	2%
Belgium	25	23	60	54	13	20	2	3
Canada	23	27	57	56	17	14	3	3
Finland	11	13	72	69	17	17	0	1
Hungary	13	22	65	55	20	21	2	2
Norway	18	19	64	65	17	15	1	1
Poland	8	14	70	66	20	17	2	3
Scotland	16	17	68	64	14	18	1	1

Table 60a
Number of close friends (Age 11)

	More than one		One		None	
Country	M	F	M	F	M	F
Austria	91%	91%	8%	8%	1%	1%
Canada	82	81	12	16	6	3
Finland	83	71	14	26	3	3
Hungary	86	83	11	14	3	3
Norway	74	60	23	34	3	6
Scotland	83	77	14	20	3	3

Table 60b
Number of close friends (Age 13)

	More than one		One		None	
Country	M	F	M	F	M	F
Austria	93%	89%	6%	10%	1%	1%
Canada	84	82	11	15	5	3
Finland	85	73	11	24	4	3
Hungary	91	85	7	11	2	4
Norway	75	67	21	30	4	3
Poland	76	67	17	28	7	5
Scotland	86	84	11	14	3	2

Table 60c
Number of close friends (Age 15)

	More than one		One		None	
Country	M	F	M	F	M	F
Austria	94%	89%	6%	10%	0%	1%
Canada	83	84	12	14	5	2
Finland	82	77	11	20	7	3
Hungary	88	83	10	14	2	3
Norway	76	81	19	17	5	2
Poland	78	65	14	28	8	7
Scotland	90	86	7	12	3	2

Table 61a
Gender of closest friend (Age 11)

Country	Same sex		Opposite sex		Don't have a close friend	
	M	**F**	**M**	**F**	**M**	**F**
Austria	74%	81%	23%	16%	3%	3%
Belgium	80	85	15	9	5	6
Canada	80	87	15	9	5	4
Hungary	86	83	9	11	5	6
Norway	89	90	7	6	4	4
Scotland	86	90	10	6	4	4

Table 61b
Gender of closest friend (Age 13)

Country	Same sex		Opposite sex		Don't have a close friend	
	M	**F**	**M**	**F**	**M**	**F**
Austria	62%	70%	32%	25%	6%	5%
Belgium	70	80	20	13	10	7
Canada	75	84	21	12	4	4
Hungary	86	80	11	15	3	4
Norway	87	90	8	6	5	4
Scotland	83	90	13	7	4	3

Table 61c
Gender of closest friend (Age 15)

Country	Same sex		Opposite sex		Don't have a close friend	
	M	**F**	**M**	**F**	**M**	**F**
Austria	56%	64%	38%	32%	6%	4%
Belgium	70	70	24	22	6	8
Canada	71	75	25	23	4	2
Hungary	78	65	15	29	7	6
Norway	83	85	12	13	5	2
Scotland	84	88	13	9	3	3

Table 62a
Students' ability to talk with their friend(s) of the same sex about things that bother them (Age 11)

Country	Very easy		Easy		Difficult		Very difficult		Don't have that problem	
	M	F	M	F	M	F	M	F	M	F
Austria	25%	30%	42%	44%	14%	15%	11%	6%	8%	4%
Belgium	38	35	41	43	13	12	5	6	3	4
Canada	38	42	38	43	16	11	6	4	2	1
Hungary	24	28	55	54	15	10	3	5	3	3
Norway	21	27	44	49	24	19	11	4	0	1
Scotland	23	31	45	48	21	15	8	4	3	1

Table 62b
Students' ability to talk with their friend(s) of the same sex about things that bother them (Age 13)

Country	Very easy		Easy		Difficult		Very difficult		Don't have that problem	
	M	F	M	F	M	F	M	F	M	F
Austria	28%	45%	47%	42%	14%	9%	7%	2%	5%	2%
Belgium	22	36	44	44	19	11	11	7	4	2
Canada	37	55	43	37	15	6	4	2	2	0
Hungary	37	36	49	53	9	7	3	2	2	2
Norway	17	36	50	49	25	13	8	2	0	0
Poland	24	37	55	51	12	9	5	2	4	2
Scotland	22	44	49	45	18	10	10	2	1	0

Table 62c
Students' ability to talk with their friend(s) of the same sex about things that bother them (Age 15)

Country	Very easy		Easy		Difficult		Very difficult		Don't have that problem	
	M	F	M	F	M	F	M	F	M	F
Austria	23%	50%	49%	38%	18%	9%	6%	2%	4%	1%
Belgium	34	40	45	46	12	9	7	3	2	2
Canada	38	63	43	32	14	5	4	0	1	0
Hungary	42	43	45	49	8	6	2	1	3	2
Norway	18	50	50	41	27	7	5	2	0	0
Poland	24	39	54	51	14	8	5	2	3	1
Scotland	28	59	47	33	17	7	8	1	0	0

Table 63a
**Students' ability to talk with their friend(s) of the opposite sex
about things that bother them (Age 11)**

	Very easy		Easy		Difficult		Very difficult		Don't have that problem	
Country	M	F	M	F	M	F	M	F	M	F
Austria	14%	9%	19%	22%	14%	23%	13%	14%	40%	32%
Belgium	23	10	34	36	24	27	13	21	6	6
Canada	18	8	25	25	27	35	18	24	12	8
Hungary	9	5	31	23	26	29	12	18	22	25
Norway	8	3	22	18	27	34	21	24	22	21
Scotland	8	5	25	15	28	28	22	31	16	21

Table 63b
**Students' ability to talk with their friend(s) of the opposite sex
about things that bother them (Age 13)**

	Very easy		Easy		Difficult		Very difficult		Don't have that problem	
Country	M	F	M	F	M	F	M	F	M	F
Austria	19%	15%	26%	31%	20%	27%	12%	11%	23%	15%
Belgium	17	14	32	29	27	28	19	25	6	3
Canada	22	19	36	37	28	29	10	12	4	3
Hungary	14	8	49	39	20	31	6	10	11	11
Norway	7	8	28	27	33	36	17	18	15	10
Poland	10	6	32	25	33	36	12	18	13	16
Scotland	15	9	30	29	28	33	18	19	9	11

Table 63c
**Students' ability to talk with their friend(s) of the opposite sex
about things that bother them (Age 15)**

	Very easy		Easy		Difficult		Very difficult		Don't have that problem	
Country	M	F	M	F	M	F	M	F	M	F
Austria	18%	20%	36%	40%	19%	24%	10%	7%	17%	9%
Belgium	27	21	41	34	19	27	10	14	3	3
Canada	28	30	39	40	23	22	8	6	2	2
Hungary	18	17	55	43	16	25	5	7	6	8
Norway	16	16	34	40	29	31	12	8	9	6
Poland	11	8	42	38	30	33	9	10	8	11
Scotland	15	17	42	41	26	28	13	7	4	7

Table 64a
How often students spend time with friends outside school hours (Age 11)

Country	Every day		4 - 6 days a week		2 - 3 days a week		Once/week or less		Have no friends	
	M	F	M	F	M	F	M	F	M	F
Canada	42%	30%	30%	30%	15%	20%	11%	18%	1%	1%
Finland	48	38	33	31	14	20	5	10	1	1
Hungary	44	41	45	45	6	9	3	4	2	1
Norway	52	43	29	30	14	17	4	8	1	2
Scotland	32	28	29	24	23	21	15	24	1	2
Wales	37	25	25	24	21	23	16	27	1	1

Table 64b
How often students spend time with friends outside school hours (Age 13)

Country	Every day		4 - 6 days a week		2 - 3 days a week		Once/week or less		Have no friends	
	M	F	M	F	M	F	M	F	M	F
Canada	44%	34%	27%	27%	16%	21%	11%	18%	2%	1%
Finland	44	38	32	28	17	20	7	14	0	1
Hungary	56	40	37	44	4	9	2	5	1	2
Norway	43	40	36	31	16	21	4	7	1	1
Poland	38	39	29	22	21	21	10	15	2	3
Scotland	33	25	28	26	23	28	15	20	1	1
Wales	38	28	27	23	20	27	14	22	1	1

Table 64c
How often students spend time with friends outside school hours (Age 15)

Country	Every day		4 - 6 days a week		2 - 3 days a week		Once/week or less		Have no friends	
	M	F	M	F	M	F	M	F	M	F
Canada	44%	27%	29%	29%	17%	26%	9%	16%	1%	1%
Finland	48	38	29	31	16	20	7	11	0	0
Hungary	50	38	36	37	9	15	4	8	1	2
Norway	48	41	32	31	14	21	6	6	0	1
Poland	37	31	25	22	21	27	14	18	3	2
Scotland	33	24	30	26	27	36	10	14	0	0
Wales	28	20	30	23	27	33	15	24	1	0

Table 65a
How students feel about life (Age 11)

Country	Very happy		Quite happy		Not very happy		Not happy at all	
	M	F	M	F	M	F	M	F
Austria	42%	41%	54%	50%	3%	8%	1%	1%
Belgium	47	48	46	46	5	5	1	1
Canada	46	47	43	45	8	7	3	1
Finland	39	43	57	54	3	3	1	0
Hungary	21	20	73	74	5	5	1	1
Norway	43	46	51	46	5	7	1	0
Poland	52	55	43	39	4	5	1	1
Spain	53	55	40	41	5	4	1	1
Sweden	65	59	31	36	3	4	1	1
Wales	47	44	47	48	5	5	1	2

Table 65b
How students feel about life (Age 13)

Country	Very happy		Quite happy		Not very happy		Not happy at all	
	M	F	M	F	M	F	M	F
Austria	31%	35%	64%	55%	4%	9%	1%	1%
Belgium	33	36	60	55	6	7	1	2
Canada	41	29	50	55	8	13	1	3
Finland	27	31	67	62	5	7	1	0
Hungary	16	14	79	77	5	9	0	1
Norway	40	41	53	51	6	7	1	1
Poland	32	34	59	57	8	7	1	1
Spain	40	43	55	51	4	6	1	0
Sweden	59	57	37	38	3	4	1	1
Wales	43	35	51	54	5	9	1	2

Table 65c
How students feel about life (Age 15)

Country	Very happy		Quite happy		Not very happy		Not happy at all	
	M	F	M	F	M	F	M	F
Austria	28%	33%	68%	55%	3%	10%	1%	1%
Belgium	36	29	57	55	6	15	1	1
Canada	29	25	60	57	9	16	2	2
Finland	22	25	71	67	6	7	1	1
Hungary	9	12	77	70	12	16	2	2
Norway	32	41	62	51	5	7	1	1
Poland	27	18	61	67	11	13	2	3
Spain	20	26	70	64	8	9	2	1
Sweden	47	42	47	47	4	10	2	1
Wales	35	29	57	58	6	11	2	2

Table 66a
How often students feel lonely (Age 11)

Country	Very often		Rather often		Sometimes		Never	
	M	F	M	F	M	F	M	F
Austria	5%	6%	5%	8%	44%	53%	46%	33%
Canada	5	8	12	12	64	67	19	14
Finland	4	3	6	8	67	68	23	21
Hungary	6	4	5	6	53	59	37	30
Norway	3	6	5	6	55	63	36	26
Poland	4	5	7	6	53	53	36	36
Scotland	*	*	7	10	47	60	46	30
Spain	4	3	2	3	44	46	49	48
Sweden	2	4	6	8	53	58	39	30
Wales	5	5	5	8	43	51	47	36

*Students in Scotland were only given three response choices: "Often", "Sometimes" and "Never".

Table 66b
How often students feel lonely (Age 13)

Country	Very often		Rather often		Sometimes		Never	
	M	F	M	F	M	F	M	F
Austria	3%	7%	5%	6%	54%	61%	38%	26%
Canada	5	8	7	12	65	69	23	11
Finland	2	2	5	6	56	65	36	27
Hungary	5	6	6	12	56	62	33	21
Norway	2	3	5	6	50	59	43	31
Poland	3	6	6	9	52	60	39	25
Scotland	*	*	8	7	43	57	50	36
Spain	3	3	4	4	44	48	49	46
Sweden	1	3	4	4	50	57	45	36
Wales	2	5	4	8	42	54	51	33

*Students in Scotland were only given three response choices: "Often", "Sometimes" and "Never".

Table 66c
How often students feel lonely (Age 15)

Country	Very often		Rather often		Sometimes		Never	
	M	F	M	F	M	F	M	F
Austria	3%	5%	4%	9%	56%	66%	38%	20%
Canada	6	9	11	14	59	67	24	10
Finland	2	4	3	9	60	63	35	24
Hungary	5	6	10	16	59	64	27	14
Norway	3	3	4	6	48	57	45	34
Poland	5	8	8	14	58	62	29	16
Scotland	*	*	4	7	39	58	57	35
Spain	3	7	5	8	46	52	46	33
Sweden	1	4	6	9	49	61	44	26
Wales	4	7	5	10	41	54	51	29

*Students in Scotland were only given three response choices: "Often", "Sometimes" and "Never".

Table 67a
What students perceive their teachers think about their school work (Age 11)

	Very good		Good		Average		Below average	
Country	M	F	M	F	M	F	M	F
Austria	15%	17%	40%	43%	40%	40%	5%	1%
Belgium	15	13	41	42	37	40	6	5
Canada	22	31	45	49	26	18	7	2
Finland	5	6	35	37	55	54	5	4
Norway	13	15	47	49	37	33	3	3
Poland	17	32	45	53	36	15	2	0
Scotland	12	11	29	27	51	57	9	5
Spain	14	18	50	56	33	24	4	1
Sweden	13	9	36	35	48	53	3	3
Wales	15	17	48	51	33	30	4	2

Table 67b
What students perceive their teachers think about their school work (Age 13)

	Very good		Good		Average		Below average	
Country	M	F	M	F	M	F	M	F
Austria	11%	10%	31%	36%	52%	50%	5%	4%
Belgium	11	12	36	37	44	45	9	6
Canada	20	26	44	45	29	25	7	4
Finland	4	6	31	37	59	53	6	4
Norway	9	6	46	47	41	45	4	3
Poland	12	22	40	56	45	21	3	1
Scotland	12	11	33	33	48	52	7	4
Spain	11	13	41	48	42	32	6	6
Sweden	8	2	30	30	58	64	3	4
Wales	14	11	47	46	36	39	3	4

Table 67c
What students perceive their teachers think about their school work (Age 15)

	Very good		Good		Average		Below average	
Country	M	F	M	F	M	F	M	F
Austria	9%	11%	32%	34%	53%	51%	6%	4%
Belgium	11	10	34	34	43	47	11	9
Canada	17	20	44	48	34	30	5	2
Finland	8	10	26	37	57	47	9	6
Norway	10	10	40	44	40	39	10	7
Poland	7	7	42	49	48	43	3	0
Scotland	13	9	30	34	51	54	6	3
Spain	8	6	35	38	46	50	11	6
Sweden	6	5	27	28	54	60	13	6
Wales	11	9	43	40	40	47	5	4

Table 68a
How students feel about school (Age 11)

Country	I like it a lot		I like it a little		I don't like it much		I don't like it at all	
	M	F	M	F	M	F	M	F
Austria	32%	32%	46%	54%	15%	10%	7%	3%
Belgium	23	30	44	47	23	19	10	5
Canada	18	35	55	53	16	10	11	3
Finland	7	11	43	55	40	29	10	5
Hungary	2	5	33	49	55	43	10	3
Norway	33	39	48	45	14	11	5	5
Poland	19	34	60	56	13	7	8	3
Scotland	31	49	52	39	11	8	6	4
Spain	18	21	50	52	22	23	10	4
Sweden	21	26	57	63	14	10	8	1
Wales	27	39	49	47	13	10	11	4

Table 68b
How students feel about school (Age 13)

Country	I like it a lot		I like it a little		I don't like it much		I don't like it at all	
	M	F	M	F	M	F	M	F
Austria	11%	13%	50%	63%	24%	18%	15%	6%
Belgium	13	20	44	44	32	29	11	8
Canada	17	25	55	54	18	15	10	6
Finland	4	5	39	50	47	38	10	6
Hungary	1	2	37	50	53	44	9	3
Norway	33	40	53	49	11	9	4	2
Poland	10	27	61	59	19	10	10	3
Scotland	26	30	51	55	12	10	10	5
Spain	8	14	53	53	29	28	9	4
Sweden	17	23	62	66	15	9	6	3
Wales	20	28	52	52	17	13	11	7

Table 68c
How students feel about school (Age 15)

Country	I like it a lot		I like it a little		I don't like it much		I don't like it at all	
	M	F	M	F	M	F	M	F
Austria	7%	17%	56%	56%	24%	18%	13%	9%
Belgium	10	13	41	49	35	30	14	8
Canada	15	22	55	58	19	16	11	4
Finland	1	4	31	46	56	45	12	5
Hungary	2	3	46	56	43	36	8	5
Norway	19	24	55	54	19	17	7	5
Poland	19	21	64	61	14	15	3	3
Scotland	17	26	53	51	20	16	10	7
Spain	6	9	51	69	35	19	8	3
Sweden	8	13	56	61	26	22	10	4
Wales	18	24	51	46	20	20	11	10

Table 69
CANADA ONLY
Students' ability to talk with their teacher about things that bother them

Age	Very easy		Easy		Difficult		Very difficult		Don't have that person	
	M	F	M	F	M	F	M	F	M	F
Age 11	11%	8%	21%	25%	29%	32%	29%	34%	3%	1%
Age 13	5	3	18	17	30	39	44	40	3	1
Age 15	5	2	15	16	31	38	45	42	4	2

Table 70a
Importance of having free time to spend on one's own (Age 11)

Country	Very important		Quite important		Not important Don't like time on own		Not important Never thought about it	
	M	F	M	F	M	F	M	F
Austria	31%	26%	26%	34%	32%	29%	11%	11%
Belgium	23	20	28	33	40	38	9	9
Canada	45	41	38	45	13	7	5	7
Hungary	22	26	38	31	31	33	8	10
Norway	13	11	29	29	24	22	34	39
Scotland	27	23	41	47	15	15	17	15

Table 70b
Importance of having free time to spend on one's own (Age 13)

Country	Very important		Quite important		Not important Don't like time on own		Not important Never thought about it	
	M	F	M	F	M	F	M	F
Austria	38%	36%	32%	35%	23%	22%	7%	7%
Belgium	31	27	30	31	35	36	4	6
Canada	49	44	34	40	9	8	8	8
Hungary	34	38	36	37	25	20	5	5
Norway	12	13	32	35	19	18	37	34
Poland	62	67	34	31	2	2	2	1
Scotland	39	30	39	50	12	12	10	8

Table 70c
Importance of having free time to spend on one's own (Age 15)

Country	Very important		Quite important		Not important Don't like time on own		Not important Never thought about it	
	M	F	M	F	M	F	M	F
Austria	41%	39%	29%	35%	22%	23%	8%	4%
Belgium	37	38	29	30	31	30	3	2
Canada	50	48	34	37	9	8	7	7
Hungary	32	38	36	37	27	22	5	3
Norway	19	20	32	39	18	16	31	25
Poland	70	80	28	18	1	1	1	1
Scotland	46	42	40	42	9	10	5	6

Brief Descriptions of 11 Participating Countries

1. Austria

Austria is a relatively small country in central Europe with a population of about seven and a half million. The population includes communities of Hungarians and Yugoslavians. German is the official language.

Attendance at school is compulsory between the ages of 6 and 15. The most common pattern of schooling is four years in primary school (Volksschule), four years in middle school (Hauptschule), which is organized in two streams differentiated by curricula and academic requirements and then four years of high school (Gymnasium) — some high schools are technical, leading to work and apprenticeships; others are more academically oriented leading to university entrance. Education is federally administered.

Physical education classes are compulsory throughout school for between two and four hours per week. Health education is not offered systematically; curricula are mainly teacher determined. Health professionals are not used in the classroom at this time.

2. Belgium

A small country on the North Sea bordering the Netherlands, France and Germany, Belgium has a population of about 10 million. It is officially bilingual (French and Flemish) and the presence of two language groups has created a profound duality in modern Belgium affecting every facet of national life.

School is compulsory for 12 years or from ages 6 to 18. However, students can leave at age 15, but must continue with part-time studies for three years. The primary level lasts six years, three cycles of two years each; the secondary level is also six years with two cycles of three years each. There are official schools and free schools, most of which are religious and all are funded by the state, province and municipality.

3. Canada

Geographically, Canada is the second largest country in the world, but has just over 26 million people in its 10 provinces and 2 territories. It comprises the northern half of North America, bordering the Pacific, Arctic and Atlantic oceans and the United States. Canada is officially bilingual — English and French — with education offered in both languages where the population warrants, and, in recent years, many French-immersion programs have been implemented across Canada.

As education is provincially controlled, there are many structural variations across the country. School is compulsory for students between the ages of 6 and 16. Children attend primary school from grades 1 to 6 or grades 1 to 8 depending on the province or territory, and secondary school from grades 7 to 11, 7 to 12 or 9 to 12. Some provinces and territories provide middle schools that offer various combinations of grades — 6 to 9, 7 to 9, or 8 and 9. Secondary schools offer programs leading to work or community college as well as to university. Education is funded by the provincial and territorial Department (Ministry) of Education and through municipal property taxes.

In most of Canada, physical education classes are compulsory up to Grade 9 (ages 14-15). Formal health education is usually taught in conjunction with these classes, often by specialist teachers from Grade 7.

4. Finland

Finland lies in the northern reaches of Europe bordering Norway, Sweden and Russia, and has approximately five million people. About 5% of the population is Swedish-speaking and both Finnish and Swedish are considered official languages.

Attendance at school is compulsory between the ages of 7 and 16. Education is available in Swedish where there are sufficient numbers. There are two school cycles, lower and upper. The lower cycle, taught by a classroom teacher, is six years and the upper cycle of three years is taught by subject teachers. After the upper cycle students can enter a senior secondary school for three years which leads to a university entrance examination about age 19. The results of these examinations are very important in ranking students for higher education. About half of the students continue to higher education upon completion of senior secondary school, partly because the number of places available is less than the number of those who qualify for higher education.

Physical education classes are compulsory for two to three hours per week throughout school in Finland.

5. Hungary

Hungary is a landlocked country on the eastern edge of Europe with a population of ten and one-half million. The population is relatively homogenous and the official language is Hungarian.

Children between the ages of 6 and 16 must attend school. The first level, or basic school, is divided into four lower years with a classroom teacher and four upper years with subject teachers. At age 14 students graduate to a grammar school (gymnazium), technical school or other specialized secondary school (e.g., arts) or they continue in an apprenticeship training school. While the gymnazia are predominately academically oriented, the technical schools give practical training and each school is allied with an industrial or agricultural concern. Special schools concentrate on music or art. All secondary schools are four years in length. Students from the gymnazia and technical schools write a matriculation examination to qualify for university entrance. Outstanding students in the special schools may apply for higher education.

Schools offer physical education at least three times per week; many schools have daily lessons. These classes are compulsory throughout school. Health education is more sporadically taught — sometimes by classroom teachers, but sometimes by biology teachers, and nurses and doctors often participate. The standard of the health education is generally low.

6. Norway

Norway shares the northern Scandinavian peninsula with Sweden and Finland. Geography has been a crucial factor in shaping the Norwegian character. Norway gets little sunshine for several months and then almost constant light in the summer. The population is approximately 4 215 000. Most Norwegians now live in urban areas in the eastern part of the country.

Basic education is compulsory for nine years, from ages 7 to 16, and is divided into two stages — junior classes, 1 to 6, and youth classes, 7 to 9. Most school children use the form of Norwegian called "bokmäl" or book language as the language of instruction. English is the most prevalent second language. There is a common curriculum for the first seven years with limited options in year eight and more options in year nine. After

nine years students must write compulsory examinations in Norwegian (nynorsk), mathematics and English. Secondary education is offered for three years and allows some flexibility in subject choice. Work-oriented, practical vocational courses are offered, but most students follow the general studies option which leads to higher education.

Schools offer physical education classes two to three times per week in all grades and they are compulsory. Health education is not taught separately, but an effort is made to integrate it in other subjects.

7. Poland

Poland is situated on the North Sea and borders Germany, Czechoslovakia, Lithuania and Russia, and has over 38 million people. Poland is one of the largest countries in Europe. It has a fairly homogenous population with one official language, Polish.

School attendance is compulsory between ages 7 and 15. Basic education is offered for these eight years. If students are not able to complete their basic education by the time they are 15, they must remain in school until the age of 17. Secondary education is offered in general, vocational or basic vocational secondary schools. Technical education may be pursued after students graduate from basic vocational secondary schools. Students who expect to attend university attend a lycée for four years to prepare for matriculation examinations.

8. Scotland

Scotland is part of the islands that comprise the United Kingdom and lies to the north of England. Geographically, it is situated quite far north, but the climate is tempered by the Gulf Stream. Scotland comprises several large islands as well as the mainland. Its population is approximately two and one-half million and is quite homogenous. English is the official language, but there has been, in recent years, some emphasis placed on the native Gaelic.

School structure is basically the same throughout the United Kingdom. Compulsory attendance is from ages 5 to 16. Children attend primary school from ages 5 to 11, then enter a secondary school which may be comprehensive; that is, academic and vocational or strictly academic. The secondary

school offers six years of instruction for those who wish to continue to higher education. Education is financed by the central government with additional funds from local taxes. The elected local education authorities have substantial control over their local school jurisdiction.

In Scotland, physical education is compulsory up to age 14 and is optional after. Health eduction is taught in elementary school and is optional after age 15.

9. Spain

Spain is part of the Iberian peninsula which lies on the western edge of Europe bordering Portugal and France, the Atlantic Ocean and the Mediterranean Sea. The population is 39 million and Spanish is the official language. There are several regions where local languages are spoken by part of the population. At present, the country is divided into 17 autonomous communities; each of them has its own parliament and governor.

The central government defines the basis for the school system, which in some areas is governed by the regional government, but not yet in all. An "old" and a "new" school system operate at present: the new one, considered to be more progressive, has been recently approved and is just beginning to be implemented. Schooling is compulsory from ages 6 to 14, which for the most part covers primary school.

Physical education is offered for one or two hours a week in primary school. Health education is neither compulsory nor systematic. Whether it is taught or not often depends on the motivation and abilities of particular teachers. However, school curricula are being changed and it is expected that health education will be included for some grades, but not as a separate subject.

10. Sweden

Sweden shares the northern part of the Scandinavian peninsula with Norway and Finland. It is the largest of these countries geographically and in population with almost eight and one-half million people. Over 90% live in the southern half of the country. The population is extremely homogenous with 95% of the people sharing the same language, religion and culture. The Swedes have been considered by much of the world to be an extremely fit population.

Education in Sweden is compulsory between the ages of 7 and 16 and consists of three levels of three years each — junior which comprises grades 1 to 3; intermediate, grades 4 to 6; and senior, grades 7 to 9. Up to Grade 6, students are taught by classroom teachers and in the senior level by subject teachers. Students who continue their education may attend one of four types of upper secondary. These are two-, three- and four-year general secondary schools or two-year vocational schools. Students must take either a three-or four-year general secondary program to continue to higher education.

11. Wales

Wales is part of the United Kingdom and borders the Irish Sea on the west and England on the east. It has a population of approximately 2 800 000. Although English is the predominate language, Welsh is spoken extensively with all areas offering instruction in Welsh as well as English. There has been a strong nationalistic trend toward maintaining the Welsh language.

School attendance is compulsory between ages 5 and 16. Children attend primary school until age 11 and then enter a comprehensive secondary school that offers both academic and vocational programs. Education is financed by the Welsh Home Office in combination with local education authorities.

Physical education is compulsory, but the number of weekly lessons varies. All students receive some health education, but there is no national curriculum.

Bibliography

Ajzen, I., & Fishbein, M. (1980). *Understanding attitudes and predicting social behavior.* Englewood Cliffs, NJ: Prentice-Hall.

Ajzen, I. (1985). From intentions to actions: A theory of planned behavior. In J. Kuhl, & J. Beckmann (Eds.), *Action control: From cognition to behavior* (pp. 11-39). Berlin: Springer-Verlag.

Bandura, A. (1989). Perceived self-efficacy in the exercise of control over AIDS infection. In V. M. Mays, G. W. Albee, & S. F. Schneider (Eds.), *Primary prevention of AIDS.* Newbury Park: Sage Publications.

Barlow, C. F. (1984). *Headaches and migraine in childhood.* London: Spastics International Medical Publications.

Becker, M. (Ed.). (1974). *The health belief model and personal health behavior.* Thorofare, NJ: Charles B. Slack.

Briggs, G. M., & Colloway, D. H. (1984). *Nutrition and physical fitness.* Toronto: Holt, Rinehart & Winston of Canada.

Del Rio, C. et al. (1989). Patterns of alcohol use among university students in Spain. *Alcohol and Alcoholism, 24*(5), 465-71.

Eder, A. (1990). Risk factor loneliness. On the interrelations between social integration, happiness and health in 11-, 13- and 15-year-old schoolchildren in 9 European countries. *Health Promotion International, 5*(1), 19-33.

Ferber, R. (1987). The Sleepless Child. In C. Guilleminault (Ed.), *Sleep and its disorder in children* (pp. 159-160). New York: Raven Press.

Fleming, I. E., Offord, D. R., & Boyle, M. (1989). Prevalence of childhood and adolescent depression in the community — Ontario Health Study. *British Journal of Psychiatry, 155*, 647-654.

Gochman, D. S. (1982). Labels, systems and motives. Some perspectives for future research and programs. In D. S. Gochman & G. S. Parcel (Eds.), Children's health beliefs and health behaviors. *Health Education Quarterly, 9*, 167-174. (Special issue).

Government of Canada. (1989). *Because they're young: Active living for Canadian children and youth. Blueprint for Action.* Ottawa: Fitness and Amateur Sport.

Health and Welfare Canada. (1989a). *Alcohol in Canada.* Ottawa: Supply and Services Canada.

Health and Welfare Canada. (1989b). *The active health report on fitness, nutrition and safety.* Ottawa: Supply and Services Canada.

Health and Welfare Canada. (1989c). *Knowledge development for health promotion: A call for action.* Ottawa: Supply and Services Canada.

Health and Welfare Canada. (1989d). *Licit and illicit drugs in Canada.* Ottawa: Supply and Services Canada.

Health and Welfare Canada. (1989e). *National survey on drinking and driving, 1988: Overview Report.* Ottawa: Supply and Services Canada.

Health and Welfare Canada. (1990). *National alcohol and other drugs survey. Highlights report.* Ottawa: Supply and Services Canada.

Health and Welfare Canada. (1990f). *Nutrition recommendations: A call for action.* Ottawa: Supply and Services Canada.

Holmes, B. (Ed.). (1983). *International Handbook of Education Systems. Vol. 1., Europe and Canada.* Chichester, GB: John Wiley and Sons.

Human development report. (1990). Published for the United Nations Development Programme. New York: Oxford University Press.

Jessor, S., & Jessor, R. (1977). *Problem behavior and psychosocial development.* New York: Academy Press.

Johnson, L., & Barnhorst, R. (Eds.). (1991). *The state of the child in Ontario: Child youth and family policy research centre.* Don Mills, ON: Oxford University Press.

King, A. J. C. (1986). *The adolescent experience.* Toronto: Ontario Secondary School Teachers' Federation.

King, A. J. C., Beazley, R. P., Warren, W. K., Hankins, C. A., Robertson, A. S., & Radford, J. L. (1988). *Canada youth and AIDS study*. Kingston, ON: Social Program Evaluation Group, Queen's University.

King, A. J. C., & Peart, M. J. (1990). *The good school*. Toronto: Ontario Secondary School Teachers' Federation.

King, A. J. C., Robertson, A. S., Warren, W. K., & Fuller, K. R. (1984). *Summary Report: Canada health knowledge survey: 9, 12 and 15 year olds (1982-83)*. Ottawa: Health and Welfare Canada.

King, A. J. C., Robertson, A. S., & Warren, W. K. (1985). *Summary Report: Canada health attitudes and behaviours survey: 9, 12 and 15 year olds (1984-85)*. Ottawa: Health and Welfare Canada.

Kurian, G. T. (1988). *Education encyclopedia. Vol. 1*. New York: Facts on File Publications.

Leviton, L. C. (1989). Theoretical foundations of AIDS-prevention programs. In R. O. Valdiserri (Ed.), *Preventing AIDS: The design of effective programs*. New Brunswick: Rutgers University Press.

Matthews, M. (1991). *The prediction and modification of health behaviours of young adults*. Unpublished doctoral thesis, Queen's University, Kingston, ON.

Mendoza, R., Batista-Foguet, J. M., & Oliva, A. (1991). *Health-related behaviour in European school children: Findings of the second cross-national survey on health-related behaviour in school-children (1985-86)*. Vol. 1. Copenhagen: World Health Organization.

Nilssen, O. (1991). The Tromoo study: Identification of and a controlled intervention on a population of early-stage risk drinkers. *Preventive Medicine, 20*, 518-528.

Offord, D., Boyle, M., & Racine, Y. (1986). *Ontario child health study*. Toronto: Queen's Printer.

Offord, D., Boyle, M., & Racine, Y. (1989). *Ontario Child Health Study: Children at risk*. Toronto: Queen's Printer.

Olweus, D. (1991). Bully/victim problems among school children: Basic facts and effects of a school-based intervention program. In Pepler, D. J. & Rubin, K. H. (Eds.), *The development and treatment of childhood aggression* (pp. 411-448). Hillsdale, NH: Erlbaum.

A pack of trouble. *Toronto Star*. October 22, 1991.

Perry, C. L., & Jessor, R. (1985). The concept of health promotion and the prevention of adolescent drug abuse. *Health Education Quarterly, 12*, 169-184.

Pinich, W. J., Heck, M., & Vinal, D. (1986). Health needs and concerns of male adolescents. *Adolescence, 21*, 961-969.

Posterski, D., and R. Bibby. (1988). *Canada's youth "Ready for today": A comprehensive survey of 15-24 year olds*. Ottawa: Canadian Youth Foundation.

Postlethwaite, T. N. (Ed.). (1988). *The encyclopedia of comparative education and national systems of education*. Oxford: Pergamon Press.

Smart, R. G., Adlaf, E. M., & Walsh, G. (1991). *The Ontario student drug use survey*. Toronto: Addiction Research Foundation.

Social indicators of development 1989. A World Book Publication. (1989). Baltimore, MD: The John Hopkins University Press.

Stare, F. J., & McWilliams, M. (1984). *Living nutrition*. 4th ed. Rexdale, ON: John Wiley & Sons.

Statistical yearbook. (1990). Paris: UNESCO.

Student drug use down. *Toronto Star*. November 20, 1991.

World tables. A World Book Publication. (1991). Baltimore, MD:The John Hopkins University Press.